no LC

457

D1488898

POLITICAL TRACTS
1713—1719

June 1715

1

An Enquiry
into the Behaviour of the Queen's
last Ministry, with Relation to their
Quarrells among themselves, and the
Design charged upon them of
altering the Succession of the Crown

Since the Death of the Queen it was
reasonable enough for me to conclude that
I had done with all publick Affairs and
Speculations; Besides, the Scene and Station
I am in have reduced my Thoughts into a
narrow Compass; and being wholly
excluded from any View of Favour under
the present Administration upon that
invincible Reason of having been in some
Degree of Trust and Confidence with the
former; I have not found the Transition
very difficult into a private Life, for which
I am better qualifyed both by Nature and
Education.

The reading and enquiring after
News having not been one of my
Diversions, having always detested a mixed
and generall Conversation, which however
it fell to my lott is now in my
Power to avoyd, and being placed by
Function at a great
Distance from the Seat of Business, I am
altogether ignorant of many common
Events which happen in the
World. Onely from the little I know
and hear, it is manifest that most mens
Breasts are filled with Doubts, Fears,
and Iealosyes, or else with Hatred and
Rage to a degree that there seems to be
an end of all amicable Commerce between
People of different Partyes, and what
the Consequences of this may be let those
consider who have contributed to the
Causes; which I thank God, is no
Concern of mine.

There are two Points with Reference
to the Conduct of the late Ministry, much
insisted on, and little understood by those
who write or talk upon that Subject
wherein I am sufficiently qualifyed to
give Satisfaction, and would gladly do it
because I see very much Weight layd
upon each, and most mens Opinions
of Persons and Things regulated accordingly.

About

OPENING PAGE OF *An Enquiry* (FOUL COPY), IN STELLA'S HAND,
CORRECTED BY SWIFT
(*By kind permission of Lord Rothschild*)

71641

JONATHAN SWIFT

POLITICAL TRACTS
1713—1719

Edited by
Herbert Davis and Irvin Ehrenpreis

828
597 1po

BASIL BLACKWELL · OXFORD
1964

Alverno College Library
Milwaukee, Wisconsin

First published 1953
Reprinted 1964

PRINTED IN GREAT BRITAIN FOR
BASIL BLACKWELL & MOTT LTD. BY
THE COMPTON PRINTING WORKS (LONDON) LTD. LONDON, N.1.
AND BOUND BY
THE KEMP HALL BINDERY, OXFORD

ACKNOWLEDGEMENT

THE editors wish to make special acknowledgement to Lord Rothschild for his generosity, kindness and patience in allowing them on many occasions to examine the manuscripts of Swift in his library and to make full use of them in preparing the text and illustrations for this volume. The fragment in Swift's hand of *A Discourse concerning the Fears from the Pretender* has already been printed by Professor Nichol Smith, who found it among the Ford papers and included it in the *Letters to Ford*, 1935; but now it takes its proper place among Swift's works. The corrected fair copy of *Some free Thoughts upon the present State of Affairs* has provided a text which contains for the first time passages like the Memorandum and the criticism of the Tory leadership, hitherto suppressed. And, of incomparable importance, there are the two manuscripts of *An Enquiry into the Behaviour of the Queen's last Ministry*. The first, labelled by Swift 'Foul Copy,' is the original draft in his own hand, except for the first leaf, which is in the hand of Stella; here are to be seen his first thoughts and his earliest corrections, with some passages, such as the violent attack upon George I, which were afterwards discarded. The second, a fair copy made by an amanuensis, has his later revisions and a few notes in the hand of Mrs. Whiteway. These give us a text in the final form as Swift had carefully left it, and material which will be found in the textual notes, showing all the stages of a composition which he worked over during a period of twenty years.

The CONTENTS

ACKNOWLEDGEMENT   *page* v

THE INTRODUCTION   ix

POLITICAL TRACTS

The Importance of the Guardian Considered   1

The Publick Spirit of the Whigs   27

A Discourse concerning the Fears from the Pretender   69

Some free Thoughts upon the present State of Affairs   73

Some Considerations upon the Consequences hoped
  and feared from the Death of the Queen   99

Memoirs, relating to That Change which happened
  in the Queen's Ministry in the Year 1710   105

An Enquiry into the Behaviour of the Queen's last
  Ministry   129

APPENDIXES

A. A Modest Enquiry into . . . a Report of Her
   Majesty's Death   183

B. The Humble Address Of the . . . Lords   198

C. A Copy of Dr. Swift's Memorial to the Queen   200

TEXTUAL NOTES   201

INDEX   233

ILLUSTRATIONS

Opening Page of *An Enquiry* (Foul Copy)   *frontispiece*

The Proclamation against *The Publick Spirit of the Whigs*

facing page xxii

Opening Page of *Some free Thoughts*   *facing page* xxiv

Title Page of *Some free Thoughts*   *facing page* xxv

First Page of *Some Considerations*   *facing page* 101

FACSIMILES OF TITLE-PAGES

The Importance of the Guardian Considered   *page* 3

The Publick Spirit of the Whigs   29

Some free Thoughts   75

The INTRODUCTION

THE pamphlets included in this volume belong to the first six or seven years after Swift's installation in June 1713 as Dean of St. Patrick's. On that occasion he had stayed in Dublin only a fortnight and had then retired to his country living at Laracor owing to the ill state of his health. On July 8 he wrote to Vanessa:

> I design to pass the greatest part of the time I stay in Ireland here in the cabin where I am now writing; neither will I leave the kingdom till I am sent for; and if they have no further service for me, I will never see England again. At my first coming I thought I should have died with discontent, and was horribly melancholy while they were installing me; but it begins to wear off, and change to dulness.
>
> . . . I will say so much to you that I verily think, if the thing you know of had been published just upon the peace, the Ministry might have avoided what hath since happened. But I am now fitter to look after willows, and to cut hedges, than to meddle with affairs of state. I must order one of the workmen to drive those cows out of my island, and make up the ditch again; a work much more proper for a country vicar, than driving out factions, and fencing against them. And I must go and take my bitter draught to cure my head, which is spoilt by the bitter draughts the public hath given me.[1]

'The thing you know of' was his *History* of the negotiations leading to the Peace of Utrecht, which he had written at Windsor the previous spring in order to print it in justification of the treaty immediately after the terms were known. When he realized that the Ministry were not willing to use it, he left them, as there was nothing else he could do. But he was not allowed to remain untroubled, enjoying the 'felicity of being among his willows.' A few days later came an appeal from

---

[1] *Corr.*, ii, 53–4.

his friend Erasmus Lewis, the Earl of Dartmouth's secretary, to return to London:

> you might certainly be of great use to us, by your endeavours to reconcile, and by representing to them the infallible consequences of these divisions.[1]

This was followed on July 30 by an urgent message:

> My Lord Treasurer desires you will make all possible haste over, for we want you extremely.[2]

Still he made excuses, and finally tried to put off his return until October; but on August 6, Lewis wrote again in such a way as to persuade him to return at once. He left Dublin on August 29 and arrived in London on September 9. But he did not find it the cure for the spleen, as they had promised him; within a month he is complaining that he is 'heartily weary of Courts and Ministers, and politics' and he has a mind to be at home, since the Queen has been pleased that Ireland should be his home. Nevertheless he stayed on in England until the death of the Queen and soon found himself involved in the violent political controversies that were then taking place. These were connected with the treaty arrangements with France, such as the demolition of Dunkirk and the trade agreements, and the more dangerous problems relating to the Hanoverian Succession.

The first of these matters led to the beginning of the controversy with Steele, who was to be his chief antagonist during the winter. In the *Guardian* of August 7 Steele had printed a vigorous reply to the memorial which had been presented to the Queen on behalf of the inhabitants of Dunkirk. In a letter signed 'English Tory' he had urged the editor to let it be known that the British people were not willing to consider any delay in so urgent a matter, and expected the immediate demolition of Dunkirk:

> Pray, Mr. IRONSIDE, repeat this last Particular, and put it in a different Letter, *That the Demolition of* Dunkirk *will remove* France *many hundred Miles further off from us;* and then repeat again, *That the* British *Nation expects the Demolition of* Dunkirk.

---

[1] *Corr.*, ii, 55.   [2] *Corr.*, ii. 57.

And when reports continued to appear in the papers, coming from Antwerp or from Dunkirk, that the demolition of the fortifications and the harbour had been deferred, the *Flying Post* took up the cry and printed this refrain at the end of each number in the latter part of August and September, after the quotations of Bank and South Sea Stock:

> Dunkirk is not yet demolish'd. The Pretender is not yet remov'd from Lorrain.

On the other side two pamphlets were published by Morphew, attacking Steele for his insolence to the Queen. The first was entitled *The Honour and Prerogative of the Queen's Majesty Vindicated and Defended Against The Unexampled Insolence of the Author of the Guardian: In a Letter from a Country Whig to Mr. Steele.* It pointed out that the *Guardian* had hitherto been read in the country by Whigs and Tories alike, as expressing the old moderate loyal view, and that such Whigs would regard it as the greatest satire upon them if it was supposed that they could be pleased by such threats against the best of sovereigns. The second was entitled *Reasons concerning the immediate Demolishing of Dunkirk: Being a Serious Enquiry into the State and Condition of that Affair*, etc. and contained, besides the attack on Steele, a fuller discussion of the whole question of the importance of Dunkirk. Steele's naïve protest is put aside and the real point at issue between the Whigs and the Tories in this matter is frankly disclosed:

> If they had said they would have it demolished, because the Dutch were not willing we should keep it; because the Flemings are not willing to have us be so much their Masters; because the Emperor does not care to trust us with it; because by it you are able to establish the English Trade in Flanders, whether the States-General approve it or no.

Whatever the final arrangements, the immediate importance of Dunkirk was not its demolition but that it should be held 'as a pledge that France would perform her part in the Treaty and as a means of insuring that British commerce in the Low Countries might not be so much at the Mercy either of the Dutch, or the Emperor, as otherwise it would be.' Another pamphlet of little importance was also published by Morphew with the title *A Second Whigg-Letter, from William Prynne to Nestor Ironside Esq.* in which Steele is complimented by 'one of the Destroyers of Monarchy' for continuing to do their job so well.

Meanwhile the *Examiner* on August 21 charged him with threatening the Queen, while still a servant of hers, under a salary, and favoured in spite of all his ill behaviour; and attacked him again on August 24, repeating some of the arguments of the pamphlet, *The Honour and Prerogative of the Queen's Majesty Vindicated,* the first and second editions of which were advertised in these numbers. The controversy continued in the newspapers on both sides and other pamphlets appeared in support of Steele, who was now at work on a more elaborate examination of the whole matter, which he entitled *The Importance of Dunkirk consider'd,* and announced in the *Guardian* of September 8. It was published on September 22, and a second and third edition came out within the week. Having just been elected a Member of Parliament for the borough of Stockbridge, Steele had chosen to reply to his critics in the form of a letter to the worshipful Mr. John Snow, the Bailiff of Stockbridge. He sends him all the papers that have appeared since the dissolution of the last Parliament, including those containing attacks upon himself:

> you will find your Humble Servant no small Man, but spoken of more than once in Print: You will find I take up whole Pages in the *Examiner*, and that there is a little Pamphlet written wholly upon me, and directed to me. As you are the Magistrate of the Town wherein, of all Places in the World, it concerns me most to appear a different Man, from the Person whom these Writers represent me; I address my Vindication to you, and at the same time to the whole Borough.[1]

Swift had arrived in London just at the time when the newspapers were making full play with the topic of Steele and the demolition of Dunkirk. He could not help recalling their quarrel during the previous summer and realizing that

[1] See *Tracts and Pamphlets by Richard Steele*, ed. Rae Blanchard, Baltimore, 1944, p. 87.

the opportunity was now being offered him to settle matters
between them. He had particularly disliked Steele's unwillingness to accept his kindness in influencing the Ministers
not to replace him as Gazetteer; though he had tried to bring
the incident to a close by writing with great dignity and
restraint a letter of farewell before leaving for Ireland.[1]
Nevertheless it is doubtful whether Swift's attack should be
regarded as the fruit of personal bitterness. For Steele's
pamphlet was not merely a justification of himself; it was
also an important statement of the Whigs' point of view in
the matter of foreign trade, which had led them to oppose the
commercial treaty with France.

Swift's reply, *The Importance of the Guardian Considered*,
finally appeared on November 2, 1713.[2] In his Preface he
takes up Steele's challenge; he will not attack him as an honest
man, he will not bother to answer his arguments, he will
simply treat him as 'our brother-scribbler' by considering his
pamphlet partly as a critic and partly as a commentator.
He is indeed restrained in his detraction; at least, if he had
wished to be malicious, he could have said more. In referring
to Steele's original letter to the *Guardian* of August 7, he is
almost playful:

> Mr. English Tory, the very same person with Mr. Steele,
> writes a letter to Nestor Ironside, Esq; who is the same person
> with English Tory, who is the same person with Mr. Steele
> ... This letter [was] written and published by these three
> gentlemen who are *one* of your representatives.

He adopts throughout an attitude of amused contempt—
the argument is not worth discussing, the French memorial
is 'as idle a one as ever I read,' and all Mr. Steele's talk of a
reply to be laid before Her Majesty's ministry means no more
than that he will write about it in a penny paper which he
publishes every day to be read in coffee houses and to get him
a little money. There is surely nothing very 'terrible,' as
some have called it, in all this. Steele had been strutting about

---

[1] See *Correspondence of Richard Steele*, ed. Rae Blanchard, Oxford, 1941, pp.
70–8.
[2] See Advertisements in the *Examiner*, October 30 and November 2, 1713.

before his constituents, a little vain of his new dignity as a member of Parliament, imagining himself as a public figure of some importance, who proposed as a gentleman of liberal education and wide knowledge of the world to 'direct Her Majesty in the weightiest matters of government.' These pretensions are swept aside as easily as his pretensions to superior virtue; this gentleman of the Horse Guards with a few sprinklings of rudimentary literature and a few common-places from some canting moralist is shown up as being capable of schoolboy offences against grammar, and as a writer of meaningless cadence 'filling up niches with words before he has adjusted his conceptions to them.' And finally Mr. Snow, the bailiff of Stockbridge, is reminded that in the matter of Dunkirk 'it is not altogether impossible that there may be some few reasons of state which have not been yet communicated to Mr. Steele.' This paper should not be regarded as a serious political pamphlet; the occasion did not warrant it. An almost trivial tone is maintained deliberately, as befitting an attempt merely to expose a rather foolish impostor, a half-educated and irresponsible journalist, posing as a patriot and enlightened politician.

Swift has been suspected of having written another paper published by Morphew at this time, dated from Will's Coffee-House, October 27, and advertised in the *Examiner* of November 13, 1713, as 'published yesterday'—*The Character of Richard St——le, Esq; With some Remarks. by Toby, Abel's Kinsman, or according to Mr. Calamy, A.F. & N. In a Letter to his God-father*.[1] Steele assumed that he had written it, and later it was attributed to him by Dean Smedley.[2] More recently the case has been argued by C. W. Dilke, in his attempt to show that it is very unlikely that Dr. William Wagstaffe, of St. Bartholomew's Hospital, was really responsible for this and other pamphlets included in the *Miscellaneous Works* of William Wagstaffe, published in 1726. But though, like Swift's

---

[1] *A. F. & N.* was a parody of Edmund Calamy, the nonconformist historian and preacher, who, before he could add D.D. to his name, used on the title-pages of his books the formula, *Edm. Fil. & Nepos*, or simply *E. F. & N.*

[2] See *Gulliveriana* (1728), pp. 236–7.

pamphlet, it attempts to make fun of Steele's claim to 'Public
Spirit, Charity, Benevolence to Mankind and Disinterest' and
to demonstrate with examples the badness of his writing, there
is no evidence whatever that Swift had anything to do with it,
and the style and quality of the writing show that he did not.
The author of the introductory Life of Dr. Wagstaffe felt
that this particular paper needed apology and was careful to
explain that it was written without any feeling of personal
enmity against Steele, who was unknown to Wagstaffe, but
to oblige 'some Friends in the Ministry . . . by thus shewing his
Dislike to a Gentleman who had so much endeavour'd, on
all occasions, to oppose them.'[1]

Steele was not silenced or much disturbed by these attacks.
He had, indeed, before they appeared, committed himself to a
much more important undertaking, which was advertised in
the *Englishman* of October 22. This work, for which subscriptions were invited, was entitled *The Crisis . . . with some
Seasonable Remarks on the danger of a Popish Successor.* In the
preparation of it he had sought assistance, and in the Preface
he states that Addison, Hoadly and other Whig friends had
collaborated with him. At the same time members of the
party and of the Hanover Club undertook to insure its circula-
tion throughout the country, with the result that forty
thousand copies were said to have been sold.[2] Swift made fun
of all this excitement in *The First Ode of the Second Book of
Horace Paraphras'd: And Address'd to Richard St——le, Esq;*
which he printed on January 7, 1714.

> DICK, thour't resolv'd, as I am told,
> Some strange *Arcana* to unfold,

---

[1] *Miscellaneous Works of Dr. William Wagstaffe* (1726), p. xiii. An authorita-
tive reply to Dilke is to be found in Sir Norman Moore's *History of St. Bartholomew's Hospital* (1918), II, 523–9. It may be added here that some of the other
tracts in this volume could not have been written by any member of the
Scriblerus Club, nor printed with their approval, e.g., *The State and Condition
of our Taxes considered* (1714) which refers to the Earl of Oxford as 'that
Hypocrite in Business, that mighty Trifler of the Tr—sury, . . . whose Merit
is Tricking, and who justly is the Contempt of both Parties' (p. 180).

[2] It was also reprinted at Edinburgh and Dublin, and French and German
translations were published at Amsterdam and at Hamburg. See *Tracts and
Pamphlets*, ed. Rae Blanchard, pp. 126 and 641.

For this is exactly the method that Swift uses, after boldly and unreservedly denying that there was any cause for alarm, or that the Ministry by any single act had done anything 'tending towards bringing in the Pretender, or to weaken the Succession in the House of Hanover.' Although we now know that this was not true,[1] it seems clear from all that Swift wrote at this time and later, that he was himself innocent of any thought of tampering with the succession and had no suspicion that the Queen or her ministers were guilty of having any dangerous dealings with the Pretender.

He allows himself, therefore, to ridicule all the fuss that had been made over this pamphlet, the advertisements and the subscriptions and the efforts of the party to distribute it all over the country:

> At the destined Period, the first News we hear, is of a huge Train of Dukes, Earls, Viscounts, Barons, Knights, Esquires, Gentlemen, and others, going to *Sam. Buckley*'s the Publisher of the *Crisis*, to fetch home their Cargoes, in order to transmit them by Dozens, Scores, and Hundreds, into the several Counties, and thereby to prepare the Wills and Understandings of their Friends against the approaching Sessions.

He is angry at the insolent Dedication to the Clergy, and asks by what authority Steele dares to direct the clergy what to preach and to constitute himself a Vicar-General of the Church of England. He provides a suitable answer for the clergy to return to such counsellors as the Bishop of Sarum and the author of the *Crisis*. He then proceeds to a candid examination of the style and erudition of 'this very solemn Writer,' 'this child of Obscurity,' 'this Politician' with his Insinuations, his Solecisms and his Absurdities. But when he comes to expose the errors in Steele's account of the Union, he forgets for a moment his main purpose of discrediting the author and permits himself some observations which had to be subsequently modified,[2] and some comments on the Scottish

---

[1] See G. N. Clark, *The Later Stuarts*, Oxford, 1949, p. 233.

[2] In a Postscript to the *Examiner*, March 1, 1713–14: I had a Letter on *Friday* last, which I suppose to have come from the Author of *The Public Spirit of the Whigs*, &c., wherein he desires I would let the World know, That he owns

nobles, which were to rouse much resentment in the House of Lords and to provide an opportunity for his enemies to cause him a good deal of trouble.

In the second half of his reply Swift changes his tactics, though he maintains his tone of contempt even when he deigns to examine Steele's arguments. He is concerned here to answer the chief charges which the Whigs had brought against the Ministry, namely, that the Treaty of Utrecht had produced disastrous consequences and that the negotiations had been carried out in a way which was both dishonourable and ignominious. Steele and his associates had brought up many of the points which were later to appear in the impeachments of Oxford, Bolingbroke and Ormonde. In his defence of the government Swift made use of some of the material already embodied in his *History* of the negotiations, which he had hoped to publish the previous summer. I do not think it has been pointed out that only a few days before Swift's *Public Spirit of the Whigs* was first announced, a curious rumour was put abroad that Swift's *History* was about to appear. On January 29, the *Examiner* had printed the following Postscript:

> Tho' I am sorry to find my Self an Instrument (however Innocent) of drawing the frequent Scurrilities of the *Flying-Post* and his Brethren, upon a very *Deserving Gentleman*, whom, against their Conscience, they will suppose to be concerned in this Paper; yet my Sorrow is mixt with some Pleasure, when I am encouraged to hope, that the unjust Attacks of these Underlings, since they are supposed to act by the Command of their Superiors, may provoke that Worthy and Able Writer to publish a *Great Work* which the World hath long expected, and I hear hath been long finished; wherein the whole History of their Iniquity will probably be laid in so clear a Light, that neither I, nor any other Friend of the Publick, will have need to hold the Pen any longer in their Service.

This sounds as though Swift may have talked of printing his

himself in a Mistake in the 22d *Page*, where he says, *He doth not remember that an Union was ever thought on by any, except King* James I. *and the late King* William; for he hath been since told, That some Overtures were made to that End, in the Reigns of other Princes.' And see below, pp. 48-9.

History since his return from Dublin; but he was evidently
persuaded that a direct reply to Steele's *Crisis* was more
necessary. It was probably planned that this should be ready
for the opening of the new Parliament to prepare the way for
the attack on Steele to be made in the House. Just as he was
finishing his pamphlet, the printer brought him another to
answer 'written by the same Author, and entituled, *The
Englishman, being the Close of the Paper so called.*' But he refused
to do more than add a few contemptuous sentences attacking
Steele again for his insolence and sedition. He must have
known of the reference to such 'insolent papers' which was
to be made in the Queen's speech to Parliament on March 2,
1713–14, whether he had actually suggested it or not:

> There are some who have arrived to that Height of Malice as
> to insinuate, that the Protestant Succession in the House of
> *Hanover* is in Danger under my Government:
> Those who go about thus to distract the Minds of Men with
> imaginary Dangers, can only mean to disturb the present Tran-
> quillity, and to bring real Mischiefs upon us.
> After all I have done to secure our Religion, and your Liberties,
> and to transmit both safe to Posterity, I cannot mention these
> Proceedings without some Degree of Warmth; and I must hope,
> you will all agree with me, That Attempts to weaken my
> Authority, or to render the Possession of my Crown uneasy to
> me, can never be proper Means to strengthen the Protestant
> Succession.

In their *Address of Thanks* the Commons replied that they
would

> on all Occasions shew their just Abhorrence of the licentious
> Practices, in publishing scandalous Papers, and spreading
> seditious Rumours . . . they cannot but be astonished at the
> malicious Insinuations of any, who would suggest that Suc-
> cession to be in Danger under your Majesty's most auspicious
> Government. . . . and must look upon such Insinuations to be
> groundless in themselves, and affronting to your Majesty, and
> your Government.[1]

Then in due course on March 12, a complaint was made
to the House of three printed pamphlets by Richard Steele,

[1] *Journals of the House of Commons*, XVII, 474 and 483.

namely, *The Englishman*, from Saturday, January 16, to Tuesday, January 19, 1713–14, another entitled *The Crisis*, and the other entitled *The Englishman: Being the Close of the Paper so called*. Steele appeared on March 18, owned that he had written and published these pamphlets, and proceeded to make his defence; whereupon it was voted that for his offence in writing and publishing the said scandalous and seditious libels, he should be expelled the House.

But while the government had succeeded in their case against Steele, a complaint against the very pamphlet in which Swift had come to their aid had been brought before the House of Lords, on account of the paragraphs, already referred to, where he had spoken so contemptuously of the Scottish nobility, and of the Union of the two Kingdoms. On March 2, the House had come to the following Resolution:

> That the said Pamphlet is a false, malicious, and factious Libel, highly dishonourable and scandalous to the *Scotch* Nation, tending to the Destruction of the Constitution, and most injurious to Her Majesty, who has often declared from the Throne, That the Union of the Two Kingdoms of *England* and *Scotland* was the peculiar Happiness of Her Reign, in making so full a Provision for the Peace and Quiet of Her People, and the Security of our Religion, by so firm an Establishment of the Protestant Succession throughout *Great Britain*.

The printer and the publisher were arrested, and a full examination of their servants was ordered to discover the author of the pamphlet.[1] These examinations took place on March 3, 5, 6, and 9, but then all further enquiries were stopped— to avoid embarrassment to the government—as a result of the prosecution which the Earl of Mar informed the House he had ordered to be undertaken against the printer, John Barber. But on March 9, it was further ordered that a humble Address be presented to Her Majesty

> That Her Majesty will be graciously pleased to issue Her Royal Proclamation, with a Promise of such Reward as Her Majesty

---

[1] See *Journals of the House of Lords*, XIX, 628–635, and MS Minute Book of the House of Lords, 1713–14, 2 March—9 March, where a detailed account of this examination is given.

shall think fit, to any Person who shall discover the Author of the Pamphlet.

This was duly issued on March 15, 1713–14.[1]

Meantime the printer had re-issued the pamphlet with the offending passages removed,[2] and Swift had been provided by the Treasurer with funds for the printer 'to answer such exigencies as their case may immediately require.'[3] This seems to indicate that the ministers were willing to share with Swift responsibility for the pamphlet. Although they had reason for their dislike of the Duke of Argyll, it is difficult to understand how they came to allow such a general attack on the Scottish peers, on whom (as Dr. Ball points out) they depended for their majority in the House of Lords. It is also difficult to explain why neither Swift nor the printer nor any of their friends had not realized that such an attack would constitute a breach of parliamentary privilege. But further evidence is provided in his comment on this affair, when writing to the Earl of Peterborough on May 18, that he regarded himself as one who had suffered for writing for the government, and presumably therefore with their knowledge and approval:

> Barber, the printer, was, some time ago, in great distress, upon printing a pamphlet, of which evil tongues would needs call me the author: he was brought before your House, which addressed the Queen in a body, who kindly published a proclamation with three hundred pounds to discover. The fault was, calling the Scots 'a fierce poor northern people.' So well protected are those who scribble for the Government; upon which, I now put one query to your Excellency: What has a man without employment to do among Ministers, when he can neither serve himself, his friends, nor the public?'[4]

After he had finished *The Public Spirit of the Whigs*, but before it was published, Swift began work upon *A Discourse concerning the Fears from the Pretender*, dating the manuscript

[1] See Appendix B.
[2] See Textual Notes, pp. 201–2.
[3] See *Corr.*, ii, 129–130 and *fn*.
[4] *Corr.*, ii, 138.

By the Queen,

A PROCLAMATION,

For Difcovering the Author of a Falfe, Malicious, and Factious Libel, Intituled,
The Publick Spirit of the Whigs, fet forth in their *Generous Encouragement of the Author of the Crifis*, with *fome Obfervations on the Seafonablenefs, Candor, Erudition,
and Style of that Treatife.*

ANNE R.

20. March 171$\frac{3}{4}$

Hereas the Lords Spiritual and Temporal in Parliament Affembled,
have, by their humble Addrefs, befought Us, That We would be
Gracioufly Pleafed to Iffue Our Royal Proclamation, with a
Promife therein of fuch a Reward, as We fhould, in Our Royal
Wifdom, think fit, to any perfon who fhall Difcover, and make due
Proof againft the Author or Authors of a Falfe, Malicious, and Fac-
tious Libel, Intituled, The Publick Spirit of the Whigs, fet forth in their
Generous Encouragement of the Author of the *Crifis*, with fome Obfervations on
the Seafonablenefs, Candor, Erudition, and Style of that Treatife, highly Dif-
honourable and Scandalous to Our Subjects of Scotland, tending
to the Deftruction of the Constitution, and (by making Falfe and
Unjuft Reflections upon the Union, and the Steps and Motives to
it) moft Injurious to Us: as alfo that We would Promife therein
Our moft Gracious Pardon to fuch perfon or perfons as fhall make fuch Difcovery, of all
Crimes and Mifdemeanors committed in relation to the Printing, Publifhing, and Difperfing
the faid Libel: We therefore, out of Our earneft Defire to have the Author or Authors of the
faid Libel Difcovered and Brought to Juftice, have Readily Inclined thereunto, and do, by
this Our Royal Proclamation, Gracioufly Promife, That if any perfon fhall Difcover, and
make due Proof againft the Author or Authors of the faid Libel, fuch perfon fhall Receive from
Us a Reward of the Sum of Three hundred pounds, which Our High Treafurer is hereby
directed to Pay accordingly, and alfo the perfon or perfons, making fuch Difcovery, fhall
have Our moft Gracious Pardon of all Crimes and Mifdemeanors committed in relation to
the Printing, Publifhing, and Difperfing the faid Libel.

Given at Our Court at St. *James's* the Fifteenth Day of *March*, 17¹³. In the Thirteenth
Year of Our Reign.

God fave the Queen.

LONDON, Printed by *John Baskett*, Printer to the Queens moft Excellent Majefty, And by the
Affigns of *Thomas Newcomb*, and *Henry Hills*, deceas'd. 17¹³.

THE PROCLAMATION AGAINST *The Publick Spirit of the Whigs*

fragment of the two opening paragraphs February 20.[1] He
knew that this was not only 'the most popular Topick of
Quarrell between the two contending Partyes' but also the
most serious cause of the growing lack of confidence in the
Queen's ministers; and it therefore needed to be discussed
more fully than he had been able to do in his reply to Steele.
He probably put it aside when he became involved in the
uneasy business arising out of the action taken against *The
Public Spirit of the Whigs*; and during the next two months
he seems to have given up hope of being able to do anything
to save the ministry. At the end of March he says in a letter
to Archdeacon Walls:

> we are in a confounded situation at present; fit only to talk of
> some years hence by the fireside.[2]

Nevertheless he continued his efforts, but must have been too
much occupied with the private quarrels of his friends to have
time to consider how he might allay the fears of the public.
Writing in April to the Duchess of Ormonde, he says:

> You cannot imagine how much I am grieved, when I find some
> people I wish well to, run counter to their own interest, and give
> their enemies such advantages, by being so hard upon their
> friends as to conclude, if they are not without fault, they are not
> to be supported, or scarce conversed with.[3]

Some time in May, however, before leaving London to
retire into the country at Letcombe Bassett, in Berkshire,
he seems to have decided to continue the 'Discourse'; at least
he still uses that title in writing to Ford on June 12, 1714—
'I am going on with the Discourse of which you saw the
beginning; but not a Word of it for your Life.' But he must
have begun afresh and have taken a new title, which would
not sound so much like a party attack, or a defence of the
ministers, but would rather offer a reasonable examination
and frank discussion of current problems, in giving *Some free*

---

[1] Now in the possession of Lord Rothschild; it was among the papers preserved by Charles Ford, and was first printed in the *Letters to Ford*, ed. D. Nichol
Smith (Oxford, 1935), pp. 216–17.
[2] *Corr.*, ii, 132. [3] *Corr.*, ii, 133.

Thoughts upon the present State of Affairs. It was finished and
sent to Ford on July 1, with these instructions:

> Here it is, read it, and send it to B[arber] by an unknown
> hand, have nothing to do with it, thô there be no Danger. . . .
> Do not send it by the Penny post, nor your Man, but by a Porter
> when you are not at your Lodgings. Get some Friend to copy
> out the little Paper, and send it inclosed with the rest, and let the
> same Hand direct it, and seal it with an unknown Seal. . . .
> I would fain have it sent on Saterday night, or Sunday because
> of the date, that it might not be suspected to come from here.
> If you think anything in the little Letter suspicious, alter it as
> you please.[1]

Ford replied on the 6th, reporting that he had sent it to the
printer on the Sunday, and hopes it will soon be ready. He
thinks it equal to anything Swift had written, and feels that it
should do great service as matters stand at present. Apart
from minor corrections of spelling and tenses, he had made
no alterations, though he had hesitated about one phrase
concerning the Queen.

> There is so great a tenderness and regard shewn all along to
> the [Queen] that I could have wish'd this expression had been
> out, [the uncertain timorous nature of the ——] But there was
> no striking it out without quite spoiling the beauty of the
> passage, and as if I had been the Author myself, I preferr'd
> beauty to discretion.[2]

The mishaps and delays which prevented the publication of
the pamphlet are mentioned in the subsequent correspondence
between Swift and Ford; but it is enough to quote here Swift's
own memorandum, which he wrote on the first page of the
manuscript copy, when he gave it to Mrs. Whiteway on
June 15, 1737:

> This discourse was written at upper Letcomb in Berkshire,
> about two months before the Queens Death during my Retire-
> ment upon finding it impossible after above two years endeavor
> to reconcile My Lord Treasurer, and My Lord Bolingbroke;
> from the quarrel between which two great men all our misfor-
> tunes proceeded.
> The Papers were sent in an unknown hand to Mr. Barber the

---

[1] *Letters to Ford*, pp. 17–18.   [2] Ibid., p. 18.

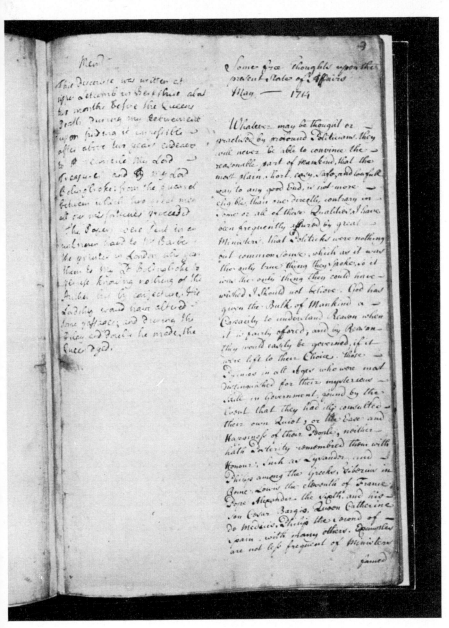

OPENING PAGE OF *Some free Thoughts*, IN SCRIBE'S HAND, WITH
MEMORANDUM ADDED BY SWIFT

(*By kind permission of Lord Rothschild*)

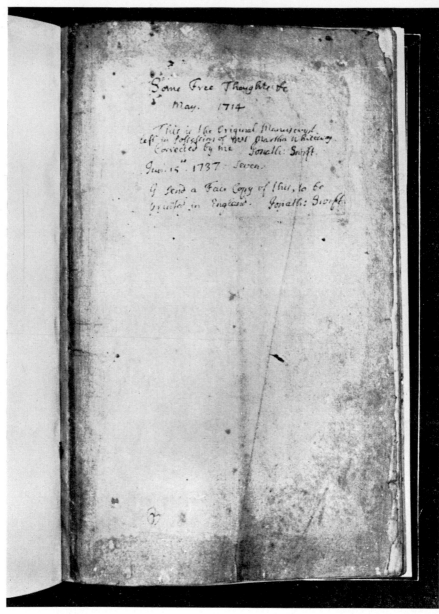

Some Free Thoughts &c
May. 1714

This is the Original Manuscript
left in Possession of Mrs Martha Whiteway.
Corrected by me Jonath: Swift.

Jun: 15th 1737 - Seven.

I send a Fair Copy of this, to be
printed in England. Jonath: Swift.

TITLE PAGE OF *Some free Thoughts* WITH ENDORSEMENT TO
MRS. WHITEWAY, IN SWIFT'S HAND
(*By kind permission of Lord Rothschild*)

printer in London who gave them to My Ld Bolingbroke to peruse, knowing nothing of the Author, but by conjecture. His Lordship would have altered some passages; and during the Delay and doubts he made, the Queen dyed.

Four years later, in May, 1741, it was printed by George Faulkner in Dublin, not from this manuscript, but from the copy which had been preserved by John Barber. It is a remarkable discourse, in which at the close of his public life in London, Swift gives his views on politics and politicians, writing in the mood of one who has already withdrawn from the centre of action, and was keeping himself aloof even before he went into the country. He begins with generalizations, in which he examines the fruits of his experience, and tries to separate the important from the trivial and to distinguish between the proper methods of reasonable statesmanship and the refinements of party politics, in order to discover if possible reasons for the strange fact that, after all that had been done in the last four years, the present Administration should be in such great distress: for 'at the minute I am now writing,' neither their Power nor Duration 'are upon any tolerable Foot of Security.' They had been put on the defensive in the House of Lords, and they were subject to the resentment of a section of their own party, the 'High Tories,' whose hopes had been disappointed. It was necessary for him to take up his old task as *Examiner*, and find out 'what Occasions the Ministry may have given for this Coldness, Inconstancy and Discontent among their Friends.' His cool analysis of the situation provides in part a defence, in part a criticism of the Treasurer:

> the want of a due Communication and Concert . . . this reserved mysterious way of acting, upon Points where there appeared not the least Occasion for it . . . was imputed to some hidden Design, which every Man conjectured to be the very Evil he was most afraid of.

The High Churchmen were led to suspect that a comprehension was intended, and others feared that there was a view of introducing the Pretender. Though obviously inconsistent, these reports weakened the support necessary to an administration concerned with the difficulties of negotiating a peace and handicapped by the exhausted condition of the country's resources. Yet with more unanimity and less refinement men of much less wisdom and ability would have come through.

Then, believing that sometimes others see better than ministers of state what are the general wishes of the people, Swift proceeds to point out what course ought to be steered. First, the Church of England must be preserved entire against its open enemies, the Dissenters, and its secret enemies, the Low Churchmen and Republicans. There must be no tampering with these factions; their friends should now be removed from all places in the army, particularly among those troops appointed to guard the Crown. Secondly, the Protestant Succession must be secured in the House of Hanover in accordance with the desire of the whole nation; it must not be allowed to become a topic of slander and suspicion. Here Swift returns to the matter which he had started to discuss in his *Discourse concerning the Fears from the Pretender* three months before. There can be no doubt that now as then he was entirely sincere in accepting the Hanoverian Succession, and equally sincere in his belief that there was no real danger that the Queen or her Ministers would take any steps to bring in the Pretender and accept a Roman Catholic as heir to the Crown. Swift must have seen clearly enough what a temptation it was for the Ministry to look for an alternative to the Hanoverian Succession; nevertheless he repeats his bold assertion:

> that excepting those who are Non-Jurers by Profession, I have not met with above two Persons who appeared to have any Scruples concerning the present Limitation of the Crown.

And later, when correcting the copy which he gave to Mrs. Whiteway, he wrote in the margin by the side of the following passage the words *The Author means himself*:

> I have likewise been assured by a Person of some Consequence, that during a very near and Constant Familiarity with the great Men at Court for four Years past, he never could observe even in those Hours of Conversation where there is usually least

Restraint, that one Word ever passed among them to shew a Dislike of the present Settlement, although they would sometimes lament that the false Representations of their's and the Kingdom's Enemies had made some Impressions in the Mind of the Successor.

And now, writing in the summer of 1714, not long before the death of the Queen, and—what is more important—not changing one word when he looked it over twenty years later, he solemnly states his conviction:

> From all these Considerations I must therefore lay it down as an uncontestible Truth, that the Succession to these Kingdoms in the illustrious House of Hannover is as firmly secured as the Nature of the Thing can possibly admit; by the Oaths of all who are entrusted with any Office, by the very Principles of those who are termed the High-Church, by the generall Inclinations of the People, by the Insignificancy of that Person who claims it either from Inheritance, and the little Assistance he can expect from Princes abroad or Adherents at home.

And, as if this were not enough, he goes further in recommending that an attempt should be made to meet the wishes of the Court of Hanover by inviting the eldest grandson of the Elector to come over to receive his maintenance and a title, and points out the advantage of having the infant Prince educated in English laws and manners and religion. At the same time he urges the Ministry to act more vigorously to lessen the power of the opposition as quickly as possible, a task which could be carried out with less difficulty, since the Queen herself was said to have lost all patience with them. Here again there is an implicit criticism of the trimming and the hesitant policy of the Treasurer, which could only lead to a weakening of the government and the certainty that they would lose their power entirely in a new reign. Nevertheless he felt that he had borne more hardly upon Bolingbroke, and when he heard that the manuscript of the pamphlet had been shown to him, he remembered some passages which he was willing to have modified. He wrote to Ford on July 18:

> Here's a Splutter with your nasty Pamphlet; I fancy, one of Ld B——'s alterations will be to soften a Particular that seems

to fall hard upon him: *Whether others have not contended for a greater Part in the Direction of Affairs* &c., *than either Friendship, Gratitude, or* &c. The Word *Gratitude* seems hard there, and may be left out; but I will not have any thing harder on the Dragon than it is.

And when he comes to the end of his letter, he adds the amusing comment:

> Upon second thoughts, how comicall a Thing was it to shew that Pamphlet to Ld Bol—— of all men living. Just as if *the Public Spirit* had been sent to Argyle for his Approbation.[1]

A week later, when there was still no sign of its being printed, Swift sent a second copy of the pamphlet to Ford, though he felt that it was then already too late to do any good; but he gave instructions that the following Preface should be printed before it:

> The annexed Papers were sen. a month ago to a very cautious Printer, with leave to shew them to any one Friend he had a Mind: The Person he shewed them to has kept them ever since in order to make some Alterations, and the time is almost lapsed wherein they might have done any Service. I shall no longer wait the Leisure either of that Printer or his Friend; If you do not think them worth a Publication, pray return them immediatly. I am Sr &c.[2]

But before Ford had time to arrange anything, on July 30, the Queen was taken ill, and died on the morning of August 1.

Oxford had been dismissed on July 27, and the Duke of Shrewsbury had taken his place on the 30th. Bolingbroke found himself entirely powerless on the death of the Queen, as he was not a member of the Privy Council nor one of the Regents who by the provision of the Act of Settlement were to act until the King arrived from Hanover.

Swift had recently applied for 'a Licence of Absence in generall, without specifying England' in case of difficulties; but Ford reminded him that he would have to take the Oaths in Ireland within three months. He therefore decided to set off for Dublin on August 16, promising Oxford and Boling-

---

[1] *Letters to Ford*, pp. 29, 31. The 'Dragon' was a nickname for the Treasurer.
[2] Ibid., pp. 38-9.

broke that he would return later if necessary. But it is clear from his letter to Ford on August 7 that he saw at once what would happen:

> I think the Regents agree pretty well in their Choice of Persons, and that we are this moment under the Height of a Whig Administration. . . . How a div—l do you gather from the List of R——ts that there will not be many removalls; they are all of the rankest Whigs, except 4 or 5 Proselytes, which is worse; at least such as quarrelled about the Peace and the Treatyes, and Danger of the Succession.
> . . . I am breeding another Pamphlet, but have not writt a Word of it. The Title will be something like this—Some Considerations upon the Consequences apprehended by the Qu——s Death. If I have humor I will write it here and upon the Road, and send it you from Ireland.[1]

He began to write two days later, as the fragment of the manuscript, now in the Forster Collection, is dated August 9, 1714. But he did not get far with it, and evidently did not continue to write when he was 'upon the Road.' The manuscript consists only of two folio leaves, written neatly in his small informal hand, on the right half of the page, ending near the top of page four. It is a short statement of what he had written more fully in his *History* about the change of ministry in 1710, and the difficult part thrust on the Treasurer between the Queen, who was 'in her own Nature extreamly dilatory and timorous' and the warm members of the party who pressed for a thorough change. Though he does not proceed far enough to come within sight of the immediate situation, it seems as though he must have started to write with the intention mainly of defending the Treasurer, prompted by his loyalty to one who had become so unpopular with both parties that there was little likelihood of his return to power, in spite of his protestations of devotion to the new king.[2]

On August 24 Swift wrote to Ford again from Ireland, and complained that he had not added one syllable to the thing he was about, which at London or Letcombe would have now been finished. He still talks of the possibility of coming over

---

[1] *Letters to Ford*, pp. 50–1.   [2] Ibid., p. 52 and *fn.*

again soon, though he says he cannot afford an idle journey
and will first be advised by Lewis and by Ford, whether it
would be of any use.[1] It was not until September 11 that the
fact of Bolingbroke's dismissal became known in Ireland, and
from the circumstances attending it Swift evidently realized
how things were moving, and that he would be left in exile
in Dublin 'to grow as stupid as the present situation of affairs
will require.' He realized also that his own efforts had been
wasted:

> The —— take this country: it has, in three weeks, spoiled
> two as good sixpenny pamphlets, as ever a proclamation was
> issued out against.[2]

Some Free Thoughts, &c. had been put aside to be printed in
better times, and *Some Considerations* was abandoned, though
the few pages of the manuscript were preserved together with
the rest of the material that Swift was keeping as a record of
the last years of the reign of the Queen.

But in his retirement he began the very next month to
write his *Memoirs*, turning back from a consideration of the
immediate situation to a time when, with the change of
ministry in 1710, he had first begun to play his part in public
affairs, and writing not as a pamphleteer to shape opinions
and influence action, but to provide 'an entertainment to
those who will have any personal regard for me or my
memory.' He may possibly have been prompted by the appearance of *The Secret History of the White Staff*, which had been
written by Defoe, using material supplied by Oxford. At any
rate, in a letter of October 19, Arbuthnot assumes that Swift
will have seen the pamphlet and would share his opinion of it,
as 'either contrived by an enemy, or by himself, to bring down
vengeance.'[3] Swift may have started to write with the intention of defending Oxford, left without a single friend among
the party; or he may have written, as he says, simply to satisfy
his particular friends—being able 'as one who was in the
secret of affairs' to explain some passages which they would
be glad to know the secret springs of.

---

[1] *Letters to Ford*, p. 60.   [2] *Corr.*, ii, 239, 240.   [3] *Corr.*, ii, 246.

He had wished to be appointed historiographer, to write the official history of her Majesty's reign, and had petitioned the Queen and the Earl of Oxford for the post and for the materials necessary for such a history;[1] but not having succeeded he determined nevertheless to give an account, though obliged to depend on his own memory of the events following the trial of Dr. Sacheverell, which led to the change of Ministry. This he is careful to indicate in the earlier part of the narrative by such phrases as 'I was told, and it was then generally reported'; 'I cannot engage for this passage, but the account he gave me was'; 'I remember, my Lord Somers complained to me.' But after he comes on the scene, he is able to give a direct and vivid account of all that he witnessed. Indeed, the chief interest of these *Memoirs* is that they are more personal than the other pamphlets in this volume. They provide an apology for Swift's political journalism, an account of his education and training in politics; and in particular they set forth the evidence that in his earlier writings on matters concerning the Church of England he had never been a 'favourer of the low-party.' They are brought to a close just at the moment of Harley's greatest influence and power, when, after Guiscard had attempted to assassinate him, and after his recovery, he was made an earl and Lord Treasurer, at the same time as St. John was made a viscount.

It was in a very different mood and under different circumstances that Swift was prompted to continue his memoirs in the form of *An Enquiry into the Behaviour of the Queen's Last Ministry*. In the middle of the winter, some time in January, 1714–15, he had received a warning from Erasmus Lewis to hide his papers, if he had not already done so. This was due to the alarm caused by the action taken against the Earl of Strafford and Prior, who had been required to surrender all their correspondence. Nevertheless Swift remained in Dublin until the usual time for his round of country visits, which lasted this year from the end of April until the middle of June. On June 10, the House of Commons had voted to impeach Oxford and Bolingbroke; and the Duke of Ormonde's impeach-

[1] See Appendix C.

ment had followed on June 21. Oxford remained and was imprisoned in the Tower, but the others fled to France. Swift himself was in some danger at this time, as letters to him from the Duke of Ormonde and from John Barber, the printer, had been intercepted. He writes from Dublin on June 21:

> I have been much entertained with news of myself since I came here: it is said there was another packet directed to me, seized by the Government, but after opening several seals it proved only plum-cake. I was this morning with the Archbishop who told me how kind he had been in preventing my being sent to etc. I said I had been a firm friend of the last Ministry, but thought it brought me to trouble myself in little parties without doing good, that I therefore expected the protection of the government, and that if I had been called before them, I would not have answered one syllable or named one person. . . . I have been named in many papers as proclaimed for five hundred pounds.[1]

And in a letter to Pope of June 28, he does not hide his anxiety:

> You know how well I loved both Lord Oxford and Boling-broke, and how dear the Duke of Ormonde is to me. Do you imagine I can be easy while their enemies are endeavouring to take off their heads? . . . Do you imagine I can be easy, when I think of the probable consequences of these proceedings, perhaps upon the very peace of the nation, but certainly of the minds of so many hundred thousand good subjects?[2]

In this mood, and at this very time Swift sat down to write his *Enquiry*. The news of the attainder of the Duke of Ormonde had only reached Dublin the day before, on June 27. But as this fact is referred to on the second page of the manuscript, Swift probably started to write at once, driven perhaps by his uneasiness, his distress and his astonishment at the news, 'which indeed neither they nor I, nor I believe any one Person in the three Kingdoms did ever pretend to foresee.'[3]

He evidently thought of leaving Dublin in July, but was

---

[1] *Corr.*, ii, 282-3.   [2] *Corr.*, ii, 286.
[3] If we may accept the endorsement made on the first page of Stella's copy, in her hand, 'begun June 1715,' Swift must have started some time between June 27 and June 30.

prevented by 'nasty foolish affairs of the Deanery,' and so stayed on during the rest of the year, going to Laracor towards the end of February, 1715–16.[1] He continued to work at the *Enquiry*, and seems even to have had in mind the possibility of printing it as a reply to some of the worst slanders on the Ministry. It might be 'of some use or satisfaction to examine' the two chief complaints. He had already done this in his *History* and again in his *Memoirs*, but they were 'neither of them fit to see the light at present.' He boldly proclaims himself the friend of the three persons accused of high treason, for he had little imagined himself to be perpetually in the company of traitors; but he promises to write with the utmost caution, and is 'resolved, for *very Materiall Reasons*, to avoyd giving the least Offence to any Party or Person in Power.' He often refers to his *History* where he had taken a good deal more liberty and realizes that it was 'consequently very unfit for present perusall.' But now he will only relate quite impartially what is safe and convenient.

He is, of course, concerned to defend the Earl of Oxford, even if it means shifting some of the responsibility for his hesitancy and delay in making appointments to the Queen who was suspicious of being advised; or placing the blame for their quarrels upon Bolingbroke's disappointed ambition, in being made only a viscount, which was the utmost the Queen was willing to allow. But he admits that Oxford had not understood the importance of Lady Masham's influence, and had lost the trust and confidence of his supporters by his unwillingness to take necessary action at the time of the great anxiety caused by the Queen's illness at Christmas, 1713. After continuing to examine the behaviour of the ministry until the time when he left them, in the spring of 1714, to retire into the country, he sums up his enquiry thus:

> I impute the Cause of these Misfortunes to the Queen, who . . . grew very difficult to be advised. The next in fault was the Treasurer. . . . However the Treasurer's Friends were yet much more to blame than Himself.

[1] *Corr.*, ii, 305.

C

Only this first chapter was finished in 1715. It is now possible, with the help of the manuscripts and the evidence provided in the letters to Ford, to give the story of the continuation of the *Enquiry*, and the corrections and changes that were made later.

Two manuscripts survive: an early draft in the hand of Swift, except the first leaf of text which was copied out by Stella, either because the outside leaves were no longer legible, or because they had been too much altered and required recopying; and a fair copy of this corrected draft, done by an amanuensis, with further corrections in the hand of Swift. With these before us we can follow the various stages of the composition, and observe the changes which Swift made from time to time as he took it out and planned for its publication; finally contenting himself with leaving these various copies carefully preserved, in the knowledge that they would ultimately be printed.

At the beginning of the second chapter Swift has written in the margin of the first draft: 'This Chapter seems to have been written about two years after the foregoing.' That would be the summer of 1717; and it is most probable that Swift resumed his enquiry soon after the trial and discharge of the Earl of Oxford. On May 27, Oxford had set forth the circumstances of his case and his long confinement in the Tower, and had petitioned the House of Lords that they would 'determine according to the rules of justice and course of Parliament.' After a report from the Committee on Precedents, the date June 6 was fixed for the trial; but in answer to a request from the House of Commons for more time for a review of all documents, it was postponed until June 24. There was a further disagreement between the two Houses of Parliament as to the order of procedure, and further delay, until finally, on July 1, Oxford was acquitted of all the articles of impeachment by a unanimous vote of all the Lords present.[1]

[1] See *Journals of the House of Lords*, XX, 472f.; *Journals of the House of Commons*, XVIII, 591f.

The next day Erasmus Lewis wrote to Swift to give him further details:

> The acclamations were as great as upon any occasion, and our friend, who seems more formed for adversity than prosperity, has at present many more friends than ever he had before, in any part of his life. I believe he will not have the fewer, from a message he received this morning from the King, by my Lord Chamberlain, to forbid him the Court. You know the prosecution was at first the resentment of a party, but it became at last a ridiculous business, weakly carried on by the impotent rage of a woman, I mean of my Lady Marlborough, who is almost distracted that she could not obtain her revenge.[1]

Swift immediately wrote to the Earl of Oxford, offering to attend him in his retirement in Herefordshire, if he should so desire. A week later on July 16, he wrote again, to say that

> if it doth not consist with your conveniency, the matter is at an end. But I imagine . . . I ought to see you and ask you some questions, and receive your instructions, concerning some things I have often spoken to you about, that might employ my leisure in the present situation of affairs, which we then easily foresaw, etc.[2]

It is clear from these letters that he was ready to continue his enquiry into the behaviour of the Queen's last ministry; and he could not have but been again stirred by the kindness of the reply he received from the Earl of Oxford in August:

> you will be welcome before anyone in the world.

This it is true was accompanied by what might be regarded as a warning:

> Our impatience to see you should not draw you into uneasiness. We long to embrace you, if you find it may be of no inconvenience to yourself.[3]

Swift was writing at this time to many of his friends in England, to Prior and to Addison and to Atterbury; and Lewis speaks of their expecting him, though they hear he is waiting for an Act of Grace.

But it was to be a long time before he would return to

---

[1] *Corr.*, ii, 391.   [2] *Corr.*, ii, 393, 395.   [3] *Corr.*, ii, 399.

England. Meanwhile we have the evidence of this manuscript
that he went on with the *Enquiry*, finishing it by 1720, when he
must have showed this original draft to Ford, who read it
and pointed out certain things in which Swift was mistaken.
Thereupon Swift made some corrections and revisions during
the winter of 1720–21, and then had a fair copy made by an
amanuensis. This is confirmed by a reference in the long
letter addressed to Pope, if I am right in dating this January,
1720–21:[1]

> These papers, at my few hours of health and leisure, I have been
> digesting into order by one sheet at a time, for I dare not venture
> any further, lest the humour of searching and seizing papers
> should revive.

And some months later in a letter to Ford of June 19, 1721,
he refers specifically to the *Enquiry*:

> I have finished that Tract you saw, where you said I was
> mistaken about some Persons; I mean Ld Poulet &c and I have
> some thoughts of sending that and the other Thing which was
> sent to you before the Qu—— died, and have them both printed
> in a Volume by some Whig Bookseller, by sending it to him at a
> venture.[2]

This mistake about Lord Poulett, whose name was originally
included in a list of ministers belonging to the low church
party, was corrected in the fair copy, the second manuscript,
which may therefore be dated as belonging to the early part
of 1721.

By that time, however, Swift had become involved in Irish
politics and was turning again from the writing of memoirs
to more direct action; and the manuscripts were put aside.
Nevertheless, later on, when the Drapier had done his work,
he picked up these manuscripts again and took pains to revise
them once more and to leave them in these various copies in
the hope that they would ultimately be printed for the instruction of posterity. For, when he was staying with his friends
the Achesons at Market Hill, in 1728, he wrote to Sheridan

---

[1] See Vol. IX of this edition, pp. xii, *fn.*, and 26.
[2] *Letters to Ford*, pp. 93–4.

on September 18, asking him to get from the Deanery the fair copies of these papers:

> I desire you will step to the Deanery, speak to Mrs. Brent, bid her open the middle great drawer of Ridgeway's escritoire in my closet, and then do you take out from thence the History in folio, marble cover; and two thin folios fairly writ, I forget the titles, but you have read them, one is an account of the proceedings of Lord Oxford's Ministry, and the other to the same purpose. There are foul copies of both in the same drawer, but do you take out the fair ones, not in my hand. Let them be packed up and brought hither by the bearer.[1]

The variety of inks and the difference in the hands still recognizable in the corrections and alterations of this fair copy show that Swift returned to it again and again, though it is not possible to follow the order in which the more important changes were introduced. But the notes in Mrs. Whiteway's hand[2] could hardly have been written before her intimacy with Swift began, about 1734; and his fresh concern with the *Enquiry* which prompted those notes was probably connected with the plans for publishing the *History*, which engaged him in 1735 and 1736, when he was considering whether to add material from the *Memoirs* and the *Enquiry* and make one work out of them all, or to print the two shorter pieces 'by way of appendix.'[3]

It was in June, 1737, that Swift presented his original manuscripts to Mrs. Whiteway, and though the leaf containing the title of this manuscript is now lost, Forster had made the following copy of it:

> An Enquiry &c. This the original Manuscript
> Corrected by Me, and Given into the Custody of
> Mrs Martha Whiteway by Me   Jonathan
> Swift. June 1737——seven.   Memdum
> I send a fair copy of this by the Earl of
> Orrery to be printed in England   Jonathan Swift.[4]

This probably refers to the first copy by an amanuensis, with the corrections in Swift's hand, and not to the original foul

---

[1] *Corr.*, iv, 43–4.   [2] See below, p. 174.   [3] *Corr.*, v, 392, 401.
[4] From a notebook in the Forster Collection, item 547, fol. 3.

copy. It was probably another copy of the corrected MS which Swift gave to Orrery to take to Dr. William King in Oxford. For Mrs. Whiteway gave the original draft and the corrected copy to her son-in-law, Deane Swift, who printed the *Enquiry* for the first time in 1765, when he edited Volume VIII of the quarto edition of Swift's *Works*, published in London. In March 1765, he announced that he intended to give these manuscripts to the British Museum, but evidently decided to keep them until he should have finished a new edition of Swift, which he had in mind. He also at one time thought of burning them. But they were still in his possession at the time of his death, and they remained in the family until they were bought by Forster about 1860, from whom they passed to his publisher John Murray, whose grandson sold them to Lord Rothschild in 1935.

A study of the two manuscripts of the *Enquiry* not only provides evidence of the manner and time of its composition, but it shows that again in this last discussion of public affairs at the end of the Queen's reign, he found no reason to change his views materially over the course of the twenty years following her death. The corrections that he made from time to time are mainly changes in a word or phrase, or slight omissions to give clarity and conciseness. Often they are made only to prevent repetition of a word or syllable; and they show again how sensitive Swift remained to the sound of his sentences when read. They show also his concern with the look of the printed page and his dislike of such abbreviated forms as *tho'*, *altho'*, etc.

A study of the textual notes will provide examples of the more important changes, where we can watch him at work on a passage which does not satisfy him, altering it several time until finally it is precisely what he wants. We can see possibilities of misunderstanding or vague suggestions being removed. For instance, in commenting on the Queen's relations with Lady Masham, he first wrote that when she made a request, the Queen would often 'refuse it, and reproach her with too much Violence.' This is ambiguous, and is therefore reduced to 'blame her as too violent,' then again still further to 'refuse, and seem displeased.' But this, in its bareness, asks for a statement of the reason for her displeasure; and so we reach the final form, which is exact and unambiguous—'refuse, and at the same time condemn her for too much Party Zeal.' Nothing is too small to escape his attention, if a blur can be removed, leaving a sharper delineation: thus 'Changes so long expected' become 'Change of Employments'; 'Paper' is altered to 'Warrant.' Sometimes he deliberately increases the weight of his disapproval: the Whigs' 'slight and mean Causes' become 'the lowest, vilest and obscurest Causes.' Rarely, he will modify his own point of view: in his final comment, after many changes, on the creation of the twelve peers, he admits that he himself 'did very much dislike' the proceeding.[1]

In general it may be said of all these memoirs, undertaken after his active participation in public affairs was over, that they were seriously written and carefully revised to provide an account of the four last years of the Queen's reign by one, who had had an unusual opportunity of observing the work of the ministry from the inside. They are none the.less valid in being the work of one whose party and personal loyalties are never disguised, and who seems to write with the intention of pursuing his enemies and witnessing against them to later generations. Though he had never been appointed historiographer, he insisted on carrying out the duties of that office and making himself an apologist of the Queen and her last ministry. For that reason, perhaps, he preferred to leave these separate documents, as he had originally written them under certain particular circumstances, rather than use them as the material for one complete account, rewritten as history.

He found a better way to use them and to enrich them with all that he had learned in his experience of public life. For seven years he had brooded over his papers and his memoirs, cut off from his English friends and 'writing nothing but Verses . . . all Panegyricks';[2] until he became involved again in the affairs of Ireland, which provided another opportunity of opposing his old enemies. But now, in 1721, at the age of fifty-four, he began work on an entirely new kind of book,

[1] See below, p. 152.   [2] *Letters to Ford*, p. 84.

which would give him full scope for all his powers as a wit, an ironist, a teller of tales, and which would be read by Whigs and Tories, by Churchmen and Dissenters, by young and old; and where under a new disguise he would be able to comment as freely as he liked on all these impeachments and the foolishness and bitterness of party politics, and as that innocent traveller, Lemuel Gulliver, voyaging about the world, indulge in all kinds of enquiries and write down his memoirs and his free thoughts on the world's affairs.

It was in June 1721, as he was packing up to leave for the country, that he reported to Ford that he had finished his work on the *Enquiry* and *Some free Thoughts* and was thinking of sending them at a venture to some Whig bookseller to have them printed together in a volume. But before then he was already beginning to use this material for his new work, which is first announced, casually in the midst of trivial gossip, in a letter of April 15:

> Are not these fine materialls for a Letter; but I have no others.—
> I am now writing a History of my Travells, which will be a large
> Volume, and gives Account of Countryes hitherto unknown.[1]

[1] *Letters to Ford*, p. 92.

The Importance of the *Guardian* Considered

THE
IMPORTANCE
OF THE
GUARDIAN

Confidered, in a Second

LETTER

TO THE

Bailiff of *Stockbridge*.

By a Friend of Mr. *St—le*.

LONDON:

Printed for *John Morphew*, near *Stationers Hall.* 1713. Price 6 *d*.

THE

PREFACE.

MR. Steele *in his Letter to the Bailiff of* Stockbridge *has given us leave to* treat him as we think fit, as he is our Brother-Scribler; but not to attack him as an honest Man. *That is to say, he allows us to be his* Criticks, *but not his* Answerers; *and he is altogether in the right, for there is in his Letter much to be* Criticised, *and little to be* Answered. *The Situation and Importance of* Dunkirk *are pretty well known,* Monsieur Tugghe's *Memorial, published and handed about by the* Whigs, *is allowed to be a very Trifling Paper: And as to the immediate Demolishment of that Town, Mr.* Steele *pretends to offer no other Argument but the* Expectations *of the People, which is a figurative Speech, naming the tenth Part for the whole: As* Bradshaw *told King* Charles I. *that the People of* England Expected *Justice against him. I have therefore entred very little into the Subject he pretends to* Treat, *but have considered his Pamphlet partly as a* Critick, *and partly as a* Commentator, *which, I think, is to treat* him only as my Brother-Scribler, *according to the Permission he has graciously allowed me.*

To the Worshipful

Mr. *JOHN SNOW.*

Bailiff of *Stockbridge.*

SIR,

I Have just been reading a Twelve-peny Pamphlet about *Dunkirk*, addressed to your Worship from one of your intended Representatives; and I find several Passages in it which want Explanation, especially to You in the Country: For we in Town have a way of Talking and Writing, which is very little understood beyond the Bills of Mortality. I have therefore made bold to send you here a second Letter, by way of Comment upon the former.

In order to this, *You Mr.* Bailiff, *and at the same time the whole Burrough*, may please to take Notice, that *London*-Writers often put Titles to their Papers and Pamphlets which have little or no Reference to the main Design of the Work: So, for Instance, you will observe in reading, that the Letter called, *The Importance of Dunkirk*, is chiefly taken up in shewing you the *Importance* of Mr. *Steele*; wherein it was indeed reasonable your Burrough should be informed, which had chosen him to Represent them.

I would therefore place the *Importance* of this Gentleman before you in a clearer Light than he has given himself the Trouble to do; without running into his early History, because I owe him no Malice.

Mr. *Steele* is Author of two tolerable Plays, (or at least of the greatest part of them) which, added to the Company he kept, and to the continual Conversation and Friendship of Mr. *Addison*, hath given him the Character of a Wit. To take the height of his Learning, you are to suppose a Lad just fit for the University, and sent early from thence into the wide World, where he followed every way of Life that might least improve or preserve the Rudiments he had got. He hath no Invention, nor is Master of a tolerable Style; his chief Talent is Humour, which he sometimes discovers both in Writing and Discourse; for after the first Bottle he is no disagreeable Companion. I never knew him taxed with Ill-nature, which hath made me wonder how Ingratitude came to be his prevailing Vice; and I am apt to think it proceeds more from some unaccountable sort of Instinct, than Premeditation. Being the most imprudent Man alive, he never follows the Advice of his Friends, but is wholly at the mercy of Fools or Knaves, or hurried away by his own Caprice; by which he hath committed more Absurdities in Oeconomy, Friendship, Love, Duty, good Manners, Politicks, Religion and Writing, than ever fell to one Man's share. He was appointed Gazetteer by Mr. *Harley* (then Secretary of State) at the Recommendation of Mr. *Mainwaring*, with a Salary of Three Hundred Pounds; was a Commissioner of Stampt-Paper of equal Profit, and had a Pension of a Hundred Pound *per Annum*, as a Servant to the late Prince *George*.

This Gentleman, whom I have now described to you, began between four and five Years ago to publish a Paper thrice a Week, called the *Tatler*; It came out under the borrowed Name of *Isaac Bickerstaff*, and by Contribution of his ingenious Friends, grew to have a great Reputation, and was equally esteemed by both Parties, because it meddled with neither. But, sometime after *Sacheverell*'s Tryal, when Things began to change their Aspect; Mr. *Steele*, whether by the Command of his Superiors, his own Inconstancy, or the Absence of his Assistants, would needs corrupt his Paper with Politicks; published one or two most virulent Libels, and chose for his Subject even that individual Mr. *Harley*, who had made him Gazetteer. But his Finger and Thumb not proving strong enough to stop the general Torrent, there was an universal Change made in the Ministry; and the Two new Secretaries, not thinking it decent to employ a Man in their Office who had acted so infamous a Part; Mr. *Steele*, to avoid being dis-carded, thought fit to resign his Place of Gazetteer. Upon which occasion I cannot forbear relating a Passage *to You Mr. Bailiff, and the rest of the Burrough*, which discovers a very peculiar Turn of Thought in this Gentleman you have chosen to Represent you. When Mr. *Mainwaring* recommended him to the Employment of Gazetteer, Mr. *Harley* out of an Inclination to encourage Men of Parts, raised that Office from Fifty Pound to Three Hundred Pound a Year; Mr. *Steele* according to form, came to give his new Patron Thanks; but the Secretary, who had rather confer a hundred Favours than receive Acknowledgments for one, said to him in a most obliging manner: Pray Sir, do not thank me, but thank Mr. *Mainwaring*. Soon after Mr. *Steele's* quitting that Employment, he complained to a Gentleman in Office, of the Hardship put upon him in being forced to quit his Place; that he knew Mr. *Harley* was the Cause; that he never had done Mr. *Harley* any Injury, nor received any Obligation from him. The Gentleman amazed at this Discourse, put him in mind of those Libels published in his *Tatlers:* Mr. *Steele* said, he was only the Publisher, for they had been sent him by other Hands. The Gentleman thinking this a very monstrous kind of Excuse, and not allowing it, Mr. *Steele* then said, Well, I have Libelled him, and he has turned me out, and so we are equal. But neither would this be granted: And he was asked whether the Place of Gazetteer were not an Obligation? No, said he, not from Mr. *Harley*; for when I went to thank him, he forbad me, and said, I must only thank Mr. *Mainwaring*.

But I return, Mr. Bailiff, to give you a further Account of this Gentleman's Importance. In less, I think, than Two Years, the Town and He grew weary of the *Tatler:* He was silent for some Months; and then a daily Paper came from him and his Friends under the Name of *Spectator*, with good Success: This being likewise dropt after a certain Period, he hath of late appeared under the Style of *Guardian*, which he hath now likewise quitted for that of *Englishman*; but having chosen other Assistance, or trusting more to himself, his Papers have been very coldly received, which hath made him fly for Relief to the never-failing Source of Faction.

On the . . . . . of *August* last, Mr. *Steele* writes a Letter to *Nestor Ironside*, Esq; and subscribes it with the Name of *English Tory*. On the 7th the said *Ironside* publishes this Letter

in the *Guardian*. How shall I explain this Matter to you, Mr.
Bailiff, and your Brethren of the Burrough? You must know
then, that Mr. *Steele* and Mr. *Ironside* are the same Persons,
because there is a great Relation between *Iron* and *Steel*;
and *English Tory* and Mr. *Steele* are the same Persons, because
there is no Relation at all between Mr. *Steele* and an *English
Tory*; so that to render this Matter clear to the very meanest
Capacities, Mr. *English Tory*, the very same Person with Mr.
Steele, writes a Letter to *Nestor Ironside*, Esq; who is the same
Person with *English Tory*, who is the same Person with Mr.
Steele: And Mr. *Ironside*, who is the same Person with *English
Tory*, publishes the Letter written by *English Tory*, who is the
same Person with Mr. *Steele*, who is the same Person with Mr.
Ironside. This Letter written and published by these *Three*
Gentlemen who are *One* of your Representatives, complains
of a printed Paper in *French* and *English*, lately handed about
the Town, and given *gratis* to Passengers in the Streets at
Noon-day; the Title whereof is, *A most humble Address or
Memorial presented to Her Majesty the Queen of* Great Britain, *by
the Deputy of the Magistrates of* Dunkirk. This Deputy, it seems,
is called the Sieur *Tugghe*. Now, the Remarks made upon this
Memorial by Mr. *English Tory*, in his Letter to Mr. *Ironside*,
happening to provoke the *Examiner*, and another Pamphleteer,
they both fell hard upon Mr. *Steele*, charging him with
Insolence and Ingratitude towards the Queen. But Mr. *Steele*
nothing daunted, writes a long Letter *to you Mr. Bailiff, and at
the same time to the whole Burrough*, in his own Vindication: But
there being several difficult Passages in this Letter, which may
want clearing up, I here send you and the Burrough my
Annotations upon it.

Mr. *Steele* in order to display his *Importance* to your Bur-
rough, begins his Letter by letting you know *he is no small
Man*; because in the Pamphlets he hath sent you down, you
will *find him spoken of more than once in Print*. It is indeed a great
Thing to be *spoken of in Print*, and must needs make a mighty
Sound at *Stockbridge* among the Electors. However, if Mr.
Steele has really sent you down all the Pamphlets and Papers
printed since the Dissolution, you will find he is not the only

Person of Importance; I could Instance *Abel Roper*, Mr. *Marten* the Surgeon, Mr. *John Moor* the Apothecary at the Pestle and Mortar, Sir *William Read*, Her Majesty's Oculist, and of later Name and Fame, Mr. *John Smith* the Corncutter, with several others who are *spoken of more than once in Print.* Then he recommends to your Perusal, and sends you a Copy of a printed Paper given *gratis* about the Streets, which is the Memorial of Monsieur *Tugghe* (above-mentioned) *Deputy of the Magistrates of Dunkirk,* to desire Her Majesty not to demolish the said Town. He tells you how insolent a Thing it is, that such a Paper should be publickly distributed, and he tells you true; but these Insolences are very frequent among the Whigs: One of their present Topicks for Clamour is *Dunkirk:* Here is a Memorial said to be presented to the Queen by an obscure *Frenchman:* One of your Party gets a Copy, and immediately Prints it by Contribution, and delivers it *gratis* to the People; which answers several Ends. *First,* It is meant to lay an Odium on the Ministry; *Secondly,* If the Town be soon demolished, Mr. *Steele* and his Faction have the Merit, their Arguments and Threatnings have frighted my Lord Treasurer' *Thirdly,* If the Demolishing should be further deferred, the Nation will be fully convinced of his Lordship's Intention to bring over the *Pretender.*

Let us turn over fourteen Pages, which contain the Memorial it self, and which is indeed as idle a one as ever I read; we come now to Mr. *Steele*'s Letter under the Name of *English Tory,* to Mr. *Ironside.* In the Preface to this Letter, he hath these Words, *It is certain there is not much danger in delaying the Demolition of* Dunkirk *during the Life of his present most Christian Majesty, who is renowned for the most inviolable Regard to Treaties; but that pious Prince is Aged, and in case of his Decease,* &c. This Preface is in the Words of Mr. *Ironside* a professed Whig, and perhaps you in the Country will wonder to hear a Zealot of your own Party celebrating the *French* King for his Piety and his religious Performance of Treaties. For this I can assure you is not spoken in jest, or to be understood by contrary; There is a wonderful resemblance between that Prince and the Party of Whigs among us. Is he for arbitrary Government?

D

So are they: Hath he persecuted Protestants? So have the
Whigs: Did he attempt to restore King *James* and his pretended Son? They did the same. Would he have *Dunkirk* surrendred to him? This is what they desire. Does he call himself
the *Most Christian*? The Whigs assume the same Title, though
their Leaders deny Christianity: Does he break his Promises?
Did they ever keep theirs?

From the 16th to the 38th Page Mr. *Steele*'s Pamphlet is
taken up with a Copy of his Letter to Mr. *Ironside*, the Remarks
of the *Examiner*, and another Author upon that Letter; the
Hydrography of some *French* and *English* Ports, and his
Answer to Mr. *Tugghe*'s Memorial. The Bent of his Discourse
is in appearance to shew of what prodigious Consequence
to the Welfare of *England*, the Surrendry of *Dunkirk* was.
But here, Mr. Bailiff, you must be careful; for all this is said in
Raillery; for you may easily remember, that when the Town
was first yielded to the Queen, the Whigs declared it was of no
Consequence at all, that the *French* could easily repair it after
the Demolition, or fortify another a few Miles off, which
would be of more Advantage to them. So that what Mr. *Steele*
tells you of the prodigious Benefit that will accrue to *England*
by destroying this Port, is only suited to present Junctures and
Circumstances. For if *Dunkirk* should now be represented as
insignificant as when it was first put into Her Majesty's Hands,
it would signify nothing whether it were demolished or no,
and consequently one principal Topick of Clamour would fall
to the Ground.

In Mr. *Steele*'s Answer to Monsieur *Tugghe*'s Arguments
against the Demolishing of *Dunkirk*, I have not observed any
thing that so much deserves your peculiar Notice, as the great
Eloquence of your new Member, and his wonderful Faculty
of varying his Style, which he calls, *proceeding like a Man of
great Gravity and Business*. He has Ten Arguments of *Tugghe*'s
to answer; and because he will not go in the old beaten Road,
like a Parson of a Parish, *First*, *Secondly*, *Thirdly*, &c. his manner
is this,

> In answer to the Sieur's *First*.
> As to the Sieur's *Second*.

As to his *Third*.
As to the Sieur's *Fourth*.
As to Mr. Deputy's *Fifth*.
As to the Sieur's *Sixth*.
As to this Agent's *Seventh*.
As to the Sieur's *Eighth*.
As to his *Ninth*.
As to the Memorialist's *Tenth*.

You see every Second Expression is more or less diversified to avoid the Repetition of, *As to the Sieur's*, &c. and there is the Tenth into the Bargain: I could heartily wish Monsieur *Tugghe* had been able to find Ten Arguments more, and thereby given Mr. *Steele* an Opportunity of shewing the utmost Variations our Language would bear in so momentous a Tryal.

Mr. *Steele* tells you, That having now done *with his foreign Enemy Monsieur* Tugghe, *he must face about to his Domestick Foes, who accuse him of Ingratitude and insulting his Prince, while he is eating her Bread.*

To do him Justice, he acquits himself pretty tolerably of this last Charge: For he assures You, he gave up his Stampt-Paper-Office, and Pension as Gentleman-Usher, before he writ that Letter to himself in the *Guardian*, so that he had already received his Salary, and spent the Money, and consequently the *Bread was eaten* at least a Week before he would offer to *insult his Prince:* So that the Folly of the Examiner's objecting Ingratitude to him upon this Article, is manifest to all the World.

But he tells you, he has quitted those Employments to render him more useful to his Queen and Country in the Station you have honoured him with. That, no doubt, was the principal Motive; however, I shall venture to add some others. *First,* The *Guardian* apprehended it impossible, that the Ministry would let him keep his Place much longer, after the Part he had acted for above two Years past. *Secondly,* Mr. *Ironside* said publickly, that he was ashamed to be obliged any longer to a Person (meaning Lord *Treasurer*) whom he had used so ill: For it seems, a Man ought not to use his Benefactors ill above two Years and a half. *Thirdly*, The *Sieur Steele* appeals for Protection to you, Mr. Bailiff, from *others* of your *Denomination*, who would have carried him *some where else*, if you had not removed him by your *Habeas Corpus* to St. *Stephen*'s Chapel. *Fourthly*, Mr. *English Tory* found, by calculating the Life of a Ministry, that it hath lasted above three Years, and is near expiring; he resolved therefore to *strip off the very Garments spotted with the Flesh*, and be wholly regenerate against the Return of his old Masters.

In order to serve all these Ends, your Burrough hath honoured him (as he expresses it) with chusing him to represent you in Parliament, and it must be owned, he hath equally honoured you. Never was Burrough more happy in suitable Representatives, than you are in Mr. *Steele* and his Collegue, nor were ever Representatives more happy in a suitable Burrough.

When Mr. *Steele* talk'd of *laying before Her Majesty's Ministry, that the Nation has a strict Eye upon their Behaviour with relation to* Dunkirk, Did not you, Mr. Bailiff, and your Brethren of the Burrough presently imagine, he had drawn up a sort of Counter-Memorial to that of Monsieur *Tugghe*'s, and presented it in form to my Lord *Treasurer*, or a Secretary of State? I am confident you did; but this comes by not understanding the Town: You are to know then, that Mr. *Steele* publishes every Day a Peny-paper to be read in Coffee-houses, and get him a little Money. This by a Figure of Speech, he calls, *laying Things before the Ministry*, who seem at present a little too busy to regard such Memorials; and, I dare say, never saw his Paper, unless he sent it them by the Peny-Post.

Well, but he tells you, he *cannot offer against the* Examiner *and his other Adversary, Reason and Argument without appearing void of both*. What a singular Situation of the Mind is this! How glad should I be to hear a Man *offer Reasons and Argument, and yet at the same time appear void of both*! But this whole Paragraph is of a peculiar strain; the Consequences so Just and Natural, and such a Propriety in Thinking, as few Authors ever arrived to. *Since it has been the Fashion to run down Men of much greater Consequence than I am; I will not bear the Accusation.*

This I suppose is, *to offer Reasons and Arguments, and yet appear void of both*. And in the next Lines; *These Writers shall treat me as they think fit, as I am their Brother-Scribler, but I shall not be so unconcerned when they attack me as an honest Man*. And how does he defend himself? *I shall therefore inform them that it is not in the Power of a private Man, to hurt the Prerogative*, &c. Well; I shall *treat* him *only as a Brother-Scribler:* And I guess he will hardly be attacked as an honest Man: But if his meaning be that his Honesty ought not to be attacked, because he *has no Power to hurt the Honour and Prerogative of the Crown without being punished*; he will make an admirable Reasoner in the House of Commons.

But all this wise Argumentation was introduced, only to close the Paragraph by haling in a Fact, which he relates to you and your Burrough, in order to quiet the Minds of the People, and express his Duty and Gratitude to the Queen. The Fact is this; That *Her Majesty's Honour is in danger* of being lost *by Her Ministers tolerating Villains without Conscience to abuse the greatest Instruments of Honour and Glory to our Country, the most Wise and Faithful Managers, and the most Pious, disinterested, generous, and self-denying Patriots*; And the Instances he produces, are the Duke of *Marlborough*, the late Earl of *Godolphin*, and about two Thirds of the Bishops.

Mr. Bailiff, I cannot debate this Matter at length, without putting you and the rest of my Countrymen, who will be at the Expence, to Six-pence Charge extraordinary. The Duke and Earl were both removed from their Employments; and I hope you have too great a Respect for the Queen, to think it was done for nothing. The former was *at the Head* of many great Actions; and he has received plentiful Oblations of Praise and Profit: Yet having read all that ever was objected against him by the *Examiner*, I will undertake to prove every Syllable of it true, particularly that famous Attempt to be General for Life. The Earl of *Godolphin* is dead, and his Faults may sojourn with him in the Grave, 'till some Historian shall think fit to revive part of them for Instruction and Warning to Posterity. But it grieved me to the Soul, to see so many good Epithets bestowed by Mr. *Steele* upon the Bishops: Nothing has done more hurt to that Sacred Order for some Years past, than to hear some Prelates extolled by Whigs, Dissenters, Republicans, Socinians, and in short by all who are Enemies to Episcopacy. God, in his Mercy, for ever keep our Prelates from deserving the Praises of such Panegyrists!

Mr. *Steele* is discontented that the Ministry have not *called the* Examiner *to Account as well as the* Flying-Post. I will inform you, Mr. Bailiff, how that Matter stands. The Author of the *Flying-Post* has thrice a Week for above Two Years together, published the most impudent Reflections upon all the present Ministry, upon all their Proceedings, and upon the whole Body of *Tories*. The *Examiner* on the other side, writing in Defence of those whom Her Majesty employs in her greatest Affairs, and of the Cause they are engaged in, hath always borne hard upon the Whigs, and now and then upon some of their Leaders. Now, Sir, we reckon here, that supposing the Persons on both Sides to be of equal Intrinsick Worth, it is more Impudent, Immmoral, and Criminal to reflect on a *Majority* in Power, than a *Minority* out of Power. Put the Case, that an odd Rascally Tory in your Borough should presume to abuse your Worship who, in the Language of Mr. *Steele*, is first Minister, and the Majority of your Brethren, for sending Two such Whig-Representatives up to Parliament: And on the other side, that an honest Whig should stand in your Defence, and fall foul on the Tories; would you equally resent the Proceedings of both, and let your Friend and Enemy sit in the Stocks together? Hearken to another Case, Mr. Bailiff; suppose your Worship, during your Annual Administration, should happen to be kick'd and cuff'd by a parcel of Tories, would not the Circumstance of your being a Magistrate, make the Crime the greater, than if the like Insults were committed on an ordinary Tory Shopkeeper, by a Company of honest Whigs? What Bailiff would venture to Arrest Mr. *Steele*, now he has the Honour to be your Representative? and what Bailiff ever scrupled it before?

You must know, Sir, that we have several Ways here of abusing one another, without incurring the Danger of the Law. First, we are careful never to print a Man's Name out at length;

but as I do that of Mr. *Steele:** So that although every Body alive knows whom I mean, the Plaintiff can have no Redress in any Court of Justice. Secondly, by putting Cases; Thirdly, by Insinuations; Fourthly, by celebrating the Actions of others, who acted directly contrary to the Persons we would reflect on; Fifthly, by Nicknames, either commonly known or stamp'd for the purpose, which every Body can tell how to apply. Without going on further, it will be enough to inform you, that by some of the ways I have already mentioned, Mr. *Steele* gives you to understand, that the Queen's Honour is blasted by the Actions of Her present Ministers; that Her *Prerogative is disgraced by erecting a dozen Peers, who, by their Votes, turned a Point upon which Your All depended;* That *these Ministers made the Queen lay down Her conquering Arms, and deliver Her Self up to be vanquish'd; That they made Her Majesty betray Her Allies, by ordering Her Army to face about, and leave them in the Moment of Distress; That the present Ministers are Men of poor and narrow Conceptions, Self-Interested, and without Benevolence to Mankind; and were brought into Her Majesty's Favour for. the Sins of the Nation, and only think what they may do, not what they ought to do.* This is the Character given by Mr. *Steele* of those Persons, whom Her Majesty has thought fit to place in the highest Stations of the Kingdom, and to trust them with the Management of Her most weighty Affairs: And this is the Gentleman who cries out, *Where is Honour? Where is Government? Where is Prerogative?* Because the *Examiner* has sometimes dealt freely with those, whom the Queen has thought fit to *Discard,* and the Parliament to *Censure.*

But Mr. *Steele* thinks it highly dangerous to the Prince, *that any Man should be hindered from offering his Thoughts upon public Affairs;* and resolves to do it, *tho' with the Loss of Her Majesty's Favour.* If a Clergy-man offers to preach Obedience to the higher Powers, and proves it by Scripture, Mr. *Steele* and his Fraternity immediately cry out, What have Parsons to do with Politicks? I ask, What shadow of a Pretence has he to offer his crude Thoughts in Matters of State? to Print and Publish them? *to lay them before the Queen and Ministry?* and to

* The name in the original edition was regularly spelled with a dash, *St——.*

reprove Both for Male-Administration? How did he acquire these Abilities of directing in the Councils of Princes? Was it from 𝔓𝔲𝔟𝔩𝔦𝔰𝔥𝔦𝔫𝔤 *Tatlers* and *Spectators*, and Writing now and then a *Guardian?* Was it from his being a Soldier, Alchymist, Gazetteer, Commissioner of Stampt Papers, or Gentleman-Usher? No; but he insists it is every Man's Right to find fault with the Administration in Print, whenever they please: And therefore you, Mr. Bailiff, and as many of your Brethren in the Borough as can Write and Read, may publish Pamphlets, and *lay them before the Queen and Ministry,* to shew your utter dislike of all their Proceedings; and for this Reason, because you *can certainly see and apprehend with your own Eyes and Understanding, those Dangers which the* Ministers *do not.*

One thing I am extreamly concerned about, that Mr. *Steele* resolves, as he tells you, when he comes into the House, *to follow no Leaders, but Vote according to the Dictates of his Conscience;* He must, at that rate, be a very useless Member to his Party, unless his Conscience be already cut out and shaped for their Service, which I am ready to believe it is, if I may have leave to judge from the whole Tenor of his Life. I would only have his Friends be cautious, not to reward him too liberally: For, as it was said of *Cranmer, Do the Archbishop an ill Turn, and he is your Friend for ever:* So I do affirm of your Member, *Do Mr.* Steele *a good Turn, and he is your Enemy for ever.*

I had like to let slip a very trivial Matter (which I should be sorry to have done). In reading this Pamphlet, I observed several Mistakes, but knew not whether to impute them to the Author or Printer; till turning to the end, I found there was only one *Erratum*, thus set down, *Pag.* 45. *Line* 28. *for* Admonition *read* Advertisement. This (to imitate Mr. *Steele*'s Propriety of Speech) is a very *old* Practice among *new* Writers, to make a wilful Mistake, and then put it down as an *Erratum.* The Word is brought in upon this Occasion: To convince all the World that he was not guilty of Ingratitude, by reflecting on the Queen, when he was actually under Sallary, as the *Examiner* affirms; he assures you, he *had resign'd and divested himself of all, before he would presume to write any thing which was so apparently an* ADMONITION *to those employed in Her Majesty's Service.* In

case the *Examiner* should find fault with this Word, he might
Appeal to the *Erratum*; and having formerly been *Gazetteer*,
he conceived he might very safely venture to *Advertise*.

You are to understand, Mr. Bailiff, that in the great Rebellion
against King *Charles* I. there was a Distinction found out
between the *Personal* and *Political* Capacity of the Prince; by
the help of 'which, those Rebels professed to Fight for the
King, while the great Guns were discharging against *Charles
Stuart*. After the same manner Mr. S*teele* distinguishes between
the *Personal* and *Political* Prerogative. He does not care to trust
this Jewel *to the Will, and Pleasure, and Passion of Her Majesty*.
If I am not mistaken, the Crown-Jewels cannot be alienated
by the Prince; but I always thought the Prince could *wear*
them during his Reign, else they had as good be in the Hands of
the Subject: So, I conceive, Her Majesty may and ought to
wear the Prerogative; that it is Her's during Life; and She ought
to be so much the more careful, neither to soil nor diminish it,
for that very Reason, because it is by Law unalienable. But
what must we do with this Prerogative, according to the
notion of Mr. *Steele?* It must not be trusted with the Queen,
because Providence has given Her *Will, Pleasure, and Passion*.
Her Ministers must not act by the Authority of it; for then Mr.
Steele will cry out, What? *Are Majesty and Ministry consolidated?
And must there be no Distinction between the one and the other?* He
tells you, *The Prerogative attends the Crown*; and therefore, I
suppose, must lie in the *Tower* to be shewn for Twelve pence,
but never produced, except at a Coronation, or passing an Act.
Well; but says he, *A whole Ministry may be Impeached and condemned by the House of Commons, without the Prince's suffering by it:*
And what follows? Why, therefore a single Burgess of *Stockbridge*, before he gets into the House, may at any time Revile a
whole Ministry in Print, before he knows whether they are
guilty of any one Neglect of Duty, or Breach of Trust.

I am willing to join Issue with Mr. *Steele* in one Particular;
which perhaps may give you some Diversion. He is taxed by
the *Examiner* and others, for an insolent Expression, that the
British Nation *Expects* the immediate Demolition of *Dunkirk*.

He says, the Word E X P E C T, was meant to the *Ministry*, and not to the *Queen*; *but that however, for Argument sake, he will suppose those Words were addressed immediately to the Queen.* Let me then likewise for Argument sake, suppose a very ridiculous Thing, that Mr. *Steele* were admitted to Her Majesty's Sacred Person, to tell his own Story, with his Letter to You, Mr. Bailiff, in his Hand to have recourse to upon Occasion. I think his Speech must be in these Terms.

M A D A M,

I Richard Steele *Publisher of the* Tatler *and* Spectator, *late* Gazetteer, *Commissioner of Stampt Papers, and Pensioner to Your Majesty, now Burgess Elect of* Stockbridge, *do see and apprehend with my own Eyes and Understanding, the imminent Danger that attends the Delay of the Demolition of* Dunkirk, *which I believe Your Ministers, whose greater Concern it is, do not: For, Madam, the Thing is not done, My Lord* Treasurer *and Lord* Bolingbroke, *my Fellow-Subjects, under whose immediate Direction it is, are careless, and overlook it, or something worse; I mean, they design to sell it to* France, *or make use of it to bring in the* Pretender. *This is clear from their suffering Mr.* Tugghe's *Memorial to be published without punishing the Printer. Your Majesty has told us, that the Equivalent for* Dunkirk *is already in the* French King's *Hands; therefore all Obstacles are removed on the Part of* France; *and I, though a mean Fellow, give Your Majesty to understand in the best Method I can take, and from the Sincerity of my* G R A T E - F U L *Heart, that the British Nation* E X P E C T S *the* I M M E D I A T E *Demolition of* Dunkirk; *as you hope to preserve Your Person, Crown, and Dignity, and the Safety and Welfare of the People committed to Your Charge.*

I have contracted such a Habit of treating Princes familiarly, by reading the Pamphlets of Mr. *Steele* and his Fellows, that I am tempted to suppose Her Majesty's Answer to this Speech might be as follows.

MR. Richard Steele, *late Gazetteer*, &c. *I do not conceive that any of your Titles empower you to be my Director, or to report to me the Expectations of my People. I know their Expectations better than you; they love me, and will trust me. My Ministers were of my own free Choice; I have found them Wise and Faithful; and whoever calls them Fools or Knaves, designs indirectly an Affront to my Self. I am under no Obligations to demolish* Dunkirk, *but to the Most Christian King; if you come here as an* Orator *from that Prince to demand it in his Name, where are your Powers? If not, let it suffice you to know, that I have my Reasons for deferring it; and that the Clamours of a* Faction *shall not be a Rule by which I or my Servants are to proceed.*

Mr. *Steele* tells you; his *Adversaries are so unjust, they will not take the least Notice of what led him into the Necessity of writing his Letter to the* Guardian. And how is it possible, any Mortal should know all his *Necessities?* Who can guess, whether this *Necessity* were imposed on him by his *Superiours*, or by the Itch of Party, or by the meer want of other Matter to furnish out a *Guardian?*

But Mr. *Steele* has *had a Liberal Education*, and *knows the World as well as the Ministry does*, and *will therefore speak on whether he offends them or no, and though their Cloaths be ever so New; when he thinks his Queen and Country is*, (or as a Grammarian would express it, *are*) *ill treated.*

It would be good to hear Mr. *Steele* explain himself upon this Phrase of *knowing the World*; because it is a Science which maintains abundance of Pretenders. Every idle young Rake, who understands how to pick up a Wench, or bilk a Hackney-Coachman, or can call the Players by their Names, and is acquainted with five or six Faces in the Chocolate-House, will needs pass for a Man that *knows the World*. In the like manner Mr. *Steele* who from some few Sprinklings of rudimental Literature, proceeded a Gentleman of the Horse-Guards, thence by several Degrees to be an Ensign and an Alchymist, where he was wholly conversant with the lower Part of Mankind, thinks he *knows the World* as well as the Prime

Minister; and upon the Strength of that Knowledge, will needs direct Her Majesty in the weightiest Matters of Government.

And now, Mr. Bailiff, give me Leave to inform you, that this long Letter of Mr. *Steele* filled with Quotations and a Clutter about *Dunkirk*, was wholly written for the sake of the six last Pages, taken up in vindicating himself directly, and vilifying the Queen and Ministry by Innuendo's. He apprehends, that *some Representations have been given of* him *in your Town, as, that a Man of so small a Fortune as* he *must have secret Views or Supports, which could move him to leave his Employments,* &c. He answers, by owning he *has indeed very particular Views*; *for he is animated in his Conduct by Justice and Truth, and Benevolence to Mankind.* He has given up his Employments, because he *values no Advantages above the Conveniencies of Life, but as they tend to the Service of the Publick.* It seems, he could not *serve the Publick* as a Pensioner, or Commissioner of Stamp'd Paper, and therefore gave them up to sit in Parliament out of *Charity to his Country*, and *to contend for Liberty.* He has transcribed the common Places of some canting Moralist *de contemptu mundi, & fuga seculi*, and would put them upon you as Rules derived from his own Practice.

Here is a most miraculous and sudden Reformation, which I believe can hardly be match'd in History or *Legend.* And Mr. *Steele*, not unaware how slow the World was of Belief, has thought fit to anticipate all Objections; he foresees that *prostituted Pens will entertain a Pretender to such Reformations with a Recital of his own Faults and Infirmities, but he is prepared for such Usage, and gives himself up to all nameless Authors, to be treated as they please.*

It is certain, Mr. Bailiff, that no Man breathing can pretend to have arrived at such a sublime pitch of Virtue as Mr. *Steele* without some Tendency in the World, to suspend at least their Belief of the Fact, till Time and Observation shall determine. But I hope few Writers will be so *prostitute* as to trouble themselves with *the Faults and Infirmities* of Mr. *Steele*'s past Life, with what he somewhere else calls *the Sins of his Youth*, and in one of his late Paper's confesses to have been *numerous* enough. A shifting scambling Scene of Youth, attended with Poverty and ill Company, may put a Man of no ill Inclinations upon many Extravagancies, which as soon as they are left off, are easily pardoned and forgot. Besides, I think Popish Writers tell us, that the greatest Sinners make the greatest Saints; but so very quick a Sanctification, and carried to so prodigious a Height, will be apt to rouze the Suspicion of Infidels, especially when they consider that this Pretence of his to so Romantick a Virtue, is only advanced by way of Solution to that difficult Problem, *Why has he given up his Employments?* And according to the new Philosophy, they will endeavour to solve it by some easier and shorter way. For Example, the Question is put, Why Mr. *Steele* gives up his Employment and Pension at this Juncture? I must here repeat with some Enlargement what I said before on this Head. These unbelieving Gentlemen will answer, First, That a new Commission was every day expected for the Stamp'd Paper, and he knew his Name would be left out; and therefore his Resignation would be an Appearance of Virtue cheaply bought.

Secondly, He dreaded the Violence of Creditors, against which his Employments were no manner of Security.

Thirdly, being a Person of great Sagacity, he hath some Foresight of a Change from the usual Age of a Ministry, which is now almost expired; from the little Misunderstandings that have been reported sometimes to happen among the Men in Power; from the Bill of Commerce being rejected, and from some *HORRIBLE EXPECTATIONS*, wherewith his Party have been deceiving themselves and their Friends *Abroad* for two Years past.

Fourthly, He hopes to come into all the Perquisites of his Predecessor *R I D P A T H*, and be the principal Writer of his Faction, where every thing is printed by Subscription, which will amply make up the Loss of his Place.

But it may be still demanded, Why he affects those exalted Strains of Piety and Resignation? To this I answer, with great probability, That he hath resumed his old Pursuits after the *Philosopher's Stone*, towards which it is held by all *Adepts* for a most essential Ingredient, that a Man must seek it meerly for the Glory of God, and without the least Desire of being rich.

Mr. *Steele* is angry that some of our Friends have been reflected on in a Pamphlet, because they left us in a Point of the greatest Consequence; and upon that Account he runs into their Panegyrick against his Conscience, and the Interest of his Cause, without considering that those Gentlemen have reverted to us again. The Case is thus: He never would have praised them, if they had remained firm, nor should we have railed at them. The one is full as honest, and as natural as the other: However, Mr. *Steele* hopes (I beg you Mr. Bailiff to observe the Consequence) that notwithstanding this Pamphlets reflecting on some Tories who opposed the Treaty of Commerce, *the Ministry will see* Dunkirk *effectually demolished.*

Mr. *Steele* says something in Commendation of the Queen; but stops short, and tells you (if I take his meaning right) that he *shall leave what he has to say on this Topick*; *till he and Her Majesty are both dead.* Thus, he defers his *Praises* as he does his *Debts*, after the manner of the *Druids*, to be paid in another World. If I have ill interpreted him, it is his own Fault, for studying Cadence instead of Propriety, and filling up Nitches with Words before he has adjusted his Conceptions to them. One part of the Queen's Character is this, *that all the Hours of her Life, are divided between the Exercises of Devotion, and taking Minutes of the Sublime Affairs of Her Government.* Now, if the Business of *Dunkirk* be one of the *Sublime Affairs of Her* Majesty*'s Government,* I think we ought to be at ease, or else she *takes Her Minutes* to little Purpose. No, says Mr. *Steele*, the Queen is a *Lady*, and unless a Prince will now and then get drunk with his Ministers, *he cannot learn their Interests or Humours*; but this being by no means proper for a *Lady*, she can know nothing but what they think fit to tell her when they are Sober. And therefore *all the Fellow-Subjects* of these Ministers must watch their Motions and *be very solicitous for what passes beyond the ordinary Rules of Government*; For while we are foolishly *relying upon Her Majesty's Virtues*; These Ministers are *taking the Advantage of encreasing the Power of* France.

There is a very good Maxim, I think it is neither *Whig* nor *Tory*, that the Prince can do no wrong; which I doubt is often applied to very ill Purposes. A Monarch of *Britain* is pleased to create *a Dozen Peers*, and to make a Peace; both these Actions are, (for instance,) within the undisputed Prerogative of the Crown, and are to be reputed and submitted to as the Actions of the Prince: But as a King of *England* is supposed to be guided in Matters of such Importance, by the Advice of those he employs in his Councils; whenever a Parliament thinks fit to complain of such Proceedings, as a publick Grievance, then this Maxim takes Place, that the Prince can do no wrong, and the Advisers are called to Account. But shall this empower such an Individual as Mr. *Steele* in his *Tatling* or *Pamphleteering* Capacity, to fix *the ordinary Rules of Government*, or to affirm that *Her Ministers, upon the Security of Her Majesty's Goodness, are labouring for the Grandeur of* France? What ordinary Rule of Government is transgressed by the Queen's delaying the Demolition of *Dunkirk?* Or what Addition is thereby made to the Grandeur of *France?* Every Taylor in your Corporation is as much a *Fellow-Subject* as Mr. *Steele*, and do you think in your Conscience that every Taylor of *Stockbridge* is fit to direct Her Majesty and Her Ministers in *the sublime Affairs of her Government?*

But He *persists in it, that it is no manner of Diminution of the Wisdom of a Prince, that he is obliged to act by the Information of others.* The Sense is admirable; and the Interpretation is this, that what a Man is forced to *is no diminution of his Wisdom:* But if he would conclude from this Sage Maxim, that, because a Prince *acts by the Information of others*, therefore those Actions may lawfully be traduced in Print by every Fellow-Subject; I hope there is no Man in *England*, so much a *Whig*, as to be of his Opinion.

Mr. *Steele* concludes his Letter to you with a Story about King *William* and his *French Dog-keeper, who gave that Prince a Gun loaden only with Powder, and then pretended to wonder how his Majesty could miss his Aim: Which was no Argument against the King's Reputation for Shooting very finely.* This he would have you apply, by allowing Her Majesty to be a Wise Prince, but deceived by wicked Counsellors, who are in the Interest of *France*. Her Majesty's Aim was Peace, which, I think, She hath not miss'd; and, God be thanked, She hath got it, without any more Expence, either of SHOT or POWDER. Her *Dog-keepers*, for some Years past, had directed Her *Gun* against Her *Friends*, and at last *loaded* it so deep, that it was in danger to *burst* in Her Hands.

You may please to observe, that Mr. *Steele* calls this *Dog-keeper* a *Minister*, which, with humble Submission, is a gross Impropriety of Speech. The Word is derived from *Latin*, where it properly signifies a *Servant*; but in *English* is never made use of otherwise, than to denominate those who are employ'd in the Service of Church or State: So that the Appellation, as he directs it, is no less absurd, than it would be for you, Mr. Bailiff, to send your 'Prentice for a Pot of Ale, and give him the Title of your *Envoy*; to call a Petty-Constable a *Magistrate*, or the Common Hangman a *Minister* of Justice. I confess, when I was choqued at this Word in reading the Paragraph, a Gentleman offer'd his Conjecture, that it might possibly be intended for a Reflection or a Jest: But if there be any thing further in it, than a want of Understanding our Language, I take it to be only a Refinement upon the old levelling Principle of the Whigs. Thus, in their Opinion, a *Dog-keeper* is as much a *Minister* as any Secretary of State: And thus Mr. *Steele* and my Lord *Treasurer* are both *Fellow-Subjects*. I confess, I have known some *Ministers*, whose Birth, or Qualities, or both, were such that nothing but the Capriciousness of Fortune, and the Iniquity of the Times, could ever have raised them above the Station of *Dog-keepers*; and to whose Administration I should be loath to entrust a Dog I had any Value for: Because, by the Rule of Proportion, they who treated their *Prince* like a *Slave*, would have used their *Fellow-Subjects* like *Dogs*; and how they would treat a *Dog*, I can find no Similitude to express; yet I well remember, they maintained a large Number, whom they taught to *Fawn* upon themselves, and *Bark* at their Mistress. However, while they were in Service, I wish they had only kept Her Majesty's DOGS, and not been trusted with Her GUNS. And thus much by way of Comment upon this worthy Story of King *William* and his *Dog-keeper*.

I have now, Mr. Bailiff, explained to you all the difficult Parts in Mr. *Steele*'s Letter. As for the Importance of *Dunkirk*, and when it shall be Demolished, or whether it shall be Demolished or not, neither he, nor you, nor I, have any thing to do in the Matter. Let us all say what we please, Her Majesty will think Her self the best *Judge*, and Her Ministers the best *Advisers*; neither hath Mr. *Steele* pretended to prove that any Law Ecclesiastical or Civil, Statute or Common, is broken, by keeping *Dunkirk* undemolished, as long as the Queen shall think best for the Service of Her Self and Her Kingdoms; and it is not altogether impossible, that there may be some few Reasons of State, which have not been yet communicated to Mr. *Steele*. I am, with Respect to the Borough and Your self,

> *SIR,*
>> *Your most Humble*
>>> *and most Obedient Servant,*
>>>> &c.

FINIS.

E

The Publick Spirit
of the Whigs

THE
PUBLICK SPIRIT
OF THE
WHIGS:
Set forth in their Generous
Encouragement of the Author
OF THE
CRISIS:
WITH SOME
OBSERVATIONS
ON THE
SEASONABLENESS, CANDOR, ERUDITION, and STYLE of that Treatise.

LONDON:
Printed for *John Morphew,* near *Stationers-Hall.*
MDCCXIV.

Price One Shilling.

ADVERTISEMENT.

*U*PON *the first Publication of this Pamphlet, all the* Scotch *Lords, then in* London, *went in a Body, and complained to Queen* ANNE *of the Affront put on them and their Nation, by the Author of this Treatise. Whereupon, a Proclamation was published by her Majesty, offering a Reward of three hundred Pounds to discover him. The Reason for offering so small a Sum was, that the Queen and Ministry had no Desire to have our supposed Author taken into Custody.*

THE
PUBLICK SPIRIT

OF THE

WHIGS, *&c.*

I CANNOT without some Envy, and a just Resentment
against the opposite Conduct of others, reflect upon that
Generosity and Tenderness, wherewith the Heads and
principal Members of a struggling Faction treat those who
will undertake to hold a Pen in their Defence. And the
Behaviour of these Patrons is yet the more laudable, because
the Benefits they confer are almost *gratis*: If any of their
Labourers can scratch out a Pamphlet, they desire no more;
there is no Question offered about the Wit, the Style, the
Argument. Let a Pamphlet come out upon Demand in a
proper Juncture, you shall be well and certainly paid; you
shall be paid before-hand; every one of the Party who is able
to read, and can spare a Shilling shall be a Subscriber: Several
Thousands of each Production shall be sent among their
Friends through the Kingdom: The Work shall be reported
admirable, sublime, unanswerable; shall serve to raise the
sinking Clamours, and confirm the Scandal of introducing
Popery and the Pretender, upon the QUEEN and her Ministers.

AMONG the present Writers on that Side, I can recollect
but three of any great Distinction, which are the *Flying-Post*,
Mr. *Dunton*, and the Author of the *Crisis*: The first of these
seems to have been much sunk in Reputation since the sudden
Retreat of the *only true genuine original Author*, Mr. Ridpath,
who is celebrated by the *Dutch* Gazeteer, as *one of the best Pens
in* England. Mr. *Dunton* hath been longer and more conversant
in Books than any of the three, as well as more voluminous in
his Productions: However, having employed his Studies in so
great a Variety of other Subjects, he hath, I think, but lately

turned his Genius to Politicks. His famous Tract, entitled, *Neck or Nothing*, must be allowed to be the shrewdest Piece, and written with the most Spirit of any which hath appeared from that Side since the Change of the Ministry: It is indeed a most cutting Satire upon the Lord Treasurer and Lord *Bollingbroke*, and I wonder none of our Friends ever undertook to answer it. I confess, I was at first of the same Opinion with several good Judges, who, from the Style and Manner, supposed it to have issued from the sharp Pen of the Earl of *Nottingham*; and I am still apt to think it might receive his Lordship's last Hand. The Third and Principal of this Triumvirate is the Author of the *Crisis*; who, although he must yield to the *Flying-Post* in Knowledge of the World, and Skill in Politicks, and to Mr. *Dunton* in Keenness of Satire, and Variety of Reading; hath yet other Qualities enough to denominate him a Writer of a superior Class to either; provided he would a little regard the Propriety and Disposition of his Words, consult the Grammatical Part, and get some Information in the Subject he intends to handle.

OMITTING the generous Countenance and Encouragement that have been shewn to the Persons and Productions of the two former Authors, I shall here only consider the great Favour conferred upon the last. It hath been advertised for several Months in *The Englishman*, and other Papers, that a Pamphlet, called, *The Crisis*, should be published at a proper Time, in order to open the Eyes of the Nation. It was proposed to be printed by Subscription, Price a Shilling. This was a little out of Form; because Subscriptions are usually begged only for Books of great Price, and such as are not likely to have a general Sale. Notice was likewise given of what this Pamphlet should contain; only an Extract from certain Acts of Parliament relating to the Succession, which at least must sink ninepence in the Shilling, and leave but three Pence for the Author's political Reflections; so that nothing very wonderful or decisive could be reasonably expected from this Performance. But, a Work was to be done, a hearty Writer to be encouraged, and accordingly many thousand Copies were bespoke: Neither could this be sufficient; for when we expected to have our

Bundles delivered us, all was stopt; the Friends to the Cause sprang a new Project, and it was advertised that the *Crisis* could not appear till the Ladies had shewn their Zeal against the *Pretender*, as well as the Men; against the *Pretender* in the Bloom of his Youth, reported to be handsome, and endued with an Understanding exactly of a Size to please the Sex. I should be glad to have seen a printed List of the fair Subscribers prefixed to this Pamphlet; by which the *Chevalier* might know he was so far from *pretending* to a Monarchy here, that he could not so much as *pretend* to a Mistress.

AT the destined Period, the first News we hear, is of a huge Train of Dukes, Earls, Viscounts, Barons, Knights, Esquires, Gentlemen, and others, going to *Sam. Buckley*'s the Publisher of the *Crisis*, to fetch home their Cargoes, in order to transmit them by Dozens, Scores, and Hundreds, into the several Counties, and thereby to prepare the Wills and Understandings of their Friends against the approaching Sessions. Ask any of them whether they have read it? They will answer, No; but they have sent it every where, and it will do a World of Good: It is a Pamphlet, and a Pamphlet they hear against the Ministry; talks of Slavery, *France*, and the Pretender; they desire no more; it will settle the Wavering, confirm the Doubtful, instruct the Ignorant, inflame the Clamorous, although it never be once looked into. I am told by those who are expert in the Trade, that the Author and Bookseller of this Twelve-Penny Treatise, will be greater Gainers, than from one Edition of any Folio that hath been published these twenty Years. What needy Writer would not sollicite to work under such Masters, who will pay us before-hand, take off as much of our Ware as we please at our own Rates, and trouble not themselves to examine either before or after they have bought it, whether it be staple or no?

BUT, in order to illustrate the implicite Munificence of these noble Patrons, I cannot take a more effectual Method than by examining the Production it self; by which we shall easily find that it was never intended, further than from the Noise, the Bulk, and the Title of *Crisis*, to do any Service to the factious Cause. The entire Piece consists of a Title Page, a

Dedication to the Clergy, a Preface, an Extract from certain Acts of Parliament, and about ten Pages of dry Reflections on the Proceedings of the QUEEN and her Servants; which his Coadjutors, the Earl of *Nottingham*, Mr. *Dunton*, and the *Flying-Post*, had long ago set before us in a much clearer Light.

IN Popish Countries, when some Impostor cries out, *A Miracle! A Miracle!* it is not done with a Hope or Intention of converting Hereticks, but confirming the deluded Vulgar in their Errors; and so the Cry goes round without examining into the Cheat. Thus the Whigs among us give about the Cry, *A Pamphlet! A Pamphlet!* The *Crisis!* The *Crisis!* Not with a View of convincing their Adversaries, but to raise the Spirits of their Friends, recal their Stragglers, and unite their Numbers by Sound and Impudence; as Bees assemble and cling together by the Noise of Brass.

THAT no other Effect could be imagined or hoped for, by the Publication of this timely Treatise, will be manifest, from some obvious Reflections upon the several Parts of it; wherein the Follies, the Falshoods, or the Absurdities, appear so frequent, that they may boldly contend for Number with the Lines.

WHEN the Hawker holds this Pamphlet towards you, the first Words you perceive are, The *Crisis:* Or, *A Discourse*, &c. The Interpreter of *Suidas* gives four Translations of the Word *Crisis*; any of which may be as properly applied to this Author's Letter to the Bailiff of *Stockbridge*. Next, what he calls *A Discourse*, consists only of two Pages, prefixed to twenty two more, which contain Extracts from Acts of Parliament; for as to the twelve last Pages, they are provided for by themselves in the Title, under the Name of *Some Seasonable Remarks on the Danger of a* Popish *Successor*. Another Circumstance worthy of our Information in the Title-page, is, That the Crown hath been settled *by previous Acts*. I never heard of any Act of Parliament that was not *previous* to what it enacted, unless those two by which the Earl of *Strafford* and Sir *John Fenwick* lost their Heads, may pass for Exceptions. *A Discourse, representing from the most authentick Records*. He hath borrowed this Expression from some Writer, who probably understood the Words, but this Gentleman hath altogether misapplied them; and under Favour, he is wholly mistaken; for a Heap of Extracts, from several Acts of Parliament, cannot be called a Discourse; neither do I believe, he copied them from the most authentick Records, which as I take it are lodged in the *Tower*, but out of some common printed Copy. I grant there is nothing material in all this, further than to shew the Generosity of our Adversaries in encouraging a Writer, who cannot furnish out so much as a Title-page with Propriety or common Sense.

NEXT follows the Dedication to the Clergy of the Church of *England*, wherein the Modesty and the Meaning of the first Paragraphs are hardly to be matched. He tells them, he hath made *a Comment upon the Acts of* Settlement, which he *lays before them*, and *conjures them to recommend in their Writings and Discourses to their Fellow-Subjects*; and he doeth all this, *out of a just Deference to their great Power and Influence*. This is the right Whig-Scheme of directing the Clergy what to preach. The Archbishop of *Canterbury*'s Jurisdiction extends no further than over his own Province; but the Author of the *Crisis*, constitutes himself Vicar-General over the whole Clergy of the Church of *England*. The Bishops in their Letters or Speeches to their own Clergy proceed no further than to *Exhortation*; but this Writer *conjures* the whole Clergy of the Church to *recommend* his *Comment upon the Laws* of the Land *in their Writings and Discourses*. I would fain know, who made him a *Commentator upon the Laws* of the Land; after which it will be time enough to ask him, by what Authority he directs the Clergy *to recommend his* Comments from the Pulpit or the Press?

HE tells the Clergy *there are two Circumstances which place the Minds of the People under their Direction*; the first Circumstance is their Education; the second Circumstance is the Tenths of our Lands. This last, according to the *Latin* Phrase, is spoken *ad invidiam*; for he knows well enough, they have not a twentieth: But if you take it in his own Way, the Landlord has nine Parts in ten of the People's Minds under his Direction. Upon this Rock the Author before us is perpetually splitting, as often as he ventures out beyond the narrow Bounds of his

Literature. He hath a confused Remembrance of Words since he left the University, but hath lost half their Meaning, and puts them together with no Regard, except to their Cadence; as I remember a Fellow nailed up Maps in a Gentleman's Closet, some sideling, others upside down, the better to adjust them to the Pannels.

I AM sensible it is of little Consequence to their Cause, whether this Defender of it understand Grammar or no; and if what he would fain say, discovered him to be a Well-willer to Reason or Truth, I would be ready to make large Allowances. But when with great Difficulty I descry a Composition of Rancour and Falshood, intermixed with plausible Nonsense; I feel a Struggle between Contempt and Indignation, at seeing the Character of a *Censor*, a *Guardian*, an *Englishman*, a *Commentator* on the *Laws*, an *Instructor* of the *Clergy*, assumed by a Child of Obscurity, without one single Qualification to support them.

THIS Writer, who either affects, or is commanded of late to copy after the Bishop of *Sarum*, hath, out of the Pregnancy of his Invention, found out an old Way of insinuating the grossest Reflections under the Appearances of Admonitions; and is so judicious a Follower of the Prelate, that he taxes the Clergy for *inflaming their People with Apprehensions of Danger to them and* THEIR *Constitution, from Men who are innocent of such Designs*. When he must needs confess, the whole *Design* of his Pamphlet is *to inflame the People with Apprehensions of Danger* from the present Ministry, whom *we* believe to be at least as *innocent Men* as the last.

WHAT shall I say to a Pamphlet, where the Malice and Falshood of every Line would require an Answer, and where the Dulness and Absurdities will not deserve one?

BY his pretending to have always maintained an inviolable Respect to the Clergy, he would insinuate, that those Papers among the *Tatlers* and *Spectators*, where the whole Order is abused, were not his own: I will appeal to all who know the Flatness of his Style, and the Barrenness of his Invention, whether he doth not grossly prevaricate? Was he ever able to walk without Leading-strings, or swim without Bladders, without being discovered by his hobbling and his sinking?

Hath he adhered to this Character in his Paper called the *Englishman*, whereof he is allowed to be sole Author, without any Competition? What does he think of the Letter signed by himself, which relates to *Molesworth*, in whose Defence, he affronts the whole Convocation of *Ireland*.

I⊤ is a wise Maxim, that because the Clergy are no Civil Lawyers, they ought not to preach Obedience to Governors; and therefore they ought not to preach Temperance, because they are no Physicians: Examine all this Author's Writings, and then point me out a Divine who knoweth less of the Constitution of *England* than he; witness those many egregious Blunders in his late Papers, where he pretended to dabble in the Subject.

B⊔⊤ the Clergy have it seems imbibed their Notions of Power and Obedience abhorrent from our Laws, *from the pompous Ideas of Imperial Greatness, and the Submission to absolute Emperors.* This is gross Ignorance, below a School-boy in his *Lucius Florus:* The *Roman* History wherein Lads are instructed, reacheth little above eight hundred Years, and the Authors do every where instil Republican Principles; and from the Account of nine in twelve of the first Emperors, we learn to have a Detestation against Tyranny. The *Greeks* carry this Point yet a great deal higher, which none can be ignorant of, who hath read or heard them quoted. This gave *Hobbes* the Occasion of advancing a Position directly contrary, That the Youth of *England* was corrupted in their political Principles, by reading the Histories of *Rome* and *Greece*, which having been writ under Republicks, taught the Readers to have ill Notions of Monarchy: In this Assertion there was something specious, but that advanced by the *Crisis* could only issue from the profoundest Ignorance.

B⊔⊤, would you know his Scheme of Education for young Gentlemen at the University? It is, that they should spend their Time in perusing those Acts of Parliament, whereof his Pamphlet is an Extract, which, *if it had been done, the Kingdom would not be in its present Condition, but every Member sent into the World thus instructed since the Revolution, would have been an Advocate for our Rights and Liberties.*

HERE now is a Project for getting more Money by the *Crisis*, to have it read by Tutors in the Universities. I thoroughly agree with him, that if our Students had been thus employed for twenty Years past, *The Kingdom had not been in its* present *Condition*. But, we have too many of such Proficients already among the young Nobility and Gentry, who have gathered up their Politicks from Chocolate Houses, and factious Clubs, and who, if they had spent their Time in hard Study at *Oxford* or *Cambridge*, we might indeed have said, that the factious Part of this Kingdom *had not been in its present Condition*, or have suffered themselves to be taught, that a few Acts of Parliament relating to the Succession are preferable to all other *Civil Institutions* whatsoever: Neither did I ever before hear, that an Act of Parliament relating to one particular Point could be called a Civil Institution.

HE spends almost a Quarto Page in telling the Clergy, that they will be certainly perjured if they bring in the *Pretender* whom they have abjured; and he wisely reminds them, that they have sworn without Equivocation or Mental-Reservation; otherwise the Clergy might think, that as soon as they received the *Pretender*, and turned *Papists*, they would be free from their Oath.

THIS honest, civil, ingenious Gentleman, knows in his Conscience, that there are not ten Clergymen in *England* (except Non-jurors) who do not abhor the Thoughts of the *Pretender* reigning over us, much more than himself. But this is the Spittle of the Bishop of *Sarum*, which our Author licks up, and swallows, and then coughs out again, with an Addition of his own Phlegm. I would fain suppose the Body of the Clergy were to return an Answer by one of their Members to these worthy Counsellors: I conceive it might be in the following Terms.

   My Lord, and Gentleman,
   'The Clergy command me to give you Thanks for your
'Advice; and if they knew any Crimes from which either of
'you were as free, as they are from those which you so earnestly
'exhort them to avoid, they would return your Favour as near

'as possible in the same Style and Manner. However, that
'your Advice may not be wholly lost, particularly that Part of it
'which relates to the *Pretender*, they desire you would apply it to
'more proper Persons. Look among your own Leaders:
'Examine which of them engaged in a Plot to restore the late
'King *James*, and received Pardons under his Seal; examine
'which of them have been since tampering with his pretended
'Son, and to gratify their Ambition, their Avarice, their
'Malice and Revenge, are now willing to restore him at the
'Expence of the Religion and Liberty of their Country. Retire,
'good my Lord, with your Pupil, and let us hear no more of
'these hypocritical Insinuations, lest the QUEEN and Ministers,
'who have been hitherto content with only *disappointing* the
'lurking Villainies of your Faction, may be at last provoked to
'*expose* them.'

BUT his Respect for the Clergy is such, that he doth not
insinuate as if they really had these evil Dispositions; he only
insinuates, that they give *too much Cause* for such *Insinuations*.

I WILL upon Occasion, strip some of his *Insinuations* from
their Generality and Solecisms, and drag them into the Light.
This Dedication to the Clergy is full of them, because here he
endeavours to mold up his Rancor and Civility together; by
which Constraint, he is obliged to shorten his Paragraphs,
and to place them in such a Light, that they obscure one
another. Supposing therefore, that I have scraped off his good
Manners, in order to come at his Meaning which lies under;
he tells the Clergy, that the Favour of the QUEEN and her
Ministers, is but a *Colour of Zeal towards them:* That, the People
were deluded by a groundless Cry of the Church's Danger at
Sacheverell's Tryal; that, the Clergy, as they are *Men of Sense and
Honour*, ought to preach this Truth to their several Congrega-
tions; and let them know, that the true Design of the present
Men in Power in that and all their Proceedings since, in
Favour of the Church, was to bring in *Popery*, *France* and the
Pretender, and to enslave all *Europe*, contrary to the *Laws of our
Country*, *the Power of the Legislature*, *the Faith of Nations*, *and
the Honour of God*.

I CANNOT see, why the Clergy, as *Men of Sense, and Men of Honour* (for he appeals not to them as Men of Religion) should not be allowed to know when they are in Danger, and be able to guess whence it comes, and who are their Protectors. The Design of their Destruction indeed may have been projected in the dark; but when all was ripe, their Enemies proceeded to so many Overt-Acts in the Face of the Nation, that it was obvious to the meanest People, who wanted no other Motives to rouze them. On the other Side, can this Author, or the wisest of his Faction, assign one single Act of the present Ministry, any way tending towards bringing in the *Pretender*, or to weaken the Succession in the House of *Hanover?* Observe then the Reasonableness of this Gentleman's Advice: The Clergy, the Gentry, and the common People had the utmost Apprehensions of Danger to the Church under the late Ministry; yet then it was the greatest Impiety to *inflame the People with any such Apprehensions*. His Danger of a *Popish* Successor from any Steps of the present Ministry, is an artificial Calumny raised and spread against the Conviction of the Inventors; pretended to be believed only by those who abhor the Constitution in Church and State; an obdurate Faction, who compass Heaven and Earth to restore themselves upon the Ruin of their Country; yet here our Author *exhorts the Clergy* to preach up this imaginary Danger to their People, and disturb the publick Peace with his strained seditious Comments.

BUT, how comes this gracious Licence to the Clergy from the *Whigs*, to concern themselves with Politicks of any Sort, although it be only the Glosses and Comments of Mr. *Steele?* The Speeches of the Managers at *Sacheverell's* Tryal, particularly those of *Stanhope, Lechmere, King, Parker*, and some other, seemed to deliver a different Doctrine. Nay, this very Dedication complains of *some in Holy Orders, who have made the Constitution of their Country*, (in which and the *Coptick* Mr. *Steele* is equally skilled) *a very little Part of their Study, and yet made Obedience and Government the frequent Subjects of their Discourses*. This Difficulty is easily solved; for, by *Politicks*, they mean *Obedience*. Mr. *Hoadley*, who is a Champion for

Resistance, was never charged as medling out of his Function: *Hugh Peters*, and his Brethren, in the Times of Usurpation, had full Liberty to preach up Sedition and Rebellion; and so here Mr. *Steele* issues out his Licence to the Clergy to preach up the *Danger of a Popish Pretender*, in Defiance of the QUEEN and her Administration.

EVERY Whiffler in a laced Coat, who frequents the Chocolate House, and is able to spell the Title of a Pamphlet, shall talk of the Constitution with as much Plausibility as this very Solemn Writer, and with as good a Grace blame the Clergy for medling with Politicks, which they do not understand. I have known many of these able Politicians, furnished before they were of Age, with all the necessary Topicks of their Faction, and by the Help of about twenty Polysyllables capable of maintaining an Argument that would shine in the *Crisis*; whose Author gathered up his little Stock from the same Schools, and hath writ from no other Fund.

BUT, after all, it is not clear to me, whether this Gentleman addresseth himself to the Clergy of *England* in general, or only to those very few, (hardly enough in Case of a Change to supply the Mortality of those *Self-denying Prelates* he celebrates) who are in his Principles, and among these, only such as live in and about *London*, which probably will reduce the Number to about half a dozen at most. I should incline to guess the latter; because he tells them they *are surrounded by a learned, wealthy, knowing Gentry, who know with what Firmness, Self-denial, and Charity, the Bishops adhered to the publick Cause, and what Contumelies those Clergymen have undergone*, &c. *who adhered to the Cause of Truth:* By those Terms, *the publick Cause*, and *the Cause of Truth*, he understands the *Cause* of the Whigs in Opposition to the QUEEN and her Servants: Therefore by the *learned, wealthy, and knowing Gentry*, he must understand the *Bank* and *East-India Company*, and those other Merchants or Citizens within the Bills of Mortality, who have been strenuous against the Church and Crown, and whose Spirit of Faction hath lately got the better of their Interest. For, let him search all the rest of the Kingdom, he will find the *surrounded* Clergy, and the *surrounding* Gentry, wholly Strangers to the Merits of

F

Alverno College Library
Milwaukee, Wisconsin

those Prelates; and adhering to a very different *Cause of Truth*, as will soon, I hope, be manifest by a fair Appeal to the Representatives of both.

It was very unnecessary in this Writer to bespeak the Treatment of *Contempt and Derision*, which the Clergy are to expect from his Faction whenever they come into Power. I believe, that venerable Body is in very little Concern after what Manner their most mortal Enemies intend to *treat* them, whenever it shall please GOD for our Sins to visit us with so fatal an Event, which I hope it will be the united Endeavours both of Clergy and Laity to hinder. It would be some Support to this Hope, if I could have any Opinion of his predicting Talent, (which some have ascribed to People of this Author's Character) where he tells us, That *Noise and Wrath will not always pass for Zeal*. What other Instances of Zeal has this Gentleman or the rest of his Party been able to produce? If Clamour be *Noise*, it is but opening our Ears to know from what Side it comes: And, if Sedition, Scurrility, Slander and Calumny, be the Fruits of *Wrath*, read the Pamphlets and Papers issuing from the *Zealots* of that Faction, or visit their Clubs and Coffee-Houses in order to form a Judgment of the Tree.

When Mr. *Steele* tells us, WE *have a Religion that wants no Support from the Enlargement of Secular Power, but is well supported by the Wisdom and Piety of its Preachers, and its own Native Truth*; it would be good to know what Religion he professeth: For, the Clergy to whom he speaks, will never allow him a Member of the Church of *England*; they cannot agree, that the *Truth* of the Gospel, and the *Piety* and *Wisdom* of its Preachers, are a sufficient *Support* in an Evil Age, against Infidelity, Faction, and Vice, without the Assistance of *Secular Power*; unless GOD would please to confer the Gift of Miracles on those who wait at the Altar. I believe, they venture to go a little further, and think, That upon some Occasions, they want a little *Enlargement of Assistance from the Secular Power*, against *Atheists, Deists, Socinians,* and other Hereticks: Every first Sunday in *Lent*, a Part of the Liturgy is read to the People; in the Preface to which, the Church declares her Wishes for the Restoring of that Discipline she formerly had, and which for some Years past hath been more wanted than ever. But of this no more, lest it might *insinuate Jealousies between the Clergy and Laity*, which the Author tells us, is the *Policy of vain ambitious Men among the former, in Hopes to derive from their Order, a Veneration they cannot deserve from their Virtue.* If this be their Method for procuring Veneration, it is the most singular that ever was thought on; and the Clergy should then indeed have no more to do with Politicks of any sort than Mr. *Steele* or his Faction will allow them.

HAVING thus toiled through his Dedication, I proceed to consider his Preface, which half consisting of Quotation, will be so much the sooner got through. It is a very unfair Thing in any Writer to employ his *Ignorance* and *Malice* together, because it gives his Answerer double Work: It is like the Sort of Sophistry that the Logicians call *two Mediums*, which are never allowed in the same Syllogism. A Writer with a weak Head, and a corrupted Heart, is an over-match for any single Pen; like a hireling Jade, dull and vicious, hardly able to stir, yet offering at every Turn to kick.

HE begins his Preface with such an Account of the Original of Power, and the Nature of Civil Institutions, as I am confident was never once imagined by any Writer upon Government from *Plato* to Mr. *Lock.* Give me Leave to transcribe his first Paragraph. *I never saw an unruly Crowd of People cool by Degrees into Temper, but it gave me an Idea of the Original of Power, and the Nature of Civil Institutions. One particular Man has usually in those Cases, from the Dignity of his Appearance, or other Qualities known or imagined by the Multitude, been received into sudden Favour and Authority, the Occasion of their Difference has been represented to him, and the Matter referred to his Decision.*

I HAVE known a Poet, who was never out of *England,* introduce a Fact by Way of Simile, which could probably no where happen nearer than in the Plains of *Libia*; and begin with, *So have I seen.* Such a Fiction I suppose may be justified by Poetical Licence; yet *Virgil* is much more modest: This Paragraph of Mr. *Steele*'s, which he sets down as an Observation of his own, is a miserable mangled Translation of six Verses out of that famous Poet, who speaks after this Manner: *As when a Sedition arises in a great Multitude*, &c. *Then if they see a wise grave Man*, &c. *Virgil*, who lived but a little after the Ruin of the *Roman* Republick, where Seditions often happened, and the Force of Oratory was great among the People, made Use of a Simile, which Mr. *Steele* turns into a Fact, after such a Manner, as if he had seen it an hundred Times; and builds upon it a System of the Origin of Government. When the Vulgar here in *England* assemble in a riotous Manner, (which is not very frequent of late Years) the Prince takes a much more effectual Way than that of sending Orators to appease them: But Mr. *Steele* imagines such a Crowd of People as this, where there is no Government at all; their *Unruliness* quelled, and their Passions *cooled* by a particular Man, whose great Qualities they had known before. Such an Assembly must have risen suddenly from the Earth, and the *Man of Authority* dropt from the Clouds; for without some previous Form of Government, no such *Crowd* did ever yet assemble, or could possibly be acquainted with the Merits and Dignity of any *particular Man* among them. But, to pursue his Scheme. This Man of Authority who *cools* the *Crowd* by Degrees, and to whom they all Appeal, must of Necessity prove either an open or *clandestine Tyrant:* A *clandestine Tyrant* I take to be a King of *Brentford*, who keeps his Army in Disguise; and whenever he happens either to die naturally, be knockt on the Head, or deposed, the People *calmly take further Measures, and improve upon what was begun under his unlimited Power*. All this, our Author tells us, with extreme Propriety, *is what seems reasonable to common Sense*; that is, in other Words, it seems *reasonable* to *Reason*. This is what he calls *giving an Idea of the Original of Power, and the Nature of Civil Institutions*. To which I answer with great Phlegm, that I defy any Man alive to shew me in double the Number of Lines, although writ by the same Author, such a complicated Ignorance in History, human Nature, or Politicks, as well as in the ordinary Proprieties of Thought or of Style.

BUT, it seems, these profound Speculations were only premised to introduce some Quotations in Favour of *Resistance*.

What hath *Resistance* to do with the Succession of the House of *Hanover*, that the Whig-writers should perpetually affect to tag them together? I can conceive nothing else, but that their Hatred to the QUEEN and Ministry, puts them upon Thoughts of introducing the Successor by *another* Revolution. Are Cases of *extream Necessity* to be produced as common Maxims, by which we are always to proceed? Should not these Gentlemen sometimes inculcate the general Rule of Obedience, and not always the Exception of Resistance? Since the former hath been the perpetual Dictates of all Laws both Divine and Civil, and the latter is still in Dispute.

I SHALL meddle with none of the Passages he cites, to prove the Lawfulness of resisting Princes, except that from the present Lord Chancellor's Speech, in Defence of Dr. *Sacheverell:* That *there are extraordinary Cases, Cases of Necessity, which are implied although not expressed in the general Rule* [of Obedience.] These Words, very clear in themselves, Mr. *Steele* explains into Nonsense; which in any other Author I should suspect to have been intended as a Reflection upon as great a Person as ever filled or adorned that high Station: But I am so well acquainted with his Pen, that I much more wonder how it can trace out a true Quotation than a false Comment. To see him treat my Lord *Harcourt* with so much Civility looks indeed a little suspicious, and, as if he had Malice in his Heart. He calls his Lordship, *a very great Man*, and *a great living Authority*, places him in Company with General *Stanhope* and Mr. *Hoadley*; and in short, takes the most effectual Method in his Power of ruining his Lordship in the Opinion of every Man who is wise or good: I can only tell my Lord *Harcourt*, for his Comfort, that these Praises are encumbred with the Doctrine of *Resistance*, and the true Revolution-Principles; and provided he will not allow Mr. *Steele* for his Commentator, he may hope to recover the Honour of being libelled again as well as his Sovereign and Fellow-Servants.

WE come now to the *Crisis:* Where we meet with two Pages by Way of Introduction to those Extracts from Acts of Parliament that constitute the Body of his Pamphlet. This

Introduction begins with a Definition of Liberty, and then
proceeds in a Panegyrick upon that great Blessing; his Panegyrick is made up of half a dozen Shreds, like a School-Boy's
Theme, beaten, general Topicks, where any other Man alive
might wander securely; but this Politician, by venturing to
vary the good old Phrases, and give them a new Turn, commits
an hundred Solecisms and Absurdities. The weighty Truths
which he endeavours to press upon his Reader are such as
these. That, *Liberty is a very good Thing*; that, *without Liberty
we cannot be free*; that, *Health is good, and Strength is good, but
Liberty is better than either*; that, *no Man can be happy, without the
Liberty of doing whatever his own Mind tells him is best*; that, *Men
of Quality love Liberty, and common People love Liberty*; even
Women and Children love Liberty; and you cannot please them
better than by letting them do what they please. Had Mr.
Steele contented himself to deliver these and the like Maxims
in such intelligible Terms, I could have found where we
agreed and where we differed. But, let us hear some of these
Axioms as he hath involved them. *We cannot possess our Souls
with Pleasure and Satisfaction except we preserve to our selves that
inestimable Blessing which we call Liberty: By Liberty, I desire to
br understood, to mean the Happiness of Men's living,* &c.—The
true *Life of Man consists in conducting it according to his own just
Sentiments and innocent Inclinations.*——*Man's Being is degraded
below that of a free Agent, when his Affections and Passions are no
longer governed by the Dictates of his own Mind.*——*Without
Liberty, our Health* (among other Things) *may be at the Will of a
Tyrant, employed to our own Ruin and that of our Fellow Creatures.*
If there be any of these Maxims, which is not grossly defective
in Truth, in Sense, or in Grammar, I will allow them to pass
for uncontroulable. By the first, omitting the Pedantry of the
whole Expression, there are not above one or two Nations in
the World, where any one Man can *possess his Soul with Pleasure
and Satisfaction*. In the Second, He *desires to be understood to
mean*; that is, he desires to be meant to mean, or to be understood to understand. In the Third, *The Life of Man consists in
conducting* his Life. In the Fourth, he affirms, That *Men's Beings
are degraded when their Passions are no longer governed by the Dictates*

of their own Mind; directly contrary to the Lessons of all Moralists and Legislators; who agree unanimously, that the Passions of Men must be under the Government of Reason and Law; neither are Laws of any other Use than to correct the Irregularity of our Affections. By the last, *Our Health is ruinous to our selves and other Men, when a Tyrant pleases*; which I leave him to make out.

I CANNOT sufficiently commend our Ancestors for transmitting to us the Blessing of Liberty; yet having *laid out their Blood and Treasure upon the Purchase*, I do not see how they *acted Parsimoniously*; because I can conceive nothing more generous than that of employing our Blood and Treasure for the Service of others. But I am suddenly struck with the Thought, that I have found his Meaning: Our Ancestors acted Parsimoniously, because they only spent their own Treasure for the Good of their Posterity; whereas, we squandered away the Treasures of our Posterity too; but whether they will be thankful, and think it was done for the Preservation of their Liberty must be left to themselves for a Decision.

I VERILY believe, although I could not prove it in *Westminster-Hall* before a *Lord Chief Justice*, that by *Enemies to our Constitution*, and *Enemies to our present Establishment, Mr.* Steele *would desire to be understood to mean*, My Lord Treasurer, and the rest of the Ministry: By *those who are grown Supine in Proportion to the Danger to which our Liberty is every Day more exposed*, I should guess, he means the Tories: And, by *honest Men who ought to look up with a Spirit that becomes Honesty*, he understands the Whigs. I likewise believe, he would take it ill, or think me stupid, if I did not thus expound him. I say then, that according to this Exposition, the four great Officers of State, together with the rest of the Cabinet-Council, (except the Archbishop of *Canterbury*) are *Enemies to our Establishment, making artful and open Attacks upon our Constitution*, and are now *practising indirect Arts, and mean Subtilties, to weaken the Security of those Acts of Parliament* for settling the Succession in the House of *Hanover*. The first, and most notorious of these Criminals is, *Robert Harley*, Earl of *Oxford*, Lord High Treasurer, who is reputed to be Chief Minister: The second is, *James Butler*,

Duke of *Ormonde*, who commands the Army, and designs to employ it in bringing over the *Pretender:* The third is, *Henry St. John*, Lord Viscount *Bolingbroke*, Secretary of State, who must be supposed to hold a constant Correspondence with the Court at *Bar le Duc*, as the late Earl of *Godolphin* did with that of St. *Germains:* And to avoid Tediousness, Mr. *Bromley* and the rest are employed in their several Districts to the same End. These are the Opinions which Mr. *Steele* and his Faction, under the Direction of their Leaders, are endeavouring with all their Might to propagate among the People of *England*, concerning the present Ministry; with what Reservation to the Honour, Wisdom, or Justice of the QUEEN, I cannot determine; who by her own free Choice, after long Experience of their Abilities and Integrity, and in Compliance to the general Wishes of her People, called them to her Service. Such an Accusation, against Persons in so high Trust, should require, I think at least, one single Overt-Act to make it good. If there be no other Choice of Persons fit to serve the Crown without Danger from the *Pretender*, except among those who are called the Whig Party, the *Hanover* Succession is then indeed in a very desperate State; that illustrious Family will have almost nine in ten of the Kingdom against it, and those principally of the Landed Interest, which is most to be depended upon in such a Nation as ours.

I HAVE now got as far as his Extracts, which I shall not be at the Pains of comparing with the Originals, but suppose he hath got them fairly transcribed: I only think, that whoever is Patentee for printing Acts of Parliament, may have a very fair Action against him, for Invasion of Property: But this is none of my Business to enquire into.

AFTER two and twenty Pages spent in reciting Acts of Parliament, *he desires Leave to repeat the History and Progress of the Union;* upon which I have some few Things to observe.

This Work, he tells us, *was unsuccessfully attempted by several of her Majesty's Predecessors;* although I* do not remember it was ever thought on by any except King *James* the First,

---

* The Author's Memory failed him a little in this Assertion, as one of his Answerers observed.

and the late King *William.* I have read indeed, that some small Overtures were made by the former of these Princes towards an Union between the two Kingdoms, but rejected with Indignation and Contempt by the *English:* And the Historian tells us, that how degenerate and corrupt soever the Court and Parliament then were, they would not give Ear to so infamous a Proposal. I do not find that any of the succeeding Princes before the Revolution ever resumed the Design; because it was a Project for which there could not possibly be assigned the least Reason or Necessity: For I defy any Mortal to name one single Advantage that *England* could ever expect from such an Union.

BUT towards the End of the late King's Reign, upon Apprehension of the Want of Issue from him or the Princess *Anne,* a Proposition for uniting both Kingdoms was begun, because *Scotland* had not settled their Crown upon the House of *Hanover,* but left themselves at large, in hopes to make their Advantage: And, it was thought highly dangerous to leave that Part of the Island inhabited by a poor, fierce Northern People, at Liberty to put themselves under a different King. However, the Opposition to this Work was so great, that it could not be overcome until some Time after her present Majesty came to the Crown; when by the Weakness or Corruption of a certain Minister since dead, an Act of Parliament was obtained for the *Scots,* which gave them leave to arm themselves; and so the Union became necessary, not for any actual Good it could possibly do us, but to avoid a probable Evil; and, at the same Time, save an obnoxious Minister's Head, who was so wise, as to take the first Opportunity of procuring a general Pardon by Act of Parliament, because he could not with so much Decency or Safety desire a particular one for himself. These Facts are well enough known to the whole Kingdom: And, I remember, discoursing above six Years ago with the most considerable *Person of the adverse Party, and a great Promoter of the Union, he frankly owned to me, That this Necessity, brought upon us by the wrong Management of the Earl of *Godolphin,* was the only Cause of the Union.

* Lord Somers.

THEREFORE I am ready to grant two Points to the Author of the *Crisis:* First, that the Union became necessary for the Cause above related; because it prevented this Island from being governed by two Kings, which *England* would never have suffered; and it might probably have cost us a War of a Year or two, to reduce the *Scots.* Secondly, that it would be dangerous to break this Union, at least in this Juncture, while there is a *Pretender* abroad, who might probably lay hold of such an Opportunity. And this made me wonder a little at the Spirit of Faction last Summer among some People, who having been the great Promoters of the *Union*, and several of them the principal Gainers by it, could yet proceed so far, as to propose in the House of Lords, that it should be dissolved; while at the same Time, those Peers who had ever opposed it in the Beginning, were then for preserving it upon the Reason I have just assigned, and which the Author of the *Crisis* hath likewise taken Notice of.

BUT, when he tells us, *The* Englishmen *ought in Generosity to be more particularly careful in preserving this Union*, he argues like himself. *The late Kingdom of* Scotland (saith he) *had as numerous a Nobility as* England, *&c.* They had indeed; and to that we owe one of the great and necessary Evils of the Union upon the Foot it now stands. Their Nobility is indeed so numerous, that the whole Revenues of their Country would be hardly able to maintain them according to the Dignity of their Titles; and what is infinitely worse, they are never likely to be extinct until the last Period of all Things; because the greatest Part of them descend to Heirs general. I imagine, a Person of Quality prevailed on to marry a Woman much his Inferior, and without a Groat to her Fortune, and her Friends arguing, she was as good as her Husband, because she brought him as numerous a Family of Relations and Servants, as she found in his House. *Scotland* in the Taxes is obliged to contribute one Penny for every forty Pence laid upon *England*; and the Representatives they send to Parliament are about a thirteenth: Every other *Scotch* Peer hath all the Privileges of an *English* one, except that of sitting in Parliament, and even Precedence before all of the same Title that shall be created for the Time to come. The Pensions and Employments possessed by the Natives of that Country now among us, do amount to more than the whole Body of their Nobility ever spent at home; and all the Money they raise upon the Publick is hardly sufficient to defray their Civil and Military Lists. I could point out some with great Titles, who affected to appear very vigorous for dissolving the Union, although their whole Revenues before that Period would have ill maintained a *Welch* Justice of the Peace; and have since gathered more Money than ever any *Scotchman*, who had not travelled, could form an Idea of.

I HAVE only one thing more to say upon Occasion of the Union Act; which is, that the Author of the *Crisis* may be fairly proved from his own Citations to be guilty of HIGH TREASON. In a Paper of his called the *Englishman*, of *October* 29. there is an Advertisement about taking in Subscriptions for printing the *Crisis*, where the Title is published at length, with the following Clause, which the Author thought fit to drop in the Publication: [*And that no Power on Earth can bar, alter, or make void the* present Settlement of the Crown, *&c.* By *Richard Steele.*] In his Extract of an Act of Parliament made since the Union, it appears to be *High Treason* for *any Person, by Writing or Printing, to maintain and affirm, that the Kings or Queens of this Realm, with and by the Authority of Parliament, are not able to make Laws and Statutes of sufficient Force and Validity to limit and bind the Crown, and the Descent, Limitation, Inheritance, and Government thereof.* This Act being subsequent to the Settlement of the Crown confirmed at the Union; it is probable, some Friend of the Author advised him to leave out those *treasonable* Words in the printed Title Page, which he had before published in the *Advertisement*; and accordingly we find, that in the Treatise it self, he only *offers it to every good Subject's Consideration, whether this Article of the Settlement of the Crown is not as firm as the Union itself, and as the Settlement of Episcopacy in* England, *&c.* And he thinks the *Scots understood it so, that the Succession to the Crown was never to be controverted.*

THESE I take to be only *treasonable* Insinuations; but the Advertisement above-mentioned is actually *High-Treason*, for which the Author ought to be prosecuted, if that would avail any thing, under a Jurisdiction where cursing the QUEEN is not above the Penalty of twenty Marks.

NOTHING is more notorious, than that the Whigs of late Years, both in their Writings and Discourses, have affected upon all Occasions to allow the Legitimacy of the *Pretender:* This makes me a little wonder to see our Author labouring to prove the contrary, by producing all the popular Chat of those Times, and other solid Arguments from *Fuller's* Narrative: But, it must be supposed, that this Gentleman acts by the Commands of his Superiors, who have thought fit at this Juncture to issue out new Orders for Reasons best known to themselves. I wish they had been more clear in their Directions to him upon that weighty Point, whether the Settlement of the Succession in the House of *Hanover* be alterable or no: I have observed where in his former Pages he gives it in the Negative; but in the turning of a Leaf he hath wholly changed his Mind; He tells us, *He wonders there can be found any* Briton *weak enough to contend against a Power in their own Nation which is practised in a much greater Degree in other States:* And, *how hard it is, that* Britain *should be debarred the Privilege of establishing its own Security, by relinquishing only those Branches of the Royal Line which threaten it with Destruction; whilst other Nations never scruple upon less Occasions to go much greater Lengths;* of which he produceth Instances in *France, Spain, Sicily,* and *Sardinia;* and then adds, *Can* Great Britain *help to advance Men to other Thrones, and have no Power in limiting its own?* How can a Senator, capable of **doing Honour to Sir* Thomas Hanmer, be guilty of such ridiculous Inconsistencies? The Author of the *Conduct of the Allies* (says he) *hath dared to drop Insinuations about altering the Succession.* The Author of the *Conduct of the Allies* writes Sense and English, neither of which the Author of the *Crisis* understands: The former thinks it *wrong in Point of Policy to call in a Foreign Power to be Guarantee of our Succession, because it puts it out of the Power of our own Legislature to change our Succession without the Consent of that Prince or State who is Guaranty, whatever Necessity may happen in future Times.* Now, if it be

* Mr. *Steele's* Speech at the Election of a Speaker.

High Treason to affirm by Writing that the Legislature hath
no such Power; and if Mr. *Steele* thinks it strange that *Britain*
should be debarred this Privilege; what could be the Crime of
putting such a Case, that in future Ages, a Necessity might
happen of limiting the Succession, as well as it hath happened
already?

WHEN Mr. *Steele reflects upon the many solemn strong Barriers*
(to our Succession) *of Laws and Oaths*, &c. he *thinks all Fear
vanisheth before them.* I think so too; provided the Epithet
solemn goes for nothing: Because, although I have often heard
of a *solemn* Day, a *solemn* Feast, and a *solemn* Coxcomb, yet I
can conceive no Idea to my self of a *solemn Barrier.* However,
be that as it will; his *Thoughts*, it seems, *will not let him rest, but
before he is aware, he asks himself several Questions:* And since
he cannot resolve them, I will endeavour to give him what
Satisfaction I am able. The first is, *What are the Marks of a
lasting Security?* To which I answer, that the Signs of it in a
Kingdom or State are first, good Laws; and secondly those
Laws well executed: We are pretty well provided with the
former, but extremely defective in the latter. Secondly, *What
are our Tempers and our Hearts at Home?* If by *ours* he means
those of himself and his Abettors, they are most damnably
wicked; impatient for the Death of the QUEEN; ready to
gratify their Ambition and Revenge by all desperate Methods;
wholly alienate from Truth, Law, Religion, Mercy, Conscience,
or Honour. Thirdly, *In what Hands is Power lodged Abroad?*
To answer the Question naturally, *Louis* XIV. is King of
France, *Philip* V. (by the Councils and Acknowledgments of
the Whigs) is King of *Spain*, and so on. If by Power he means
Money; the Duke of *Marlborough* is thought to have more ready
Money than all the Kings of *Christendom* together; but, by
the peculiar Disposition of Providence, it is locked up in a
Trunk, to which his Ambition hath no key; and that is our
Security. Fourthly, *Are our unnatural Divisions our Strength?*
I think not; but they are the Sign of it; for, being *unnatural*,
they cannot last; and this shews, that Union, the Foundation
of all *Strength*, is more agreeable to our Nature. Fifthly, *Is it
nothing to us, which of the Princes of* Europe *has the longest Sword?*

Not much, if we can tie up his Hands, or put a strong *Shield* into those of his Neighbours: Or, if our *Sword* be as *Sharp*, as his is *Long:* Or if it be necessary for him to turn his own *Sword* into a Plow-share: Or, if such a *Sword* happeneth to be in the Hands of an *Infant*, or struggled for by two Competitors. Sixthly, *The powerful Hand that deals out Crowns and Kingdoms all around us, may it not in Time reach a King out to us too?* If the *powerful Hand* he means, be that of *France*, it may *reach out* as many Kings as it pleaseth, but we will not accept them. Whence does this Man get his Intelligence? I should think, even his Brother *Ridpath*, might furnish him with better. What *Crowns* or *Kingdoms* hath *France dealt* about? *Spain* was given by the Will of the former King, in Consequence of that infamous Treaty of Partition, the Advisers of which, will, I hope, never be forgot in *England*. *Sicily* was disposed of by her Majesty of *Great Britain*. So in Effect was *Sardinia*. *France* indeed once *reached out* a King to *Poland*, but the People would not receive him. This Question of Mr. *Steele*'s was therefore only put *in terrorem*, without any Regard to Truth. Seventhly, *Are there no Pretensions to our Crown that can ever be revived?* There may for ought I know be about a Dozen: And those in Time may possibly beget a Hundred. But we must do as well as we can: Captain *Bessus*, when he had fifty Challenges to answer, protested he could not fight above three Duels a Day. *If the Pretender should fail* (says the Writer) *the* French *King has in his Quiver a Succession of them, the Dutchess of* Savoy, *or her Sons, or the* Dauphin *her Grandson*. Let me suppose the *Chevalier* de *St. George* to be dead; the Dutchess of *Savoy* will then be a *Pretender*, and consequently must leave her Husband, because his Royal Highness (for Mr. *Steele* has not yet acknowledged him for a King) is in Alliance with her *British* Majesty: Her Sons, when they grow *Pretenders*, must undergo the same Fate. But I am at a Loss how to dispose of the *Dauphin*, if he happen to be King of *France* before the *Pretendership* to *Britain* falls to his Share; for I doubt he will never be persuaded to remove out of his own Kingdom, only because it is too near *England*.

But *the Duke of* Savoy *did some Years ago put in his Claim to the Crown of* England *in Right of his Wife*; *and he is a Prince of great Capacity*; *in strict Alliance with* France, *and may therefore very well add to our Fears of a Popish Successor.* Is it the Fault of the present, or of any Ministry, that this Prince put in his Claim? Must we give him Opium to destroy his *Capacity?* Or can we prevent his Alliance with any Prince who is in Peace with her Majesty? Must we send to stab or poison all the *Popish* Princes, who have any pretended Title to our Crown by the Proximity of Blood? What, in the Name of GOD, can these People drive at? What is it they demand? Suppose the present *Dauphin* were now a Man, and King of *France*, and next *Popish* Heir to the Crown of *England*; is he not excluded by the Laws of the Land? But what Regard will he have to our Laws? I answer; hath not the QUEEN as good a Title to the Crown of *France?* And how is she excluded but by their Law against the Succession of Females, which we are not bound to acknowledge? And is it not in our Power to exclude Female Successors as well as in theirs? If such a Pretence shall prove the Cause of a War, what human Power can prevent it? But our Cause must necessarily be good and righteous; for either the Kings of *England* have been unjustly kept out of the Possession of *France*, or the *Dauphin*, although nearest of Kin, can have no legal Title to *England*. And he must be an ill Prince indeed, who will not have the Hearts and Hands of ninety-nine in a Hundred among his Subjects against such a *Popish Pretender*.

I HAVE been the longer in answering the seventh Question, because it led me to consider all he had afterwards to say upon the Subject of the *Pretender*. Eighthly and Lastly, he asks himself *whether Popery and Ambition are become tame and quiet Neighbours?* In this I can give him no Satisfaction, because I never was in that Street where they live; nor do I converse with any of their Friends; only I find they are Persons of a very evil Reputation. But I am told for certain, that *Ambition* hath removed her Lodging, and lives the very next Door to *Faction*; where they keep such a Racket, that the whole Parish is disturbed, and every Night in an Uproar.

THUS much in Answer to those eight *uneasy Questions,*

put by the Author to himself, in order *to satisfy every Briton*, and give him an Occasion of *taking an impartial View of the Affairs of* Europe *in general, as well as of* Great Britain *in particular.*

AFTER enumerating the great Actions of the *Confederate* Armies under the Command of Prince *Eugene*, and the Duke of *Marlborough*, Mr. *Steele* observes in the Bitterness of his Soul, that the *British General, however unaccountable it may be to Posterity, was not permitted to enjoy the Fruits of his glorious Labour.* Ten Years *Fruits* it seems were not sufficient, and yet they were the *fruitfullest* Campaigns that ever any General cropt. However, I cannot but hope, that Posterity will not be left in the dark, but some Care taken both of her Majesty's Glory, and of the Reputation of those she employs. An impartial Historian may tell the World (and the next Age will easily believe what it continues to feel) that the Avarice and Ambition of a few factious insolent Subjects, had almost destroyed their Country, by continuing a ruinous War, in Conjunction with Allies, for whose Sakes principally we fought, who refused to bear their just Proportion of the Charge, and were connived at in their Refusal for private Ends. That, these factious People treated the best and kindest of Sovereigns with Insolence, Cruelty and Ingratitude (of which he will be able to produce several Instances.) That, they encouraged Persons and Principles alien from our Religion and Government, in order to strengthen their Faction. He will tell the Reasons why the *General* and *first Minister* were seduced to be Heads of this Faction, contrary to the Opinions they had always professed. Such an Historian will shew many Reasons which made it necessary to remove the *General* and his Friends, who knowing the Bent of the Nation were against them, expected to lose their Power when the War was at an End. Particularly, the Historian will discover the whole Intrigue of the Duke of *Marlborough*'s endeavouring to procure a Commission to be *General for Life*; wherein Justice will be done to a Person at that Time of high Station in the Law; who, (I mention it to his Honour) advised the Duke, when he was consulted upon it, not to accept of such a *Commission.* By these, and many other Instances which

Time will bring to Light, it may perhaps appear not very unaccountable to Posterity, why this great Man was dismissed at last; but rather why he was dismissed no sooner.

But this is entring into a wide Field. I shall therefore leave *Posterity* to the Information of better Historians than the Author of the *Crisis*, or my self; and go on to inform the present Age in some Facts, which this great Orator and Politician thinks fit to misrepresent with the utmost Degree either of natural or wilful Ignorance. He asserts, that in the Duke of *Ormonde's* Campaign, *after a Suspension of Arms between* Great Britain *and* France, *proclaimed at the Head of the Armies, the* British, *in the midst of the Enemies Garrisons, withdrew themselves from their Confederates.* The Fact is directly otherwise; for the *British* Troops were most infamously deserted by the Confederates, after all that could be urged by the Duke of *Ormonde*, and the Earl of *Strafford*, to press the Confederate Generals not to forsake them. The Duke was directed to avoid engaging in any Action until he had further Orders, because an Account of the King of *Spain's* Renunciation was every Day expected: This the *Imperialists* and *Dutch* knew well enough, and therefore proposed to the Duke in that very Juncture to engage the *French*, for no other Reason but to render desperate all the Queen's Measures towards a Peace. Was not the certain Possession of *Dunkirk* of equal Advantage to the uncertainty of a Battle? A whole Campaign under the Duke of *Marlborough*, with such an Acquisition, although at the Cost of many thousand Lives, and several Millions of Money, would have been thought very gloriously ended. Neither after all, was it a new Thing, either in the *British* General, or the *Dutch* Deputies, to refuse fighting, when they did not approve it. When the Duke of *Marlborough* was going to invest *Bouchain*, the Deputies of the *States* pressed him in vain to engage the Enemy; and one of them was so far discontented upon his Grace's Refusal, that he presently became a Partizan of the Peace; yet, I do not remember any Clamour then raised here against the Duke upon that Account. Again, when the *French* invaded *Doway*, after the Confederates had deserted the Duke of *Ormonde*, Prince *Eugene* was violently

G

bent upon a Battle, and said they should never have another so good an Opportunity: But Monsieur——, a private Deputy, rose up, and opposed it so far, that the Prince was forced to desist. Was it then more Criminal in the Duke of *Ormonde* to refuse fighting, by express Commands of the QUEEN, and in order to get Possession of *Dunkirk*, than for the Duke of *Marlborough* to give the same Refusal, without any such Orders, or any such Advantage? Or, shall a *Dutch* Deputy assume more Power than the QUEEN of *Great Britain*'s General, acting by the immediate Commands of his Sovereign?

THE *Emperor and the Empire* (says Mr. *Steele*, by way of Admiration) *continue the War!* Is his Imperial Majesty able to continue it or no? If he be, then *Great Britain* hath been strangely used for ten Years past: Then how came it to pass, That of above thirty thousand Men in his Service in *Italy*, at the Time of the Battle of *Turin*, there were not above four thousand paid by himself? If he be not able to continue it, Why does he go on? The Reasons are clear; because the War only affects the Princes of the Empire, (whom he is willing enough to expose) but not his own Dominions. Besides, the Imperial Ministers are in daily Expectation of the QUEEN's Death, which they hope will give a new Turn to Affairs, and rekindle the War in *Europe* upon the old Foot; and we know how the Ministers of that Court publickly Assign it for a Reason of their Obstinacy against Peace, that they hope for a sudden Revolution in *England*. In the mean Time, this Appearance of the *Emperor* being forsaken by his Ally, will serve to encrease the Clamour both here and in *Holland*, against her Majesty, and those she employs.

MR. *Steele* says, *There can be no Crime in affirming, (if it be a Truth) that the House of* Bourbon *is at this Juncture become more formidable, and bids fairer for an Universal Monarchy, and to engross the whole Trade of* Europe, *than it did before the War.*

No Crime in affirming it, if it be a Truth. I will for once allow his Proposition. But if it be false, then I affirm, that whoever advanceth so seditious a Falshood, deserveth to be hanged. Doth he mean by the House of *Bourbon*, the two Kings of *France* and *Spain?* If so, I reject his Meaning, which would insinuate that the Interests and Designs of both those Princes will be the same; whereas they are more opposite than those of any two other Monarchs in *Christendom*. This is the old foolish Slander so frequently flung upon the Peace, and as frequently refuted. These factious Undertakers of the Press write with great Advantage; they strenuously affirm a thousand Falshoods, without Fear, Wit, Conscience, or Knowledge; and we, who answer them, must be at the Expence of an Argument for each: After which, in the very next Pamphlet, we see the same Assertions produced again, without the least Notice of what hath been said to disprove them. By the House of *Bourbon*, doth he mean only the *French* King for the Time being? If so, and his Assertion be true, then that Prince must either deal with the Devil; or else the Money and Blood spent in our ten Years Victories against him, might as well have continued in the Purses and Veins of her Majesty's Subjects.

BUT the *particular* Assertions of this Author are easier detected than his *general* ones; I shall therefore proceed upon examining the Former. For Instance: I desire him to ask the *Dutch*, who can best inform him, *Why they delivered up* Traerback *to the* Imperialists? For, as to the QUEEN, her Majesty was never once consulted in it; whatever his Preceptors, the Politicians of *Button*'s Coffee-House may have informed him to the contrary.

MR. *Steele* affirms, that *the* French *have begun the Demolition of* Dunkirk *Contemptuously and Arbitrarily their own Way*. The Governor of the Town, and those Gentlemen entrusted with the Inspection of this Work, do assure me, that the Fact is altogether otherwise: That, the Method prescribed by those whom her Majesty employs, hath been exactly followed, and that the Works are already demolished. I will venture to tell him further, That the Demolition was so long deferred, in order to remove those Difficulties which the Barrier-Treaty hath put us under; and the Event hath shewn, that it was prudent to proceed no faster until those Difficulties were got over. The *Mole* and *Harbour* could not be destroy'd until the Ships were got out, which by Reason of some profound Secrets of State, did not happen until the other Day. Who *gave him those just Suspicions that the Mole and Harbour will never be destroyed?* What is it he would now insinuate? That the Ministry is bribed to leave the most important Part of the Work undone; or, that the Pretender is to invade us from thence; or, that the QUEEN hath entered into a Conspiracy with her Servants to prevent the good Effects of the Peace, for no other End but to lose the Affections of her People, and endanger her self.

INSTEAD of any further Information, which I could easily give, but which no honest Man can want; I venture to affirm, that the Mole and Harbour of *Dunkirk* will in a short Time be most effectually destroyed; and at the same Time, I venture to Prophesy, that neither Mr. *Steele*, nor his Faction, will ever confess they believe it.

AFTER all, it is a little hard, that the QUEEN cannot be allowed to demolish this Town in whatever Manner she pleaseth to fancy: Mr. *Steele*, must have it done his own Way, and is angry the *French* have pretended to do it theirs; and yet he wrongs them into the Bargain. For my own Part, I do seriously think, the most *Christian* King to be a much better Friend of her Majesty's than Mr. *Steele*, or any of his Faction. Besides, it is to be considered, that he is a Monarch and a Relation; and therefore, if I were a Privy-Counsellor, and my Advice to be asked, which of those two *GENTLEMEN BORN should have the Direction in the Demolition of *Dunkirk*, I would give it for the former; because I look upon Mr. *Steele*, in Quality of a Member of his Party, to be much more skilful in *demolishing at Home* than *Abroad*.

THERE is a Prospect of more Danger to the Balance of *Europe*, and to the Trade of *Britain*, from the *Emperor* over-running *Italy*, than from *France* over-running the *Empire*; that his *Imperial* Majesty entertains such Thoughts, is visible to the World: And, although little can be said to justify many Actions of the *French* King, yet the worst of them have never equalled the Emperor's arbitrary keeping the Possession of *Milan*, directly contrary to his Oath, and to the express Words of the *Golden Bull*; which oblige him to deliver up every *Fief*

* Mr. STEELE *often stiles himself so.*

that falls; or else they must all in the Course of Time lapse into his own Hands.

I WAS at a Loss who it was that Mr. *Steele* hinted at some Time ago by *the powerful Hand, that deals out Crowns and Kingdoms all around us:* I now plainly find, he meant no other Hand but his own. He hath dealt out the Crown of *Spain* to *France*; to *France* he hath given Leave to invade the *Empire* next Spring with two hundred thousand Men; and, now at last he deals to *France* the *Imperial* Dignity; *and so farewel Liberty*; Europe *will be* French. But in order to bring all this about, *the Capital of* Austria, *the Residence of his* Imperial *Majesty* must continue to be *visited by the Plague*, of which the *Emperor* must die, and so the Thing is done.

WHY should not I venture to *deal out one Sceptre* in my Turn as well as Mr. *Steele?* I therefore *deal out* the *Empire* to the *Elector* of *Saxony*, upon Failure of Issue to this *Emperor* at his Death; provided the Whigs will prevail on the *Son* to turn *Papist* to get an *Empire*, as they did upon the *Father* to get a *Kingdom*. Or, if this Prince be not approved of, I *deal out* in his Stead, the *Elector* of *Bavaria:* And, in one or the other of these, I dare engage to have all *Christendom* to second me, whatever the Spleen, in the Shape of Politicks, may dictate to the Author of the *Crisis*.

THE Design of Mr. *Steele*, in *representing the Circumstances of the Affairs of* Europe, is to signify to the World, that all *Europe* is put in the high Road to Slavery by the Corruption of her Majesty's present Ministers; and so he goes on to *Portugal*; which *having, during the War, supplied us with Gold in Exchange for our* Woollen-Manufacture, *hath only at present a Suspension of Arms for its Protection, to last no longer than until the* Catalonians *are reduced; and then the old Pretensions of* Spain *to* Portugal *will be revived:* And *Portugal*, when once enslaved by *Spain*, falls naturally with the rest of *Europe* into the Gulph of *France*. In the mean Time, let us see what Relief a little Truth can give this unhappy Kingdom. That, *Portugal* hath yet no more than a Suspension of Arms, they may thank themselves, because they came so late into the Treaty; and, that they came so late, they may thank the Whigs, whose false Representations they were so weak to believe. However, the QUEEN hath voluntarily given them a Guarantee to defend them against *Spain* until the Peace shall be made; and such Terms after the Peace, are stipulated for them, as the *Portuguese* themselves are contented with.

HAVING mentioned the *Catalonians*, he puts the Question, *Who can name the* Catalonians *without a Tear?* That can I; for he hath told so many melancholy Stories without one Syllable of Truth, that he hath blunted the Edge of my Fears, and I shall not be startled at the worst he can say. What he affirms concerning the *Catalonians* is included in the following Particulars: First, *That they were drawn into the War by the Encouragement of the Maritime Powers*; by which are understood *England* and *Holland:* But, he is too good a Friend of the *Dutch*, to give them any Part of the Blame. Secondly, That, *they are now abandoned and exposed to the Resentment of an enraged Prince.* Thirdly, That, *they always opposed the Person and Interest of that Prince*, who is their present King. Lastly, That, *the Doom is dreadful of those who shall in the Sight of God be esteemed their Destroyers.* And, if we interpret the Insinuation he makes, according to his own Mind, the Destruction of those People, must be imputed to the present Ministry.

I AM sometimes in Charity disposed to hope, that this Writer is not always sensible of the flagrant Falshoods he utters, but is either biassed by an Inclination to believe the worst, or a Want of Judgment to chuse his Informers. That the *Catalonians* were *drawn into the War by the Encouragement of her Majesty*, should not in Decency have been affirmed until about fifty Years hence; when it might be supposed there would be no living Witness left to disprove it. It was only upon the Assurances of a Revolt, given by the Prince of *Hesse* and others, and their Invitation, that the QUEEN was prevailed with to send her Forces upon that Expedition. When *Barcelona* was taken by a most unexpected Accident, of a Bomb lighting on the Magazine, then indeed the *Catalonians* revolted, having before submitted and sworn Allegiance to *Philip*, as much as any other Province of *Spain*. Upon the Peace between that Crown and *Britain*, the QUEEN, in order to ease the

Emperor, and save his Troops, stipulated with King *Philip* for a Neutrality in *Italy*, and that his Imperial Majesty should have Liberty to evacuate *Catalonia*; upon Conditions of absolute Indemnity to the *Catalans*, with an entire Restitution to their Honours, Dignities, and Estates. As this Neutrality was never observed by the *Emperor*, so he never effectually evacuated *Catalonia*; for, although he sent away the main Body, he left behind many Officers and private Men, who now spirit up and assist those obstinate People to continue in their Rebellion. It is true indeed, that King *Philip* did not absolutely restore the *Catalans* to *all* their old Privileges, of which they never made other Use than as an Encouragement to rebel; but, to the same Privileges with his Subjects of *Castille*, particularly to the Liberty of Trading, and having Employments in the *West-Indies*, which they never enjoyed before. Besides, the QUEEN reserved to her self the Power of procuring farther Immunities for them, wherein the most *Christian* King was obliged to second her: For, his *Catholick* Majesty intended no more, than to retrench those Privileges under the Pretext of which they now rebel, as they had formerly done in favour of *France. How dreadful* then *must the Doom be of those* who hindered these People from submitting to the gentle Terms offered them by their Prince! And who, although they be conscious of their own Inability to furnish one single Ship for the Support of the *Catalans*, are at this Instant spurring them on to their Ruin, by Promises of Aid and Protection.

THUS much in Answer to Mr. *Steele's* Account of the Affairs of *Europe*; from which he deduceth the Universal Monarchy of *France*, and the Danger of I know not how many *Popish Successors* to *Britain*. His political Reflections are as good as his Facts. *We must observe*, says he, *that the Person who seems to be the most favoured by the* French *King in the late Treaties, is the Duke of* Savoy. Extremely right: For, what ever that Prince got by the Peace, he owes entirely to her Majesty, as a just Reward for his having been so firm and useful an Ally; neither was *France* brought with more Difficulty to yield any one Point, than that of allowing the Duke such a Barrier as the QUEEN insisted on.

He *is become the most powerful Prince in* Italy. I had rather see *him* so, than the *Emperor. He is supposed to have entered into a secret and strict Alliance with the House of* Bourbon. This is one of those Facts wherein I am most inclined to believe the Author, because it is what he must needs be utterly ignorant of, and therefore might possibly be true.

I THOUGHT indeed we should be safe from all Popish Successors as far as *Italy*, because of the prodigious Clutter about sending the *Pretender* thither. But they will never agree where to fix their *Longitude*. The Duke of *Savoy* is the more dangerous for removing to *Sicily:* He *adds to our Fears* for being *too far off*, and the *Chevalier de St. George* for being *too near.* So, *whether* France *conquer* Germany, *or be in Peace and good Understanding with it*; either Event *will put us and* Holland *at the Mercy of* France, which hath a Quiver full of *Pretenders*, at its back, when ever the *Chevalier* shall die.

THIS was just the Logick of poor *Prince Butler*, a splenetick mad Man, whom every Body may remember about the Town. Prince *Pamphilio* in *Italy* employed Emissaries to torment *Prince Butler* here. But what if Prince *Pamphilio* die? Why then, he hath left in his Will, that his Heirs and Executors torment *Prince Butler* for ever.

I CANNOT think it a Misfortune, what Mr. *Steele* affirms, That *treasonable Books lately dispersed among us, striking apparently at the* Hanover *Succession, have passed almost without Observation from the Generality of the People*; because it seems a certain Sign that *the Generality of the People* are well disposed to that illustrious Family: But, I look upon it as a great Evil, to see seditious Books *dispersed among us, apparently striking at the* QUEEN and her Administration, at the Constitution in Church and State, and at all Religion; yet *passing without Observation from the Generality of* those in Power: But whether this Remissness may be imputed to *White-Hall*, or *Westminster-Hall*, is other Mens Business to enquire. Mr. *Steele* knows in his Conscience, that *the Queries concerning the* Pretender, issued from one of his own Party. And as for the poor Nonjuring Clergyman, who was trusted with committing to the Press a late Book *on the Subject of Hereditary Right*, by a Strain

of the *Summum Jus*, he is now, as I am told, with half a Score
Children, starving and rotting among Thieves and Pick-
pockets, in the common Room of a stinking Jail. I have never
seen either the Book or the Publisher; however, I would fain
ask *one single *Person* in the World a Question; Why he who
hath so often drank the abdicated King's Health upon his
Knees —— But the Transition is natural and frequent, and I
shall not trouble him for an Answer.

IT is the hardest Case in the World, that Mr. *Steele* should
take up the artificial Reports of his own Faction, and then put
them off upon the World, as *additional Fears of a Popish Successor*. I can assure him, that no good Subject of the QUEEN
is under the least Concern whether the *Pretender* be converted
or no, farther than their Wishes that all Men would embrace
the true Religion. But, reporting backwards and forwards
upon this Point, helps to keep up the Noise, and is a Topick
for Mr. *Steele* to enlarge himself upon, by shewing how little
we can depend on such Conversions; by collecting a List of
Popish Cruelties, and repeating, after himself and the Bishop
of *Sarum*, the dismal Effects likely to follow upon the Return
of that Superstition among us.

BUT, as this Writer is reported by those who know him,
to be what the *French* call *Journalier*, his Fear and Courage
operating according to the Weather in our uncertain Climate;
I am apt to believe, the two last Pages of his *Crisis* were
written on a *Sunshine Day*. This I guess from the general
Tenor of them, and particularly from an unwary Assertion,
which, if he believe as firmly as I do, will at once overthrow
all his Foreign and Domestick *Fears of a Popish Successor*. *As
divided a People as we are, those who stand for the House of* Hanover,
are *INFINITELY superior in Number, Wealth, Courage, and
all Arts Military and Civil, to those in the contrary Interest; besides
which, we have the Laws, I say, the Laws on our Side. The Laws, I
say, the Laws.* This elegant Repetition is, I think, a little out of
Place: For, the Stress might better have been laid upon so
great a Majority of the Nation; without which, I doubt the
Laws would be of little Weight; although they be very good

* PARKER, afterwards Lord Chancellor.

additional Securities. And, if what he here asserts be true, as it certainly is, although he assert it; (for I allow even the Majority of his own Party to be against the *Pretender*) there can be no Danger of a Popish Successor, except from the unreasonable Jealousies of the *best* among that Party, and from the Malice, the Avarice, or Ambition of the *worst*; without which, *Britain* would be able to defend her Succession against all her Enemies both at Home and Abroad. Most of the Dangers from Abroad which he enumerates as the Consequences of this very bad Peace, made by the QUEEN, and approved by Parliament, must have subsisted under any Peace at all; unless, among other Projects equally feasible, we could have stipulated to cut the Throats of every *Popish* Relation to the Royal Family.

WELL; by this Author's own Confession, a Number infinitely superior, and the best circumstantiated imaginable, are for the *Succession* in the House of *Hanover*. This *Succession* is established, confirmed, and secured by several Laws; her Majesty's repeated Declarations, and the Oaths of all her Subjects, engage both her and them to preserve what those Laws have settled. This is a *Security* indeed, a *Security* adequate at least to the Importance of the Thing; and yet, according to the Whig-Scheme, as delivered to us by Mr. *Steele*, and his Coadjutors, is altogether insufficient; and the Succession will be defeated, the *Pretender* brought in, and *Popery* established among us, without the farther Assistance of this Writer and his Faction.

AND what Securities have our Adversaries substituted in the Place of these? A Club of Politicians, where *Jenny Man* presides; A *Crisis* written by Mr. *Steele*; a Confederacy of knavish Stock-Jobbers to ruin Credit; a Report of the QUEEN's Death; an *Effigies* of the *Pretender* run twice through the Body by a valiant Peer: A Speech by the Author of the *Crisis:* And to sum up all, an unlimited Freedom of reviling her Majesty, and those she employs.

I HAVE now finished the most disgustful Task that ever I undertook: I could with more Ease have written *three* dull Pamphlets, than remarked upon the Falshoods and Absurdities of *One*. But I was quite confounded last *Wednesday* when the Printer came with another Pamphlet in his Hand, written by the same Author, and entituled, *The Englishman, being the Close of the Paper so called*, &c. He desired I would read it over, and consider it in a Paper by it self; which last I absolutely refused. Upon Perusal, I found it chiefly an Invective against *Toby*, the Ministry, the *Examiner*, the Clergy, the QUEEN, and the *Post-Boy:* Yet, at the same Time with great Justice exclaiming against those who presumed to offer the least Word against the Heads of that Faction whom her Majesty discarded. The Author likewise proposeth an *equal Division of Favour and Employments* between the Whigs and Tories: For, if the former *can have no Part or Portion in* David, *they desire no longer to be his Subjects*. He insists, that her Majesty *hath exactly followed* Monsieur *Tughe*'s *Memorial against demolishing of* Dunkirk. He reflects with *great Satisfaction on the Good already done to his Country by the* Crisis. *Non nobis Domine, non nobis*, &c.——He gives us Hopes that he will leave off Writing, *and consult his own Quiet and Happiness*; and concludes with a *Letter to a Friend at Court*. I suppose by the Style of *old Friend*, and the like, it must be some Body *there* of his own Level; among whom, his Party have indeed more *Friends* than I could wish. In this Letter he asserts, that the present Ministers were not educated in the Church of *England*, but are *new Converts from Presbytery*. Upon which I can only reflect, how blind the Malice of that Man must be, who invents a groundless Lye in order to defame his Superiors, which would be no Disgrace, if it had been a Truth. And he concludes, with making three Demands *for the Satisfaction of himself* and other *Malecontents*. First, *The Demolition of the Harbour of* Dunkirk: Secondly, *That* Great-Britain *and* France *would heartily join against the exorbitant Power of the Duke of* Lorrain, *and force the* Pretender *from his* Asylum *at* Bar le Duc: Lastly, *That his* Electoral Highness *of* Hanover *would be so grateful to signify to all the World, the perfect good Understanding he hath with the Court of* England, *in as plain Terms as her Majesty was pleased to declare she had with that House on her Part*.

As to the first of these Demands, I will venture to undertake it shall be granted; but then Mr. *Steele*, and his Brother *Male-contents*, must promise to believe the Thing is done, after those employed have made their Report; or else bring Vouchers to disprove it. Upon the second, I cannot tell whether her Majesty will engage in a War against the Duke of *Lorrain*, to *force him to remove the* Pretender; but I believe, if the Parliament should think it necessary to address upon such an Occasion, the QUEEN will move that Prince to send him away. His last Demand, offered under the Title of a *Wish*, is of so insolent and seditious a Strain, that I care not to touch it. Here he directly chargeth her Majesty with delivering a Falshood to her Parliament from the Throne; and declares he will not believe her, until the Elector of *Hanover* himself shall vouch for the Truth of what she hath so solemnly affirmed.

I AGREE with this Writer, that it is an idle Thing in his Antagonists to trouble themselves upon the *Articles of his Birth, Education, or Fortune*; for whoever writes at this Rate of his Sovereign, to whom he owes so many personal Obligations, I should never enquire whether he be a *GENTLEMAN BORN*, but whether he be a *HUMAN CREATURE*.

A Discourse concerning the Fears from the Pretender

A Discourse concerning
the Fears from the
Pretender.

Feb. 20 [1714]

THERE are some disputes between the two contending
Partyes now among us, which in reason ought no
longer to subsist, because Time and Events have put an
End to the Causes of them. For instance, Whether our Peace
with France and Spain were safe and honorable; Whether the
States Generall have a sufficient Barrier. Whether Spain
ought to be governed by a Prince of the Bourbon Family.
These Points are already determined, whether wisely or not;
and reasonable Men of both sides will, I suppose allow, that the
War can not be renewed at present to settle them better.

Other Differences there are, and of great Importance, which
still depend, and cannot speedily be brought to an Issue
without some degree of Correspondence between both
Partyes——As, whether the Treaty of Commerce with France
shall be confirmed by Parliament as beneficiall to our Trade,
or rejected as pernicious. Whether the Princess Sophia of
Hanover shall be invited to reside in England, as an Expedient
for securing the Succession to Her Family upon the Queen's
Demise. Whether the Pretender shall be forced to remove
from Bar le duc, or permitted to reside any where on this side
the Alpes. There are some other Controversyes of lesser
Moment between the two contending Partyes; but the most
popular Topick of Quarrell, is the Pretender. I have heard
many significant Persons of the side which is against the
Court, affirm with great appearance of Sincerity, that if they

could be perfectly satisfied upon this Article, they would leave it to Her Majesty to chuse her own Servants, and give her no further Uneasyness in any part of her Administration. I have therefore thought it may be worth some serious thought to examine.*

* See textual notes.

Some free Thoughts upon the present State of Affairs

SOME

Free THOUGHTS

UPON THE

Prefent STATE

OF

AFFAIRS.

Written in the YEAR 1714.

DUBLIN:

Printed by and for GEORGE FAULKNER.
M,DCC,XLI.

U

MEMORANDUM

THIS discourse was written at Upper Letcomb in Berkshire, about two months before the Queens Death, during my Retirement upon finding it impossible after above two years endeavor to reconcile My Lord Treasurer, and My Lord Bolingbroke: from the quarrel between which two great men all our misfortunes proceeded.

The Papers were sent in an unknown hand to Mr. Barber the printer in London who gave them to My Lord Bolingbroke to peruse, knowing nothing of the Author, but by conjecture. His Lordship would have altered Some passages; and during the Delay and doubts he made, the Queen dyed.

Some free Thoughts upon the present State of Affairs

May—1714

WHATEVER may be thought or practised by profound Politicians, they will never be able to convince the reasonable part of Mankind, that the most plain, short, easy, safe, and lawfull way to any good End, is not more eligible, than one directly contrary in some or all of these Qualities. I have been frequently assured by great Ministers, that Politicks were nothing but common sense; which as it was the only true Thing they spoke, so it was the only Thing they could have wished I should not believe. God has given the Bulk of Mankind a Capacity to understand Reason when it is fairly offered; and by Reason they would easily be governed, if it were left to their Choice. Those Princes in all Ages who were most distinguished for their mysterious Skill in Government, found by the Event that they had ill consulted their own Quiet, or the Ease and Happiness of their People; neither hath Posterity remembred them with Honour; such as Lysander and Philip among the Greeks, Tiberius in Rome, Lewis the eleventh of France, Pope Alexander the Sixth, and his son Cesar Borgia, Queen Catherine de Medicis, Philip the Second of Spain, with many others. Examples are not less frequent of Ministers famed for men of deep Intrigue whose Politicks have produced little more than Murmurings, Factions, and Discontents, which usually terminated in the Disgrace and Ruin of the Authors.

I can recollect but three Occasions in a State, where the Talents of such Men may be thought necessary, I mean in a State where the Prince is obeyed and loved by his Subjects: First, in the Negotiation of a peace: Secondly, in adjusting the Interests of our own Country with those of the Nations round us; watching the severall Motions of our Neighbours and Allyes, and preserving a due Ballance among them: Lastly in the Management of Parties and Factions at home. Yet in the first of these Cases I have often heard it observed, that plain good Sense, and a firm Adherence to the Point, have proved more effectual, than all those Arts which I remember a *great foreign Minister used in Contempt to call *the Spirit of Negotiating*. In the Second Case, much wisdom, and a through Knowledge in Affairs both Foreign and Domestick are certainly required; after which I know no Talents necessary besides Method and Skill in the common Forms of Business. In the last Case, which is that of Managing Parties, there seems indeed to be more Occasion for practicing this Gift of the lower Politicks; whenever the Tide runs high against the Court and those in Power; which seldom happens under any tolerable Administration; while the true Interest of the Nation is pursued. But here in England (for I do not pretend to establish Maxims of Government in general) while the Prince and Ministry, the Clergy, the Majority of landed Men, and Bulk of the People appear to have the same Views, and the same Principles, it is not obvious to me, how those at the Helm can have many Opportunities of Shewing their Skill in Mystery and Refinement, besides what themselves think fit to create.

I have been assured by Men long practiced in Business, that the Secrets of Court are much fewer than is generally supposed; and I hold it for the greatest Secret of Court that they are so few: Because the first Springs of great Events like those of great Rivers, are often so mean and so little, that in point of Credit and Reputation they ought to be hid: And therefore Ministers are so wise to leave their Proceedings to be accounted for by Reasoners at a distance, who often mould them into Systems, that do not only go down very well in the Coffee-House, but are Supplies for Pamphlets in the present Age, and may probably furnish Materials for Memoirs and Histories in the next.

Tis true indeed, that even those who are very near the Court, and supposed to have a large Share in the Management

* Monsieur Torcy.

of publick matters, are apt to deduce wrong Consequences by reasoning upon the Causes and Motives of those Actions, wherein themselves are employed. A great Minister puts you a Case, and asks your opinion, but conceals an essential Circumstance, upon which the whole Weight of the Matter turns; then he despises your Understanding for counselling him no better, and concludes he ought to trust entirely to his own Wisdom. Thus he grows to abound in Secrets, and Reserves, even towards those with whom he ought to act in the greatest Confidence and Concert; and thus the world is brought to judge, that whatever be the Issue and Event, it was all foreseen, Contrived, and brought to pass by some Master-Stroke of his Politicks.

I could produce innumerable Instances from my own Memory and Observation, of Events imputed to the profound Skill and Address of a Minister, which in reality were either the meer Effects of Negligence, Weakness, Humour, Passion or Pride; or at best, but the Natural Course of Things left to themselves.

During this very Sessions of Parliament, a most ingenious Gentleman, who has much Credit with those in Power, would needs have it, that in the late Dissensions at Court, which grew too high to be any longer a Secret; the whole Matter was carried with the utmost Dexterity on one Side, and with manifest ill Conduct on the other. To prove this he made use of the most plausible Topicks, drawn from the Nature and Dispositions of the several Persons concerned, as well as of Her Majesty, all which he knows as much of as most Men: And gave me a Detail of the whole with such an Appearance of Probability, as committed to writing would pass for an admirable Piece of secret History. Yet I am at the same time convinced by the strongest Reasons, that the Issue of those Dissensions as to the Effects they had in the Court and House of Lords, was partly owing to very different Causes, and partly to the Scituation of Affairs, from whence in that Conjuncture they could not easily terminate otherwise than they did, whatever unhappy Consequences they may have for the future.

In like manner I have heard a Physician pronounce with

great Gravity, that he had cured so many Patients of malignant Fevers, and as many more of the Small-Pox; whereas in truth nine parts in ten of those who recovered, owed their Lives to the Strength of Nature and a good Constitution, while such a one happened to be their Doctor.

But while it is so difficult to learn the Springs and Motives of Some Facts, and so easy to forget the Circumstances of others, it is no wonder they should be so grossly misrepresented to the Publick by curious inquisitive heads, who proceed altogether upon Conjectures, and in reasoning upon Affairs of State, are sure to be mistaken by searching too deep.

And as I have known this to be the frequent Errour of many others, so I am sure it hath been perpetually mine; whenever I have attempted to discover the Causes of Political Events by Refinement and Conjecture; which I must acknowledge hath very much abated my Veneration for what they call Arcana Imperij, whereof I dare pronounce, that the fewer there are in any Administration, it is just so much the better.

What I have hitherto said, hath by no means been intended to detract from the Qualities requisite in those who are trusted with the Management of publick Affairs; On the contrary, I know no Station of Life, where virtues of all kinds are more highly necessary, and where the want of any is so quickly or universally felt. A great Minister has no virtue for which the Publick may not be the better, nor any Vice by which the Publick may not be a Sufferer. I have known more than once or twice within four years past, a very small Omission in Appearance, prove almost fatal to a whole Scheam, and very hardly retrieved. It is not always sufficient for the Person at the Helm, that he is disintrepid in his Nature, free from any Tincture of Avarice or Corruption, that he hath great naturall and acquired Abilities, that he loves his Prince and Country, and the Constitution in Church and State. I have seen all these Accomplishments unable to bear up their owner by the Mixture of a few trifling Defects too inconsiderable to Mention, and almost as easy to be remedied as related.

I never thought the Reputation of much Secrecy was a Character of any Advantage to a Minister, because it put all other men upon their Guard to be as secret as he, and was consequently the Occasion that Persons and Things were always misrepresented to Him; And likewise because too great an Affectation of Secrecy, is usually thought to be attended with those little Intrigues and Refinements which among the Vulgar denominate a Man a great Politician, but among others is apt whether deservedly or no, to acquire the Opinion of Cunning; A Talent which differs as much from the true Knowledge of Government, as that of an Attorney from an able Lawyer. Neither indeed am I altogether convinced, that this Habit of multiplying Secrets may not be carried on so far as to stop that Communication which is necessary in some degree among all who have any considerable Part in the Management of Publick Affairs: Because I have observed the Inconveniencies arising from a want of Concert between those who were to give Directions, to have been of as ill Consequences, as any that could happen from the Discovery of Secrets. I suppose, when a Building is to be erected, the Model may be the Contrivance only of one Head; and it is sufficient that the under-workmen be ordered to cut Stones into certain Shapes, and place them in certain Positions; but the several Master-Builders must have some general Knowledge of the Design, without which they can give no Orders at all. And indeed I do not know a greater Mark of an able Minister, than that of rightly adapting the several Faculties of Men; nor is any thing more to be lamented than the Impracticableness of doing this in any great Degree under our present Circumstances, while so many shut themselves out by adhering to a Faction, and while the Court is enslaved to the Impatience of others, who desire to sell their Vote or their Interest as dear as they can. But whether this hath not been submitted to more than was necessary, whether it hath not been dangerous in the Example, and pernicious in the Practice, I must leave to the Enquiry of Others.

It may be matter of no little Admiration to consider in some Lights the State of Affairs among us for four years past. The Queen finding her self and the Majority of her Kingdom grown weary of the Avarice and Insolence, the mistaken

Politicks, and destructive Principles of her former Ministers, calls to the Service of the Publick, another Sett of Men, who by Confession of their Enemies had equal Abilities at least with their Predecessors; Whose Interest made it necessary for them (although their Inclinations had been otherwise) to act upon those Maxims which were most agreeable to the Constitution in Church and State; Whose Birth and Patrimonies gave them weight in the Nation; And who (I speak of the chief Managers) had long lived under the strictest Bonds of Friendship. With all these Advantages supported by a vast Majority of the landed Interest, and the Inferiour Clergy almost to a Man, we have several times seen the present Administration in the greatest Distress, and very near the Brink of Ruin, together with the Cause of the Church and Monarchy committed to their Charge; neither doth it appear to me at the minute I am now writing, that their Power or Duration are upon any tolerable Foot of Security. The Cause of all which I do not so much impute to the Address and Industry of their Enemies, the uncertain timorous Nature of the Queen, or Obstructions from any private Remora about the Court, as to some Failures which I think have been full as visible in their Causes as Effects.

Nothing hath given me greater Indignation than to behold a Ministry, which came in with the Advantages I have represented, forced ever Since to act upon the Defensive in the House of Lords with a Majority on their sides, and instead of calling others to account, as it was reasonably expected, misspending their time and losing many Opportunities of doing good, because a Strugling Faction kept them continually in play. This Courage among the Adversaries of the Court, was inspired into them by various Incidents, for every one of which I think the Ministers alone are to answer.

For, first, that Race of Politicians, who in the Cant Phrase are called the Whimsicalls, was never so numerous or at least so active, as it hath been since the great Change at Court; Many of those who pretended wholly to be *in* with the Principles upon which Her Majesty and her new servants proceeded, either absenting themselves with the utmost

Indifference, in those Conjunctures upon which the whole Cause depended, or siding directly with the Enemy. All which indeed arose from a very unjust and perhaps an affected Diffidence towards those at the Helm.

I very well remember, when this Ministry was not above a year old, there was no little murmuring among such as are called the higher Tories or Churchmen (particularly some who have since affected great Fears of the Pretender, and quarrelled very much with the Treaty's of Peace and Commerce with France) that a quicker Progress was not made in removing those of the discontented Party out of Employments; I remember likewise, the Reasonings upon this matter were various, even among many who were allowed to know a good deal of the Inside of the Court: some supposed the Queen was at first prevailed on to make this great Change with no other View than that of acting for the future upon a moderating Scheam, in order to reconcile both Parties; And I believe there might possibly have been some Grounds for this Supposition. Others conceived, that Employments were left undisposed of, in order to keep alive the Hopes of many more impatient Candidates than ever could be gratifyed. This hath since been looked on as a very high Strain of Politicks, and to have succeeded accordingly, because it is the opinion of many, that the numerous Pretenders to Places would never have been kept in order if all Expectation had been cut off. Others were yet more refined, and thought it neither wise nor safe wholly to extinguish all Opposition from the adverse Side; because in the Nature of Things it was absolutely necessary that there should be Parties in an English Parliament; and a Faction already odious to the People, might be suffered to continue with less Danger than any new one that could arise. To confirm this, it was said that the Majority in the House of Commons was too great on the side of the High Church, and began to form themselves into a Body by the Name of the October Club, in order to put the Ministry under Subjection. Lastly, the Danger of introducing too great a Number of unexperienced Men at once into Offices, was urged as an irrefragable Reason for making Changes by slow Degrees:

And that to discard an able Officer from an Employment or part of a Commission where the Revenue or Trade were concerned, for no other Reason but differing in some Principles of Government, might be of dangerous Consequence.

However, it is certain that none of these Excuses were able to pass among men who argued only from the Principles of generall Reason. For first, they looked upon all Scheams of Comprehension to be as visionary and impossible in the State as in the Church: Secondly, while the Spirit raised by the Tryall of Dr. Sacheverel continued in Motion, Men were not so keen upon coming in themselves as to see their Enemies out, and deprived of all Power to do Mischief: It was urged further, that this universall Ambition of hunting after Places, grew chiefly from seeing them so long undisposed of, and from too generall an Encouragement by Promises to all who were thought capable of doing either Good or Hurt. Thirdly, the fear of erecting another Party in case the present Faction were wholly subdued, was in the Opinion of plain Men, and in regard to the Scituation of our Affairs, too great a Sacrifice of the Nation's Safety, to the Genius of Politicks; considering how much is to be done, and how little Time may probably be allowed. Besides, the Division of a House of Commons into Court and Country Party, which was the Evil they seemed to apprehend, can be never dangerous to a good Ministry, who have the true Interest and Constitution of their Country at Heart: As for the Apprehension of too great a Majority in the House of Commons, it proved so vain, that upon some Points of Importance, the Court was hardly able to procure one: And the October Club which appeared so formidable at first to some Politicians, proved in the Sequel to be the chief Support of those who suspected them. It was likewise very well known that the greatest Part of those Men whom the former Ministry left in Possession of Employments, were loudly charged with Insufficiency or Corruption, over and above their obnoxious Tenets in Religion and Government; So that it would have been a Matter of some Difficulty to make a worse Choice: Besides, that Plea for keeping Men of factious Principles in Employment upon the Score of their Abilities, was thought to be extended a little too far, and construed to take in all Employments whatsoever although many of them required no more Abilities than would serve to qualify a Gentleman-Usher at Court. So that this last Excuse for the very slow Steps made in disarming the Adversaries of the Crown was allowed indeed to have more Plausibility, but less Truth than any of the former.

I do not here pretend to condemn the Councils or Actions of the present Ministry. Their Safety and Interest are visibly united with those of the Publick, they are Persons of unquestionable Abilities, altogether unsuspected of Avarice or Corruption, and have the Advantage to be further recommended by the Dread and Hatred of the Opposite Faction. However, it is manifest, that the Zeal of their Friends hath been cooling towards them for above two Years past. They have been frequently deserted or distressed upon the most pressing Occasions, and very near giving up in Despair. Their Characters have been often treated with the utmost Barbarity and Injustice in both Houses by scurrilous and enraged Orators, while their nearest Friends and even those who must have a Share in their Disgrace, never offered a word in their Vindication.

When I examine with my self what Occasions the Ministry may have given for this Coldness, Inconstancy, and Discontent among their Friends, I at the same time recollect the various Conjectures, Reasonings, and Suspicions, which have run so freely for three years past concerning the Designs of the Court; I do not only mean such Conjectures as are born in a Coffee-house, or invented by the Malice of a Party, but also the Conclusions, (however mistaken) of wise and good Men, whose Quality and Station fitted them to understand the Reason of publick Proceedings, and in whose Power it lay to recommend or disgrace an Administration to the People. I must therefore take the Boldness to assert, that all these Discontents, how ruinous soever they may prove in the Consequences, have most unnecessarily arisen from the want of a due Communication and Concert. Every Man must have a Light sufficient for the Length of the Way he is appointed to go; there is a Degree of Confidence due to all Stations; and a petty Constable will neither act chearfully or wisely without that Share of it which properly belongs to Him. Although the main Spring in a Watch be out of Sight, there is an intermediate Communication between it and the smallest Wheel, or else no true Motion could be performed. This reserved mysterious way of acting, upon Points where there appeared not the least Occasion for it, and towards Persons who in right of their Posts expected a more open Treatment, was imputed to some hidden Design, which every Man conjectured to be the very Evil he was most afraid of. Those who professed the Height of what is called the Church Principle, suspected that a Comprehension was intended, wherein the moderate Men on both Sides might be equally employed. Others went further, and dreaded such a Correspondence, as directly tended to bring the old exploded Principles and Persons once more into play. Again, some affected to be uneasy about the Succession, and seemed to think there was a View of introducing that Person, whatever he is, who pretends to claim the Crown by Inheritance. Others, especially of late, surmised on the Contrary, that the Demands of the House of Hannover were industriously fomented by some in Power without the Privity of the Queen or ——. Now although these Accusations were too inconsistent to be all of them true, (and I have good reason to be confident that not one of them was so) yet they were maliciously suffered to pass, and thereby took off much of that Popularity, which those at the Helm stood in need of, to support them under the Difficulties of a long perplexing Negotiation, a daily addition of publick Debts, and an exhausted Treasury.

But the Effects of this Mysticall manner of proceeding, did not end here; For the late Dissentions between the great Men at Court (which have been for some time past, the publick Entertainment of every Coffee-house) are said to have arisen from the same Fountain, while on one side too great a Reserve, and certainly too great a Resentment on the other, (if we may believe generall Report, for I pretend to know no further) have enflamed Animosities to such a Height as to make all Reconcilement impracticable: Supposing this to be true, it may serve for a great Lesson of Humiliation to Mankind, to behold the Habits and Passions of Men otherwise highly accomplished, triumphing over Interest, Friendship, Honour, and their own Personall Safety as well as that of their Country, and probably of a most gracious Princess who hath entrusted it to them. A Ship's Crew quarrelling in a Storm, or while their Enemies are within Gun Shott is but a faint Idea of this fatal Infatuation; of which (although it be hard to say enough) some People may think perhaps I have already said too much.

Since this unhappy Incident, the Desertion of Friends, and loss of Reputation have been so great, that I do not see how the Ministers could have continued many Weeks in their Stations, if their Opposers of all kinds had agreed about the Methods by which they should be ruined; And their Preservation hitherto seems to resemble his, who had two Poisons given him together of contrary Operations: However, those incoherent Slanders which before were thrown without Distinction, are now fairly divided; and the Current Censure is, that one part of the Ministry is for restoring the old Faction, and the other for Introducing the Pretender.

Whether some have not insisted upon too implicite a Resignation to their Wisdom, Abilities and good Intentions, as well as to the Merit of having been the Sole Movers in that great Change at Court about four Years ago; Whether others have not contended for a greater Part in the Direction of Affairs than might possibly belong to them, and upon Refusal have not carried their Resentments further than private Friendship or the Safety of the Publick would admit; Lastly, whether others at a greater distance, many of whom did equally share in the Advantages, though not in the Confidence of the Crown; have not been sometimes too medling and assuming, too craving and importunate; have not suffered those by whom they were preferred to be often distressed, and then taken Advantage of their Distresses; Whether some of them have not deserted their Friends and Principles upon

the Prospect of those Dangers which their own Instability
or Ambition created, and are now in hopes that their discontent will be a Foundation of Favour upon a Change they
have in View. These with some other the like obvious
Questions and Speculations may probably at this time of day
be a little of the latest; Yet I am confident upon the whole, that
a much inferiour Degree of Wisdom and Experience, joined
with more unanimity and less Refinement, might have born us
through all our Difficulties without any Suspicion of Magick.
But it is an Observation as old as Tacitus, that some men have
a Genius as much too high for publick Business, as others too
low.

It may seem very impertinent in one of my Level, to point
out to those who sit at the Helm, what Course they ought to
steer. I know enough of Courts to be sensible how mean an
Opinion great Ministers have of most mens Understanding
to a Degree that in any other Science would be called the
grossest Pedantry. However, unless I offer my Sentiments in
this Point, all I have hitherto said will be to no purpose.

The generall Wishes and Desires of a People are perhaps
more obvious to other Men than to Ministers of State. There
are two Points of the highest Importance, wherein a very great
Majority of the Kingdom appear perfectly hearty and unanimous. First, that the Church of England should be preserved
entire in all Her Rights, Powers and Priviledges; All Doctrines
relating to Government discouraged which She condemns; All
Schisms, Sects and Heresies discountenanced and kept under
due Subjection, as far as consists with the Lenity of our
Constitution. Her open Enemies (among whom I include at
least Dissenters of all Denominations) not trusted with the
smallest Degree of Civil or Military Power; and Her secret
Adversaries under the Names of Whigs, Low-Church,
Republicans, Moderation-Men, and the like, receive no
Marks of Favour from the Crown, but what they should
deserve by a sincere Reformation.

Had this point been steddily pursued in all it's Parts for
three Years past, and asserted as the avowed Resolution of the
Court, there must probably have been an End of that Faction,

which hath been able ever since with so much Vigour to disturb and insult the Administration. I know very well that some Refiners pretend to argue for the Usefullness of Parties in such a Government as ours; I have said something of this already, and have heard a great many idle wise Topicks upon the Subject. But I shall not argue that Matter at present; I suppose if a Man thinks it necessary to play with a Serpent, he will chuse one of a kind that is least Mischievous; otherwise although it appear to be crushed, it may have Life enough to sting him to Death. So, I think it is not safe tampering with the present Faction, at least in this Juncture. First, because their Principles and Practices have been formerly ruinous, and since very often dangerous to the Constitution in Church and State: Secondly, because they are highly irritated, by the Loss of their Power, full of Venom and Vengeance, and prepared to execute every Thing that Rage or Malice can Suggest. But principally because they have prevailed by Misrepresentations and other Artifices, to make the Successor look upon them as the only Persons he can trust. Upon which Account they cannot be too soon or too much disabled; Neither will England ever be safe from the Attempts of this wicked Confederacy, till their Strength and Interest shall be so far reduced, that for the future it may not be in the Power of the Crown, although in Conjunction with any rich and factious Body of Men, to chuse an ill Majority in a House of Commons.

One Step necessary to this great Work, will be to regulate the Army, and chiefly the Officers of those Troops which in their Turns have the Care of Her Majesties Person, who are many of them fitter to guard a Prince under an high Court of Justice, than seated on his Throne. The peculiar Hand of Providence hath hitherto preserved Her Majesty encompassed, whether sleeping or travelling, by her Enemies; But since Religion teacheth us, that Providence ought not to be tempted, it is ill venturing to trust that precious Life any longer to those, who by their publick Behaviour and Discourse discover their Impatience to see it at an End; that they may have Liberty to be the Instruments of glutting at once the Revenge

I

of their Patrons and their own. It should be well remembred, what a Satisfaction these Gentlemen (after the Example of their Betters) were so sanguine to express upon the Queen's last Illness at Windsor, and what threatnings they used of refusing to obey their General in Case that Illness had proved fatal. Nor do I think it a want of Charity to suspect, that in such an evil day, an enraged Faction would be highly pleased with the Power of the Sword, and with great Connivance leave it so long unsheathed till they were got rid of their most formidable Adversaries. In the mean time it must be a very melancholly Prospect, that whenever it shall please God to visit us with this Calamity, those who are paid to be Defenders of the Civil Power will stand ready for any Acts of Violence, that a Junta composed of the greatest Enemies to the Constitution shall think fit to enjoin them.

The other Point of great Importance is the Security of the Protestant Succession in the House of Hannover; not from any Partiality to that Illustrious House, further than as it hath had the Honour to mingle with the Blood Royal of England, and is the nearest Branch of our Regal Line reformed from Popery. This Point hath one Advantage over the former, that both Parties profess to desire the same Blessing for Posterity, but differ about the means of securing it. From whence it hath come to pass, that the Protestant Succession, in appearance the Desire of the whole Nation, hath proved the greatest Topick of Slander, Jealousy, Suspicion, and Discontent.

I have been so curious to ask severall Acquaintance among the opposite Party, whether they or their Leaders did really suspect there had been ever any Design in the Ministry to weaken the Succession in Favour of the Pretender or of any other Person whatsoever. Some of them freely answered in the Negative, Others were of the same Opinion, but added, they did not know what might be done in time, and upon farther Provocations. Others again would be thought to believe the Affirmative, but could never produce any plausible Grounds for their Belief. I have likewise been assured by a *Person of some Consequence, that during a very near and

* The Author means himself.

Constant Familiarity with the great Men at Court for four Years past, he never could observe even in those Hours of Conversation where there is usually least Restraint, that one Word ever passed among them to shew a Dislike of the present Settlement, although they would sometimes lament that the false Representations of their's and the Kingdom's Enemies had made some Impressions in the Mind of the Successor. As to my own Circle of Acquaintance, I can safely affirm, that excepting those who are Non-jurers by Profession, I have not met with above two Persons who appeared to have any Scruples concerning the present Limitation of the Crown. I therefore think it may very impartially be pronounced, that the Number of those who wish to see the Son of the abdicated Prince upon the Throne, is altogether inconsiderable. And further, I believe it will be found, that there are None who so much dread any Attempt he shall make for the Recovery of his imagined Rights, as the Roman-Catholicks of England, who love their Freedom and Properties too well, to desire his Entrance by a French Army, and a Field of Blood; who must continue upon the same Foot, if he changes his Religion, and must expect to be the first and greatest Sufferers if he should happen to fall.

As to the Person of this nominall Prince, he lyes under all manner of Disadvantages: The Vulgar imagin him to have been a Child imposed upon the Nation by the fraudulent Zeal of his Parents and their bigotted Councellors; who took speciall Care, against all the Rules of Common Policy, to educate him in their hatefull Superstition, suckt in with his milk and confirmed in his Manhood, too strong to be now shaken by Mr. Lesley; and, a counterfeit Conversion will be too gross to pass upon the Kingdom after what we have seen and suffered from the like Practice in his Father. He is likewise said to be of weak Intellectualls, and an unsound Constitution. He was treated contemptibly enough by the young Princes of France, even during the War; is now wholly neglected by that Crown, and driven to live in Exile upon a small Exhibition. He is utterly unknown in England, which he left in the Cradle; His Father's Friends are most of them dead, the rest antiquated or poor; Six and twenty Years have almost passed since the Revolution, and the Bulk of those who are now in Action either at Court, in Parliament, or publick Offices, were then Boys at School or the Universities; and look upon that great Change to have happened during a Period of Time for which they are not accomptable. The Logick of the highest Tories is now, that this was the Establishment they found, as soon as they arrived to a Capacity of Judging; that they had no hand in turning out the late King, and therefore have no Crime to answer for, if it were any. That the Inheritance to the Crown is in pursuance of Laws made ever since their Remembrance, by which all Papists are excluded; and they have no other Rule to go by. That they will no more dispute King William the third's Title, than King William the first's; since they must have Recourse to History for both: That they have been instructed in the Doctrines of passive Obedience, Non-Resistance and Hereditary Right, and find them all necessary for preserving the present Establishment in Church and State, and for continuing the Succession in the House of Hannover, and must in their own Opinion renounce all those Doctrines by setting up any other Title to the Crown. This I say, seems to be the Politicall Creed of all the high-principled Men, I have for some time met with of forty Years old, and under; which although I am far from justifying in every part, yet I am sure it sets the Protestant Succession upon a much firmer Foundation, than all the indigested Scheams of those who profess to act upon what they call Revolution-Principles. Neither should it perhaps be soon forgot, that during the greatest Licentiousness of the Press, while the sacred Character of the Queen was every day insulted in factious Papers and Ballads, not the least reflecting Insinuation ever appeared against the Hannover Family, whatever Occasion might have been laid hold on by intemperate Pens, from the Rashness or Indiscretion of one or two Ministers from thence.

From all these Considerations I must therefore lay it down as an uncontestible Truth, that the Succession to these Kingdoms in the Illustrious House of Hannover is as firmly secured as the Nature of the Thing can possibly admit; by the Oaths of all who are entrusted with any Office, by the very Principles of those who are termed the High-Church, by the generall Inclinations of the People, by the Insignificancy of that Person who claims it from Inheritance, and the little Assistance he can expect either from Princes abroad or Adherents at home.

However, since the virulent Opposers of the Queen and her Administration have so far prevailed by their Emissaries at the Court of Hannover, and by their Practices upon one or two ignorant unmannerly Messengers from thence, as to make the Elector desire some further Security, and send over a Memoriall here to that End: The great Question is how to give reasonable Satisfaction to His Highness, and (what is infinitely of greater Moment) at the same time, consult the Honour and Safety of the Queen, whose quiet Possession is of much more Consequence to us of the present Age, than his Reversion: The Substance of his Memoriall, if I retain it right, is to desire, that some one of his Family might live in England with such a Maintainance as is usuall to those of the Royall Blood, and that certain Titles should be confered upon the rest, according to antient Custom. The Memoriall doth not specify which of the Family should be invited to reside here; and if it had, I believe however, Her Majesty would have looked upon it as a Circumstance left to her own Choice: Wherefore since the old Electrice is lately dead, I am apt to think, that the Nation would humbly submit to their Sovereign's Pleasure, if Her Majesty conceived it proper upon certain Conditions to invite over the eldest Grandson of the present Elector, have a Maintenance allotted him by Parliament, and give him a Title.

But, as all this is most manifestly unnecessary in it self, and only in Complyance with the mistaken Doubts of a presumptive Heir; so the Nation would (to speak in the Language of Mr. Steele) *Expect* that Her Majesty should be made perfectly easy from that Side for the future; No more be alarmed with Apprehensions of Visits or Demands of Writs, where She hath not thought fit to give any Invitation. The Nation would likewise *expect* that there should be an End of all private Commerce between that Court and the Leaders of a Party here; And that His Electorall Highness should declare Himself entirely satisfied with all Her Majesties Proceedings, Her Treatyes of Peace and Commerce, Her Allyances abroad, Her Choice of Ministers at Home, and particularly in her most gracious Condescensions to his Requests. That he would upon all proper Occasions, and in the most publick Manner discover his utter Dislike of all Factious Persons and Principles, but especially of that Party which under the pretence or Shelter of his Protection, hath so long disquieted the Kingdom: And lastly that he would acknowledge the Goodness of the Queen, and Justice of the Nation in so fully securing the Succession to his Family.

It is indeed a Problem which I could never comprehend; why the Court of Hannover, who have all along thought themselves so perfectly secure in the Affections, the Principles, and the Professions of the Low-Church Party, should not have endeavoured according to the usuall Politicks of Princes, to gain over those who were represented as their Enemies; since these supposed Enemies had made so many Advances, were in Possession of all the Power, had framed the very Settlement to which that Illustrious Family owes it's Claim; had all of them abjured the Pretender, were now employed in the great Offices of State, and composed a Majority in both Houses of Parliament, not to mention that the Queen her self with the Bulk of the Landed Gentry and Commonalty throughout the Kingdom were in the same Interest. This, one would think might be a Strength sufficient not only to obstruct but to bestow a Succession; And since the presumed Heir, could not but be perfectly secure of the other Party, whose greatest avowed Grievance was the pretended Danger of his future Rights; It might therefore surely have been worth his Thoughts to have made at least one Step towards cultivating a fair Correspondence with the Power in Possession. Neither could those who are called his Friends have blamed him, or with the least Decency enter into any Engagement for defeating his Title.

But, why may not the Reasons of this Proceeding in the Elector be directly contrary to what is commonly imagined?

Methinks, I could endeavour to believe, that His Highness is thorowly acquainted with both Parties; is convinced that no true Member of the Church of England, can easily be shaken in his Principles of Loyalty, or forget the Obligation of an Oath by any Provocation: That these are therefore the People he intends to rely upon, and keeps only fair with the others from a true Notion he hath of their Doctrines, which prompt them to forget their Duty upon every Motive of Interest or Ambition. If this Conjecture be right, His Highness cannot sure but entertain a very high Opinion of such Ministers who continue to act under the Dread and Appearance of a Successor's utmost Displeasure, and the Threats of an enraged Faction, whom he is supposed alone to favour, and to be guided entirely in his Judgment of British Affairs and Persons by their Opinions.

But, to return from this Digression; the Presence of that Infant Prince among us could not I think in any Sort be inconsistent with the Safety of the Queen. He would be in no Danger of being corrupted in his Principles, or exposed in his Person by vicious Companions; He could be at the Head of no factious Clubs and Cabals, nor be attended by a hired Rabble, which his Flatterers might represent as Popularity. He would have none of that Impatience which the Frailty of human Nature gives to expecting Heirs. There would be no Pretence for Men to make their Court by affecting German Modes and Refinements in Dress or Behaviour: Nor would there be any Occasion of insinuating to him how much more his Levee was frequented than the Ante-Chambers, at St. James's. Add to all this, the Advantages of being educated in our Religion, Laws, Language, Manners, Nature of the Government, each so very different from those he would leave behind: By which likewise he might be highly usefull to His Father, if that Prince should happen to survive Her Majesty.

The late King William, who after his Marriage with the Lady Mary of England, could have no probable Expectation of the Crown, and very little even of being a Queen's Husband, (the

Duke of York having then a young Wife) was no Stranger to our Language or Manners, and went often to the Chappel of His Princess; which I observe the rather, because I could heartily wish the like Disposition were in another Court, and because it may be disagreeable to a Prince to take up new Doctrines on a sudden, or speak to His Subjects by an Interpreter.

An illnatured or inquisitive Man may still perhaps desire to press the Question further, by asking what is to be done, in Case it should so happen that this Malevolent working Party at home may have Credit enough with the Court of Hannover, to continue the Suspicion, Jealousy, and Uneasiness there against the Queen and her Ministry; to make such Demands be still insisted on, as are by no means thought proper to be complyed with; and in the mean time to stand at arms Length with her Majesty, and in close Conjunction with those who oppose Her.

I take the Answer to be easy. In all Contests the safest way is to put those we dispute with, as much in the Wrong as we can. When Her Majesty shall have offered such or the like Concessions as I have above mentioned, in order to remove those Scruples artificially raised in the Mind of the expectant Heir, and to divide him from that Faction by which he is supposed to have been misled; She hath done as much as any Prince can do, and more than any other would do in her Case; and will be justified before God and Man, whatever be the Event. The equitable part of those who now side against the Court, will probably be more temperate, and if a due Dispatch be made in placing the Civil and Military Power in the Hands of such as wish well to the Constitution; It cannot be any way for the Quiet or Interest of a Successor to gratify so inconsiderable a Faction as will then remain, at the Expence of a much more numerous and considerable Part of his Subjects. Neither do I see how the Principles of such a Party either in Religion or Government, will prove very agreeable; because I think, Luther and Calvin seem to have differed as much as any two among the Reformers: And because a German

Prince may in all likelyhood be suspicious of those who think they can never enough depress the Prerogative.

But supposing once for all, as far as possible, that the Elector should utterly refuse to be upon any Terms of Confidence with the present Ministry, and all others of their Principles, as Enemies to him and the Succession; nor easy with the Queen her self but upon such Conditions as may not perhaps be thought consistent with her Safety or Honour; and continue to place all his Hope and Trust in the discontented Party; In such an improbable Case, I think it were humbly to be wished, that whenever the Succession shall take place, the Alteration intended by the new Prince should be made by himself, and not by his Deputies. Because I am of Opinion, that the Clause empowering the Successor to appoint a latent unlimited Number additionall to the Seven Regents named in the Act, went upon a Supposition, that such a *Secret Committee* would not be of Persons whose Enmity and contrary Principles might dispose them to confound the rest. The late King William, whose Title was much more controverted than that of Her Majesty's Successor, can ever probably be, did for severall years leave the Administration of the Kingdom in the Hands of Lords Justices, during the Height of a War, and while the abdicated Prince himself was frequently attempting an Invasion. From whence we might imagine that the Regents appointed by Parliament upon the Demise of the Crown, would be able to keep the Peace during an Absence of a few Weeks, without any Colleagues. However, I am pretty confident, that the only Reason why a Power was given of chusing Dormant Viceroys, was to take away all Pretences of a necessity to invite over any of the Family here, during Her Majesty's Life, so that I do not well apprehend what Arguments the Elector can use to insist upon both.

To conclude; the only way of securing the Constitution in Church and State, and consequently this very Protestant Succession it self, will be by lessening the Power of our Domestick Adversaries as much as can possibly consist with the Lenity of our Government; and if this be not speedily done, it will be easy to point where the Nation is to fix the

Blame. For we are very well assured, that since the Account Her Majesty received of the Cabals, the Triumphs, the insolent Behaviour of the whole Faction during her last Illness at Windsor, she hath been as willing to see them deprived of all Power to do Mischief, as any of her most Zealous and Loyall Subjects can desire.

Some Considerations upon the Consequences hoped and feared from the Death of the Queen

Some Considerations upon the Consequences
hoped and feared from the Death of the Queen.

In order to sett in a clear Light what I have
to say upon this Subject, it will be convenient to
examine the State of the Nation with reference
to the two contending Partys; this cannot well
be done without some little Retrospection into
the five last Years of her late Majesty's Reign.

I have it from unquestionable Authority, that
the Dutchess of M——s Favor began to decline
very soon after the Queen's Accession to the
Throne, and that the E. of Godolphin's had not
much above two years longer, although her Majesty
(in all Conceales of her Affection) did not think
fit to deprive them of their Power till a long
time after.

The D. of Marl. and the Earl of Godolphin
having fallen early into the Interests of the
lower Party, for certain Reasons not seasonable
here to be mentioned, (but which may deserve
a Place in the History of that Reign) they made
larger Steps that way upon the Death of the
Prince of Denmark, taking in severall among
the warmest Leaders of that Side, into the chief
Employments of the State. Mr Harley, then
Secretary of State, who disliked their Proceedings,
and had very near overthrown their whole Scheame,
was removed with utmost Indignation, and about
the same time, Sr Simon Harcourt, and Mr St John
with some others voluntarily gave up their
Employments.

But the Queen, who had then a great Esteem
for the Person and Abilityes of Mr Harley (and in
Proportion of the other two, though at that time
not equally known to her) was deprived of his
Service with some Regret, and upon that and
other Motives, well known at Court, began to
think her self hardly used, and became anxious
even about, whether true or false, that her Majesty
was not otherwise treated with that Duty she might
expect. About this time the Church Party were loud
in their Complaints, surmising from the Virulence
of severall Pamphlets, from certain Bills projected
to be brought into Parlicent, from Endeavors to
repeal the Sacramentall Test, from the avowed
Principles, and from Speeches of some Persons in favor
and

Some Considerations upon the Consequences hoped and feared from the Death of the Queen.

Aug. 9. 1714

IN order to sett in a clear Light what I have to say upon this Subject, it will be convenient to examine the State of the Nation with reference to the two contending Partyes; this cannot well be done without some little Retrospection into the five last Years of her late Majesty's Reign.

I have it from unquestionable Authority, that the Dutchess of Marlborough's Favor began to decline very soon after the Queen's Accession to the Throne, and that the Earl of Godolphin's held not much above two years longer; although Her Majesty (no ill Concealer of her Affections) did not think fit to deprive them of their Power till a long time after.

The Duke of Marlborough and the Earl of Godolphin having fallen early into the Interests of the lower Party, for certain Reasons not seasonable here to be mentioned, (but which may deserve a Place in the History of that Reign) they made larger steps that way upon the Death of the Prince of Denmark, taking in severall among the warmest Leaders of that Side, into the chief Employments of the State. Mr. Harley, then Secretary of State, who disliked their Proceedings, and had very near overthrown their whole Scheam was removed with utmost Indignation, and about the same time, Sir Simon Harcourt, and Mr. St. John with some others voluntarily gave up their Employments.

But the Queen, who had then a great Esteem for the Person and Abilityes of Mr. Harley (and in Proportion of the other two, though at that time not equally known to her) was deprived of his Service with some Regret, and upon that and other Motives, well known at Court, began to think her self hardly used; and severall Storyes ran about, whether true or false, that Her Majesty was not allways treated with that Duty She might expect. Mean time the Church Party were loud in their Complaints, surmising from the Virulence of severall Pamphlets, from certain Bills projected to be brought into Parliament, from Endeavors to repeal the Sacramentall Test, from the avowed Principles, and free Speeches of some Persons in Power, and other Jealosyes needless to repeat, that ill designs were forming against the Religion established.

These Fears were all confirmed by the Tryall of Dr. Sacheverill, which drew the Populace as one Man into the Party against the Ministry and Parliament.

The Ministry were very suspicious that the Queen had still a reserve of Favor for Mr. Harley, which appeared by a Passage that happened some days after his Removal. For the Earl of Godolphins Coach and his, happening to meet near Kensington: the Earl a few hours after reproached the Queen that She privatly admitted Mr. Harley, and was not without some difficulty undeceived by Her Majesty's Asseverations to the contrary.

Soon after the Doctor's Tryall, this Gentleman by the Queen's Command, and the Intervention of Mrs. Masham was brought up the Backstairs; and that Princess, Spirited by the Addresses from all Parts, which shewed the Inclinations of her Subjects to be very averse from the Proceedings in Court and Parliament, was resolved to break the united Power of the Marlborough and Godolphin Familyes, and to begin this Work, by taking the disposall of Employments into her own Hands; for which an Opportunity happened by the Death of the Earl of Essex, Lieutenant of the Tower, whose Employment was given to the Earl Rivers, to the great discontent of the Duke of Marlborough, who intended it for the Duke of Northumberland then Collonell of the Oxford Regiment, to which the Earl of Hertford was to succeed. Some time after, the Chamberlain's Staff was disposed of to the Duke of Shrewsbury in the absence and without the Privity of the Earl of Godolphin. The Earl of Sunderland's Removal followed, and lastly that of the High Treasurer himself, whose Office was put into Commission, whereof Mr. Harley (made at the same time Chancellor of the Exchequer) was one; I need say nothing of other Removalls, which are well enough known and remembered; let it suffice, that in eight or nine Months time the whole Face of the Court was altered, and very few Friends of the former Ministry left in any great Stations there.

I have good Reasons to be assured, that when the Queen began this Change, she had no Intentions to carry it so far as the Church Party expected, and have since been so impatient to see. For although She were a true Professor of the Religion established Yet the first Motives to this Alteration did not arise from any Dangers she apprehended to that or the Government; but from a desire to get out of the Dominion of some who she thought had kept her too much and too long in Pupillage. She was in her own Nature extreamly dilatory and timorous; yet upon some Occasions, positive to a great degree: And when she had got rid of those who had as she thought given her the most uneasyness, she was inclined to stop, and entertain a fancy of acting upon a moderating Scheam, from whence it was very difficult to remove her. At the same time I must confess my Belief, that this Imagination was put into her Head, and made use of as an Encouragement to begin that work, after which her Advisers might think it easyer to prevail with her to go as far as they thought fit. That these were Her Majesty's dispositions in that Conjuncture, may be confirmed by many Instances. In the very Height of the Change, she appeared very loth to part with two great Officers of State of the other Party, and some whose Absence the new Ministers most earnestly wished held in for above two years after.

Mr. Harley who acted as first Minister before he had the Staff, as he was a Lover of gentle Measures, and inclined to Procrastination, so he could not with any decency press the Queen too much against her Nature, because it would be like running upon the Rock where his Predecessors had Split. But violent Humors running both in the Kingdom and the new Parliament against the Principles and Persons of the low Church Party, gave this Minister a very difficult Part to play.

The Warm Members in both Houses, especially among the Commons pressed for a thorow Change, and so did almost all the Queen's new Servants, especially after Mr. Harley was made an Earl and High-Treasurer. He could not in good Policy own his want of Power nor fling the Blame upon his Mistress; And as too much Secrecy was one of his Faults, he would often upon these Occasions keep his nearest Friends in the dark. The Truth is, he had likewise other Views, which were better suited to the Maxims of State in generall, than to that Scituation of Affairs. By leaving many Employments in the Hands of the discontented Party, he fell in with the Queen's Humor, he hoped to acquire the Reputation of Lenity, and kept a great Number of Expectants in order, who had Liberty to hope, while any thing remained undisposed of. He seemed also to think, as other Ministers have done, that since Factions are necessary in such a Government as ours it would be prudent not altogether to lay the present one prostrate, lest another more plausible, and therefore not to easy to grapple with might arise in it's Stead.

However, it is certain that a great Part of the Load he bore was unjustly laid on him. He had no Favorites among the Whig Party, whom he kept in upon the Score of old Friendship or Acquaintance, and he was a greater Object of their Hatred than all the rest of the Ministry together.

Memoirs, Relating to That Change Which Happened in the Queen's Ministry in the Year 1710

MEMOIRS,
RELATING TO
That Change which happened in the
QUEEN'S MINISTRY
in the Year 1710.

Written in OCTOBER, MDCCXIV.

HAVING continued, for near the space of four years, in a good degree of confidence with the ministry then in being, though not with so much power as was believed, or at least given out, by my friends as well as my enemies, especially the latter, in both houses of parliament: And this having happened during a very busy period of negotiations abroad, and management or intrigue at home, I thought it might probably, some years hence, when the present scene shall have given place to many new ones that will arise, be an entertainment to those who will have any personal regard for me or my memory, to set down some particularities which fell under my knowledge and observation, while I was supposed, whether truly or no, to have part in the secret of affairs.

One circumstance I'm a little sorry for, that I was too negligent (against what I had always resolved, and blamed others for not doing) in taking hints or journals of every thing material as it passed, whereof I omitted many that I cannot now recollect, though, by a thousand instances, I was convinced of the weakness of my memory. But, to say the truth, the nearer knowledge any man has in the affairs at Court, the less he thinks them of consequence, or worth regarding. And those kind of passages, which I have with greatest curiosity found or searched for in Memoirs, I wholly neglected when they were freely communicated to me from the first hand, or were such wherein I acted myself. This I take to be one among other reasons why great ministers seldom give themselves the trouble of recording the important parts of that administration, where themselves are at the head. They have extinguished all that vanity which usually possesses men during their first acquaintance at courts; and, like the masters of a puppet-show, they despise those motions which fill common spectators with wonder and delight.

However, upon frequently recollecting the course of affairs during the time I was either trusted or employed; I am deceived, if in history there can be found any period more full of passages, which the curious of another age would be glad to know the secret springs of; or, from whence more useful instructions may be gathered for directing the conduct of those, who shall hereafter have the good or ill fortune to be engaged in business of the state.

It may probably enough happen, that those who shall at any time hereafter peruse these papers, may think it not suitable to the nature of them, that, upon occasion, I sometimes make mention of myself; who, during these transactions, and ever since, was a person without titles or public employment. But, since the chief leaders of the faction then out of power, were pleased in both houses of parliament to take every opportunity of shewing their malice, by mentioning me (and often by name) as one who was in the secret of all affairs, and without whose advice or privity, nothing was done, or employment disposed of, it will not, perhaps, be improper to take notice of some passages, wherein the public and myself were jointly concerned; not to mention that the chief cause of giving myself this trouble, is to satisfy my particular friends; and, at worst, if, after the fate of manuscripts, these papers shall, by accident or indiscretion, fall into the public view, they will be no more liable to censure than other memoirs, published for many years past, in English, French, and Italian. The period of time I design to treat on, will commence with September 1710, from which time, till within two months of the Queen's death, I was never absent from court, except about six weeks in Ireland.

But, because the great change of employments in her Majesty's family, as well as the kingdom, was begun some months before, and had been thought on from the time of Dr. Sacheverel's trial, while I was absent, and lived retired in Ireland; I shall endeavour to recollect, as well as I am able, some particulars I learned from the Earl of Oxford, the Lord Viscount Bolingbroke, the Lady Masham, and Doctor Atterbury, who were best able to inform me.

I have often with great earnestness pressed the Earl of Oxford, then Lord Treasurer, and my Lady Masham, who were the sole persons which brought about that great change, to give me a particular account of every circumstance and passage during that whole transaction: Nor did this request proceed from curiosity, or the ambition of knowing and publishing important secrets; but, from a sincere honest design of justifying the Queen, in the measures she then took, and after pursued, against a load of scandal which would certainly be thrown on her memory, with some appearance of truth. It was easy to foresee, even at that distance, that the Queen could not live many years; and it was sufficiently known, what party was most in the good graces of the successor; and, consequently, what turns would be given by historians to her Majesty's proceedings, under a reign, where direct contrary measures would probably be taken. For instance, what would be more easy to a malicious pen than to charge the Queen with inconstancy, weakness, and ingratitude, in removing and disgracing the Duke of Marlborough, who had so many years commanded her armies with victory and success; in displacing so many great officers of her court and kingdom, by whose counsels she had in all appearance so prosperously governed; in extending the marks of her severity and displeasure towards the wife and daughters, as well as relations and allies, of that person she had so long employed and so highly trusted; and all this by the private intrigues of a woman of her bed-chamber, in concert with one artful man, who might be supposed to have acted that bold part only from a motive of revenge upon the loss of his employments, or of ambition to come again into power?

These were some of the arguments I often made use of with great freedom, both to the Earl of Oxford and my Lady Masham, to incite them to furnish me with materials for a fair account of that great transaction, to which they always seemed as well disposed as myself. My Lady Masham did likewise assure me, that she had frequently informed the Queen of my request, which her Majesty thought very reasonable, and did appear upon all occasions as desirous of preserving her reputation with posterity, as might justly become a great Prince to be.

But, that incurable disease, either of negligence or procrastination, which influenced every action both of the Queen and the Earl of Oxford, did in some sort infect every one who had credit or business in court: For, after soliciting near four years, to obtain a point of so great importance to the Queen and her servants, from whence I could propose nothing but trouble, malice, and envy to myself, it was perpetually put off.

The scheme I offered was to write her Majesty's reign; and, that this work might not look officious or affected, I was ready to accept the historiographer's place, though of inconsiderable value, and of which I might be sure to be deprived upon the Queen's death.

This negligence in the Queen, the Earl of Oxford, and my Lady Masham, is the cause that I can give but an imperfect account of the first springs of that great change at court, after the trial of Doctor Sacheverel, my memory not serving me to retain all the facts related to me; but what I remember I shall here set down.

There was not, perhaps, in all England, a person who understood more artificially to disguise her passions than the late Queen. Upon her first coming to the throne, the Duchess of Marlborough had lost all favour with her, as her Majesty hath often acknowledged to those who have told it me. That Lady had long preserved an ascendant over her Mistress, while she was Princess, which her Majesty, when she came to the crown, had neither patience to bear, nor spirit to subdue. This Princess was so exact an observer of forms, that she

seemed to have made it her study, and would often descend
so low, as to observe, in her domesticks of either sex, who
came into her presence, whether a ruffle, a periwig, or the
lining of a coat, were unsuitable upon certain times. The
Duchess, on the other side, who had been used to great
familiarities, could not take it into her head, that any change
of station should put her upon changing her behaviour, the
continuance of which was the more offensive to her Majesty,
whose other servants, of the greatest quality, did then treat
her with the utmost respect.

The Earl of Godolphin held in favour about three years
longer, and then declined, though he kept his office till
the general change. I have heard several reasons given for her
Majesty's early disgust against that Lord. The Duchess, who
had long been his mistress, often prevailed on him to solicit
the Queen upon things very unacceptable to her, which her
Majesty liked the worse, as knowing from whence they
originally came; and his Lordship, though he endeavoured
to be as respectful as his nature would permit him, was,
upon all occasions, much too arbitrary and obtruding.

To the Duke of Marlborough she was wholly indifferent
(as her nature in general prompted her to be), till his own
restless, impatient behavior, had turned her against him.

The Queen had not a stock of amity to serve above one
object at a time; and further than a bare good or ill opinion,
which she soon contracted and changed, and very often upon
light grounds, she could hardly be said either to love or to
hate any body. She grew so jealous upon the change of her
servants, that often, out of a fear of being imposed upon, by
an over-caution, she would impose upon herself; she took a
delight in refusing those who were thought to have greatest
power with her, even in the most reasonable things, and such
as were necessary for her service; nor would let them be done
till she fell into the humour of herself.

Upon the grounds I have already related, her Majesty had
gradually conceived a most rooted aversion for the Duke and
Duchess of Marlborough, and the Earl of Godolphin; which
spread, in time, through all their allies and relations, particu-

larly to the Earl of Sunderland, whose ungovernable temper had made him fail in his personal respects to her Majesty.

This I take to have been the principal ground of the Queen's resolutions to make a change of some offices both in her family and kingdom; and that these resolutions did not proceed from any real apprehension she had of danger to the church or monarchy. For, though she had been strictly educated in the former, and very much approved its doctrine and discipline, yet she was not so ready to foresee any attempts against it by the party then presiding. But, the fears that most influenced her, were such as concerned her own power and prerogative, which those nearest about her were making daily encroachments upon, by their undutiful behaviour and unreasonable demands.

The deportment of the Duchess of Marlborough, while the Prince lay expiring, was of such a nature, that the Queen, then in the heights of grief, was not able to bear it; but, with marks of displeasure in her countenance, she ordered the Duchess to withdraw, and send Mrs. Masham to her.

I forgot to relate an affair that happened, as I remember, about a twelvemonth before Prince George's death. This Prince had long conceived an incurable aversion for that party, and was resolved to use his utmost credit with the Queen, his wife, to get rid of them. There fell out an incident which seemed to favour this attempt; for the Queen, resolving to bestow a regiment upon Mr. Hill, brother to Mrs. Masham, signified her pleasure to the Duke of Marlborough; who, in a manner not very dutiful, refused his consent, and retired in anger to the country. After some heats, the regiment was given to a third person: But the Queen resented this matter so highly, which she thought had been promoted by the Earl of Godolphin, that she resolved immediately to remove the latter. I was told, and it was then generally reported, that Mr. St. John carried a letter from her Majesty to the Duke of Marlborough, signifying her resolutions to take the staff from the Earl of Godolphin, and that she expected his Grace's compliance; to which the Duke returned a very humble answer. I cannot engage for this passage, it having never come into my head to ask Mr. St. John about it: But, the account Mr. Harley and he gave me, was, That the Duke of Marlborough and the Earl of Godolphin had concerted with them and their friends upon a moderating scheme, wherein some of both parties should be employed, but with a more favourable aspect towards the church: That a meeting was appointed for compleating this work: That, in the mean-time, the Duke and Duchess of Marlborough, and the Earl of Godolphin, were secretly using their utmost efforts with the Queen to turn Mr. Harley, (who was then Secretary of State) and his friends, out of their employments: That the Queen, on the other side, who had then a great opinion of Mr. Harley's integrity and abilities, would not consent, and was determined to remove the Earl of Godolphin. This was not above a month before the season of the year when the Duke of Marlborough was to embark for Flanders; and, the very night in which Mr. Harley and his friends had appointed to meet his Grace and the Earl of Godolphin, George Churchill the Duke's brother, who was in good credit with the Prince, told his Highness, that the Duke was firmly determined to lay down his command, if the Earl of Godolphin went out, or Mr. Harley and his friends suffered to continue in. The Prince, thus intimidated by Churchill, reported the matter to the Queen; and the time and service pressing, her Majesty was unwillingly forced to yield. The two great Lords failed the appointment; and, the next morning, the Duke at his levee said aloud in a careless manner, to those who stood round him, That Mr. Harley was turned out.

Upon the Prince's death, November 1708, the two great Lords so often mentioned, who had been for some years united with the Low-church party, and had long engaged to take them into power, were now in a capacity to make good their promises, which his Highness had ever most strenuously opposed. The Lord Sommers was made president of the council, the Earl of Wharton Lieutenant of Ireland, and some others of the same stamp were put into considerable posts.

It should seem to me, that the Duke and Earl were not very willingly drawn to impart so much power to those of that party, who expected these removals for some years before, and were always put off upon pretence of the Prince's unwillingness to have them employed. And I remember, some months before his Highness's death, my Lord Sommers, who is a person of reserve enough, complained to me with great freedom of the ingratitude of the Duke and Earl, who, after the service he and his friends had done them in making the Union, would hardly treat him with common civility. Neither shall I ever forget, that he readily owned to me, that the Union was of no other service to the nation, than by giving a remedy to that evil, which my Lord Godolphin had brought upon us, by persuading the Queen to pass the Scotch act of security. But, to return from this digression.

Upon the admission of these men into employments, the court soon ran into extremity of Low-church measures; and although, in the House of Commons, Mr. Harley, Sir Simon Harcourt, Mr. St. John, and some others, made great and bolds stands in defence of the constitution, yet they were always borne down by a majority.

It was, I think, during this period of time that the Duke of Marlborough, whether by a motive of ambition, or a love of money, or by the rash counsels of his wife the Duchess, made that bold attempt of desiring the Queen to give him a commission to be general for life. Her Majesty's answer was, That she would take time to consider it; and, in the meanwhile, the Duke advised with the Lord Cowper, then Chancellor, about the form in which the commission should be drawn. The Chancellor, very much to his honour, endeavoured to dissuade the Duke from engaging in so dangerous an affair; and protested he would never put the great seal to such a commission.

But the Queen was highly alarmed at this extraordinary proceeding in the Duke, and talked to a person whom she had then taken into confidence, as if she apprehended an attempt upon the crown. The Duke of Argyle, and one or two more Lords, were (as I have been told) in a very private manner brought to the Queen. This Duke was under great obligations to the Duke of Marlborough, who had placed him in a high station in the army, preferred many of his friends, and procured him the garter. But, his unquiet and ambitious spirit, never easy while there is any one above him, made him, upon some trifling resentments, conceive an inveterate hatred against his general. When he was consulted what course should be taken upon the Duke of Marlborough's request to be general for life; and whether any danger might be apprehended from the refusal; I was told, he suddenly answered, That her Majesty need not be in pain; for, he would undertake, whenever she commanded, to seize the Duke at the head of his troops, and bring him away either dead or alive.

About this time happened the famous tryal of Dr. Sacheverel, which arose from a foolish passionate pique of the Earl of Godolphin, whom this divine was supposed, in a sermon, to have reflected on under the name of *Volpone*, as my Lord Sommers, a few months after, confessed to me; and, at the same time, that he had earnestly, and in vain endeavoured, to dissuade the Earl from that attempt. However, the impeachment went on in the form and manner which every body knows, and therefore there need not be any thing said of it here.

Mr. Harley, who came up to town during the time of the impeachment, was, by the intervention of Mrs. Masham, privately brought to the Queen, and, in some meetings, easily convinced her Majesty of the dispositions of her people, as they appeared in the course of that trial in favour of the church, and against the measures of those in her service. It was not without a good deal of difficulty, that Mr. Harley was able to procure this private access to the Queen, the Duchess of Marlborough, by her emissaries, watching all the avenues to the back-stairs, and upon all occasions discovering their jealousy of him; whereof he told me a passage, no otherways worth relating, than as it gives an idea of an insolent, jealous minister, who would wholly engross the power and favour of his Sovereign. Mr. Harley, upon his removal from the secretary's office, by the intrigues of the Duke of Marlborough and the Earl of Godolphin, as I have above related, going out of town, was met by the latter of these two Lords near Kensington-gate. The Earl, in a high fit of jealousy, goes immediately to the Queen, reproaches her for privately seeing Mr. Harley, and was hardly so civil to be convinced with her Majesty's frequent protestations to the contrary.

These suspicions, I say, made it hard for her Majesty and Mr. Harley to have private interviews; neither had he made use of the opportunities he met with to open himself so much to her, as she seemed to expect, and desired; though Mrs. Masham, in right of her station in the bed-chamber, had taken all proper occasions of pursuing of what Mr. Harley had begun. In this critical juncture, the Queen, hemmed in, and as it were imprisoned, by the Duchess of Marlborough and her creatures, was at a loss how to proceed. One evening a letter was brought to Mr. Harley, all dirty, and by the hand of a very ordinary messenger; he read the superscription, and saw it was the Queen's writing; he sent for the messenger, who said, he knew not whence the letter came, but that it was delivered him by an under-gardener, I forget whether of Hampton-court or Kensington. The letter mentioned the difficulties her Majesty was under, blaming him for not speaking with more freedom, and more particularly; and desiring his assistance. With this encouragement he went more frequently, though still as private as possible, to the back-stairs; and from that time began to have entire credit with the Queen. He then told her of the dangers to her crown as well as to the church and monarchy itself, from the councils and actions of some of her servants: That she ought gradually to lessen the exorbitant power of the Duke and Duchess of Marlborough, and the Earl of Godolphin, by taking the disposition of employments into her own hands: That it did not become her to be a slave to a party; but to reward those who may deserve by their duty and loyalty, whether they were such as were called of the High or Low-church. In short, whatever views he had then in his own breast; or, how far soever he intended to proceed, the turn of his whole discourse was intended, in appearance, only to put the Queen upon what they called a moderating scheme; which however made so strong an impression upon her, that when this minister, led by the necessity of affairs, the general disposition of people, and probably by his own inclinations, put her Majesty upon going greater lengths than she had first intended, it put him upon innumerable difficulties, and some insuperable; as we shall see in the progress of this change.

Her Majesty, pursuant to Mr. Harley's advice, resolved to dispose of the first great employment that fell, according to her own pleasure, without consulting any of her ministers. To put this in execution, an opportunity soon happened by the death of the Earl of Essex, whereby the lieutenancy of the Tower became vacant. It was agreed between the Queen and Mr. Harley, that the Earl Rivers should go immediately to the Duke of Marlborough, and desire his Grace's good offices with the Queen, to procure him that post. The Earl went accordingly, was received with abundance of professions of kindness by the Duke, who said the lieutenancy of the Tower was not worth his Lordship's acceptance, and desired him to think of something else. The Earl still insisted, and the Duke still continued to put him off; at length Lord Rivers desired his Grace's consent to let him go himself and beg this favour of the Queen, and hope he might tell her Majesty, his Grace had no objection to him. All this the Duke readily agreed to, as a matter of no consequence. The Earl went to the Queen, who immediately gave orders for his commission. He had not long left the Queen's presence, when the Duke of Marlborough, suspecting nothing that would happen, went to the Queen, told her that the lieutenancy of the Tower falling void by the death of the Earl of Essex, he hoped her Majesty would bestow it upon the Duke of Northumberland, and give the Oxford-regiment, then commanded by that Duke, to the Earl of Hertford. The Queen said, he was come too late; that she had already granted the lieutenancy to Earl Rivers, who had told her that he [the Duke] had no objection to him. The Duke, much surprized at this new manner of treatment, and making complaints in her Majesty's presence, was however forced to submit.

The Queen went on by slow degrees. Not to mention some changes of lesser moment, the Duke of Kent was forced to compound for his chamberlain's staff, which was given to the Duke of Shrewsbury, while the Earl of Godolphin was out of town, I think at Newmarket: His Lordship, on the first news, came immediately up to court; but the thing was done, and he made as good a countenance to the Duke of Shrewsbury as he was capable of. The circumstances of the Earl of Sunderland's removal, and the reasons alledged, are known enough. His ungovernable temper had overswayed him to fail in his respects to her Majesty's person.

Mean-time both parties stood at gaze, not knowing to what these steps would lead, or where they would end. The Earl of Wharton, then in Ireland, being deceived by various intelligence from hence, endeavoured to hide his uneasiness as well as he could. Some of his sanguine correspondents had sent him word, that the Queen began to stop her hand, and the church-party to despond. At the same time, the Duke of Shrewsbury happened to send him a letter filled with great expressions of civility: The Earl was so weak, upon reading it, as to cry out, before two or three standers-by, 'Damn him, he is making fair weather with me; but, by God, I will have his head.'

But these short hopes were soon blasted, by taking the Treasurer's staff from the Earl of Godolphin; which was done in a manner not very gracious, her Majesty sending him a letter, by a very ordinary messenger, commanding him to break it. The Treasury was immediately put into commission, with Earl Powlet at the head; but Mr. Harley, who was one of the number, and at the same time made Chancellor of the Exchequer, was already supposed to preside behind the curtain.

Upon the fall of that great minister and favourite, that whole party became dispirited, and seemed to expect the worst that could follow. The Earl of Wharton immediately desired, and obtained leave, to come for England, leaving that kingdom, where he had behaved himself with the utmost profligateness, injustice, arbitrary proceedings, and corruption, with the hatred and detestation of all good men, even of his own party.

And here, because my coming into the knowledge of the

new ministry began about this time, I must digress a little, to relate some circumstances previous to it.

Although I had been for many years before no stranger to the court, and had made the nature of government a great part of my study, yet I had dealt very little with politics, either in writing or acting, till about a year before the late King William's death; when, returning with the Earl of Berkeley from Ireland, and falling upon the subject of the five great Lords, who were then impeached for high crimes and misdemeanors, by the House of Commons, I happened to say, that the same manner of proceeding, at least as it appeared to me from the views we received of it in Ireland, had ruined the liberties of Athens and Rome, and that it might be easy to prove it from history. Soon after I went to London; and, in a few weeks, drew up a discourse, under the title of *The Contests and Dissentions of the Nobles and Commons in Athens and Rome, with the Consequences they had upon both those States.* This discourse I sent very privately to the press, with the strictest injunctions to conceal the author, and returned immediately to my residence in Ireland. The book was greedily bought, and read; and charged some times upon my Lord Sommers, and some times upon the Bishop of Salisbury; the latter of whom told me afterwards, that he was forced to disown it in a very public manner, for fear of an impeachment, wherewith he was threatened.

Returning next year for England, and hearing the great approbation this piece had received, (which was the first I ever printed) I must confess, the vanity of a young man prevailed with me, to let myself be known for the author: Upon which my Lords Sommers and Hallifax, as well as the Bishop above mentioned, desired my acquaintance, with great marks of esteem and professions of kindness: Not to mention the Earl of Sunderland, who had been of my old acquaintance. They lamented that they were not able to serve me since the death of the King, and were very liberal in promising me the greatest preferments I could hope for, if ever it came in their power. I soon grew domestic with Lord Hallifax, and was as often with Lord Sommers, as the formality of his nature (the only unconversable fault he has) made it agreeable to me.

It was then I first began to trouble myself with the difference between the principles of Whig and Tory; having formerly employed myself in other, and, I think, much better speculations. I talked often upon this subject with Lord Sommers; told him, that, having been long conversant with the Greek and Roman authors, and therefore a lover of liberty, I found myself much inclined to be what they called a Whig in politics; and that, besides, I thought it impossible, upon any other principle, to defend or submit to the Revolution: But, as to religion, I confessed myself to be an High-churchman, and that I did not conceive how any one, who wore the habit of a clergyman, could be otherwise: That I had observed very well with what insolence and haughtiness some Lords of the High-church party treated not only their own chaplains, but all other clergymen whatsoever, and thought this was sufficiently recompensed by their professions of zeal to the church: That I had likewise observed how the Whig Lords took a direct contrary measure, treated the persons of particular clergymen with great curtesy, but shewed much ill-will and contempt for the order in general: That I knew it was necessary for their party, to make their bottom as wide as they could, by taking all denominations of Protestants to be members of their body: That I would not enter into the mutual reproaches made by the violent men on either side; but, that the connivance, or encouragement, given by the Whigs to those writers of pamphlets, who reflected upon the whole body of the clergy, without any exception, would unite the church, as one man, to oppose them: And, that I doubted his Lordship's friends did not consider the consequence of this. My Lord Sommers, in appearance, entered very warmly into the same opinion, and said very much of the endeavours he had often used to redress that evil I complained of. This his Lordship, as well as my Lord Hallifax, (to whom I have talked in the same manner) can very well remember: And I have indeed been told by an honourable gentleman of the same party, that both their Lordships, about the time of Lord Godolphin's removal, did upon occasion call to mind what I had said to them above five years before.

In my journeys to England I continued upon the same foot

of acquaintance with the two Lords last mentioned, till the time of Prince George's death, when the Queen, who, as is before related, had for some years favoured that party, now made Lord Sommers President of the Council, and the Earl of Wharton Lieutenant of Ireland. Being then in London, I received letters from some Bishops of Ireland, to solicit the Earl of Wharton about the remittal of the first-fruits and tenths to the clergy there, which the Queen had long promised, and wherein I had been employed before, with some hopes of success from the Earl of Godolphin. It was the first time I was ever in company with the Earl of Wharton; he received me with sufficient coldness, and answered the request I made in behalf of the clergy with very poor and lame excuses, which amounted to a refusal. I complained of this usage to Lord Sommers, who would needs bring us together to his house, and present me to him; where he received me as drily as before.

It was every body's opinion, that the Earl of Wharton would endeavour, when he went to Ireland, to take off the Test, as a step to have it taken off here: Upon which I drew up and printed a pamphlet, by way of a letter from a member of parliament here, shewing the danger to the church by such an intent. Though I took all care to be private, yet the Lieutenant's chaplain, and some others, guessed me to be the author, and told his Excellency their suspicions; whereupon I saw him no more till I went to Ireland. At my taking leave of Lord Sommers, he desired I would carry a letter from him to the Earl of Wharton, which I absolutely refused; yet he ordered it to be left at my lodgings. I staid some months in Leicestershire; went to Ireland; and, immediately upon my landing, retired to my country-parish, without seeing the Lieutenant, or any other person; resolving to send him Lord Sommers's letter by the post. But, being called up to town, by the incessant entreaties of my friends, I went and delivered my letter, and immediately withdrew. During the greatest part of his government, I lived in the country, saw the Lieutenant very seldom when I came to town, nor ever entered into the least degree of confidence with him, or his friends,

L

except his secretary Mr. Addison, who had been my old and intimate acquaintance.

Upon the news of great changes here, he affected very much to caress me, which I understood well enough to have been an old practice with him, in order to render men odious to the church-party.

I mentioned these insignificant particulars, as it will be easily judged, for some reasons that are purely personal to myself; it having been objected by several of those poor pamphleteers, who have blotted so much paper to shew their malice against me, that I was a favourer of the low-party. Whereas it hath been manifest to all men, that, during the highest dominion of that faction, I had published several tracts in opposition to the measures then taken: For instance, A Project for the Reformation of Manners, in a letter to the Countess of Berkeley; The Sentiments of a Church-of-England man; an Argument against abolishing Christianity; and, lastly, a Letter to a Member of Parliament against taking off the Test in Ireland, which I have already mentioned to have been published at the time the Earl of Wharton was setting out to his government of that kingdom. But those who are loud and violent in coffee-houses, though generally they do a cause more hurt than good, yet will seldom allow any other merit; and it is not to such as these that I attempt to vindicate myself.

About the end of August 1710, I went for England, at the desire and by the appointment of the Archbishops and Bishops of that kingdom; under whose hands I had a commission to solicite, in conjunction with two Bishops who were then in London, the restoring the first-fruits and twentieths to the clergy, which had been many years solicited in vain. Upon my arrival in town, I found the two Bishops were gone into the country; whereupon I got myself introduced to Mr. Harley, who was then Chancellor of the Exchequer, and acted as first minister. He received me with great kindness; told me, that he and his friends had long expected my arrival; and, upon shewing my commission, immediately undertook to perform it, which he accordingly did in less than three weeks, having settled it at five meetings with the Queen, according to a scheme I offered him, and got me the Queen's promise for a further and more important favour to the clergy of Ireland; which the Bishops there, deceived by misinformation, not worth mentioning in this paper, prevented me from bringing to a good issue.

When the affair of the first-fruits was fully dispatched, I returned my humble thanks to Mr. Harley, in the name of the clergy of Ireland, and of my own, and offered to take my leave, as intending immediately to return to that kingdom. Mr. Harley told me, he and his friends knew very well what useful things I had written against the principles of the late discarded faction; and, that my personal esteem for several among them, would not make me a favourer of their cause: That there was now an entirely new scene: That the Queen was resolved to employ none but those who were friends to the constitution of church and state: That their great difficulty lay in the want of some good pen, to keep up the spirit raised in the people, to assert the principles, and justify the proceedings of the new ministers.

Upon that subject he fell into some personal civilities, which it will not become me to repeat. He added, That this province was in the hands of several persons, among whom some were too busy, and others too idle to pursue it; and concluded, that it should be his particular care, to establish me here in England, and represent me to the Queen as a person they could not be without.

I promised to do my endeavours, in that way, for some few months; to which he replied, He expected no more; and that he had other and greater occasions for me.

Upon the rise of this ministry, the principal persons in power thought it necessary, that some weekly paper should be published, with just reflections upon former proceedings, and defending the present measures of her Majesty. This was begun about the time of the Lord Godolphin's removal, under the name of the Examiner. About a dozen of these papers, written with much spirit and sharpness, some by Mr. Secretary St. John, since Lord Bolingbroke; others by Dr. Atterbury, since Bishop of Rochester; and others again by Mr. Prior, Doctor Freind, &c. were published with great applause. But these gentlemen, grown weary of the work, or otherways employed, the determination was, that I should continue it, which I did accordingly for about eight months. But, my stile being soon discovered, and having contracted a great number of enemies, I let it fall into other hands, who held it up in some manner till her Majesty's death.

It was Mr. Harley's custom, every Saturday, that four or five of his most intimate friends, among those he had taken in upon the great change made at court, should dine at his house; and, after about two months acquaintance, I had the honour always to be one of the number. This company, at first, consisted only of the Lord-keeper Harcourt, the Earl Rivers, the Earl of Peterborow, Mr. Secretary St. John, and myself: And here, after dinner, they used to discourse, and settle matters of great importance. Several other Lords were afterwards, by degrees, admitted; as, the Dukes of Ormond, Shrewsbury, and Argyle; the Earls of Ailesbury, Dartmouth, and Powlet; the Lord Berkeley, &c. These meetings were always continued, except when the Queen was at Windsor; but, as they grew more numerous, became of less consequence; and ended only in drinking and general conversation; of which I may, perhaps, have occasion to speak hereafter.

My early appearance at these meetings, which many thought to be of greater consequence than really they were, could not be concealed, though I used all my endeavours to that purpose. This gave the occasion to some great men, who thought me already in the secret, to complain to me of the suspicions entertained by many of our friends in relation to Mr. Harley, even before he was Lord Treasurer; so early were sown those seeds of discontent, which afterwards grew up so high. The cause of their complaint was, That so great a number of the adverse party continued in employment; and some, particularly the Duke of Somerset and Earl of Cholmondely, in great stations at court. They could not believe Mr. Harley was in earnest; but, that he designed to constitute a motley comprehensive administration, which they said the kingdom would never endure. I was once invited to a meeting of some lords and gentlemen, where these grievances were at large related to me, with an earnest desire that I would represent them in the most effectual manner to Mr. Harley, upon a supposition that I was in high credit with him. I excused myself from such an office upon the newness of my acquaintance with Mr. Harley; however, I represented the matter fairly to him; against which he argued a good deal, from the general reasons of politicians; the necessity of keeping men in hopes, the danger of disobliging those who must remain unprovided for, and the like usual topicks among statesmen. But, there was a secret in this matter which neither I, nor indeed any of his most intimate friends, were then apprised of; neither did he, at that time, enter with me further than to assure me very solemnly, That it was his opinion and desire, that no person should have the smallest employment, either civil or military, whose principles were not firm for the church and monarchy.

However, these over-moderate proceedings in the court gave rise to a party in the House of Commons, which appeared under the name of the October-club; a fantastic appellation, found out to distinguish a number of country gentlemen, and their adherents, who professed in the greatest degree what was called the High-church principle. They grew in number to almost a third part of the house, held their meetings at certain times and places, and there concerted what measures they were to take in parliament. They professed their jealousy of the court and ministry; declared, upon all occasions, their desire of a more general change, as well as of a strict enquiry into former mismanagements; and seemed to expect, that those in power should openly avow the old principles in church and state. I was then of opinion, and still continue so, that if this body of men could have remained some time united, they would have put the crown under a necessity of acting in a more steady and strenuous manner. But Mr. Harley, who best knew the dispositions of the Queen, was forced to break their measures; which he did by that very obvious contrivance of dividing them among themselves, and rendering them jealous of each other. The ministers gave every where out, that the October-club were their friends, and acted by their directions; to confirm which Mr. Secretary St. John and Mr. Benson, afterwards Chancellor of the Exchequer, publicly dined with them at one of their meetings. Thus were eluded all the consequences of that assembly; though a remnant of them, who conceived themselves betrayed by the rest, did afterwards meet under the denomination of the March club, but without any effect.

The parliament which then sat had been chosen without any endeavours from the court, to secure elections; neither, as I remember, were any of the lieutenancies changed throughout the kingdom. For, the trial of Doctor Sacheverel had raised, or discovered, such a spirit in all parts, that the ministers could very safely leave the electors to themselves, and thereby gained a reputation of acting by a free parliament. Yet this proceeding was, by some refiners of both parties, numbered among the strains of Mr. Harley's politicks, who was said to avoid an over-great majority, which is apt to be unruly, and not enough under the management of a ministry. But, from the small experience I have of courts, I have ever found refinements to be the worst sort of all conjectures; and from this one occasion I take leave to observe, That of some hundreds of facts, for the real truth of which I can account, I never yet knew any refiner to be once in the right. I have already told, that the true reason why the court did not interpose in matter of elections, was because they thought themselves sure of a majority, and therefore could acquire reputation at a cheap rate. Besides it afterwards appeared upon some exigencies, which the court had much at heart, that they were more than once like to fail for want of numbers. Mr. Harley, in order to give credit to his administration, resolved upon two very important points; first, to secure the unprovided debts of the nation; and, secondly, to put an end to the war. Of the methods he took to compass both those ends, I have treated at large in another work: I shall only observe, that while he was preparing to open to the House of Commons his scheme for securing the public debts, he was stabbed by the Marquis de Guiscard, while he was sitting in the Council-chamber at the

Cock-pit, with a Committee of nine or ten Lords of the cabinet, met on purpose to examine the Marquis upon discovery of a treasonable correspondence he held with France.

This fact was so uncommon in the manner and circumstances of it, that although it be pretty well known at the time I am now writing, by a printed account, toward which I furnished the author with some materials, yet I thought it would not be proper wholly to omit it here. The assassin was seized, by Mr. Harley's order, upon the eighth of March 1710–11; and, brought before the committee of Lords, was examined about his corresponding with France: Upon his denial, Mr. Harley produced a letter, which he could not deny to be his own hand. The Marquis, prepared for mischief, had conveyed a penknife into his pocket, while the messenger kept him attending in one of the offices below. Upon the surprize of his letter appearing against him, he came suddenly behind Mr. Harley, and reaching his arm round, stabbed that minister into the middle of the breast, about a quarter of an inch above the *cartilago ensiformis*; the penknife striking upon the bone, and otherwise obstructed by a thick embroidered waistcoat, broke short at the handle, which Guiscard still grasped, and redoubled his blow. The confusion upon this accident is easier conceived than described: The result was, that the Marquis, whether by the wounds given him by some of the Lords, or the bruises he received from the messengers while they were seizing him, or the neglect of his chirurgeon; or, that being unwilling to live, he industriously concealed one of his wounds; he died in a few days after. But Mr. Harley, after a long illness, and frequent ill symptoms, had the good fortune to recover.

Guiscard was the younger brother of the Count of that name, a very honourable and worthy person, formerly Governor of Namur. But this Marquis was a reproach to his family, prostitute in his morals, impious in religion, and a traitor to his Prince: As to the rest, of a very poor understanding, and the most tedious, trifling talker, I ever conversed with. He was grown needy, by squandering upon his vices, was become contemptible both here and in Holland, his regiment taken from him, and his pension retrenched; the despair of which first put him upon his French correspondence; and the discovery of that drove him into madness. I had known him some years; and, meeting him upon the Mall a few hours before his examination, I observed to a friend then with me, that I wondered to see Guiscard pass so often by without taking notice of me. But although, in the later part of his life, his countenance grew cloudy enough, yet I confess I never suspected him to be a man of resolution, or courage, sufficient to bear him out in so desperate an attempt.

I have some very good reasons to know, that the first misunderstanding between Mr. Harley and Mr. St. John, which afterwards had such unhappy consequences upon the public affairs, took it's rise during the time that the former lay ill of his wounds, and his recovery doubtful. Mr. St. John affected to say in several companies, that Guiscard intended the blow against him; which, if it were true, the consequence must be, that Mr. St. John had all the merit, while Mr. Harley remained with nothing but the danger and the pain. But, I am apt to think, Mr. St. John was either mistaken, or mis-informed: However, the matter was thus represented in the weekly paper called the Examiner, which Mr. St. John perused before it was printed, but made no alteration in that passage.

This management was looked upon, at least, as a piece of youthful indiscretion in Mr. St. John; and, perhaps, was represented in a worse view to Mr. Harley: Neither am I altogether sure, that Mr. St. John did not entertain some prospect of succeeding as first minister, in case of Mr. Harley's death; which, during his illness, was frequently apprehended. And, I remember very well, that, upon visiting Mr. Harley, as soon as he was in a condition to be seen, I found several of his nearest relations talk very freely of some proceedings of Mr. St. John; enough to make me apprehend, that their friendship would not be of any long continuance.

Mr. Harley, soon after his recovery, was made an Earl, and Lord Treasurer; and Lord Keeper, a Baron.

An Enquiry
into the Behaviour of the
Queen's Last Ministry

AN ENQUIRY

into the Behaviour of the Queen's last Ministry, with Relation
to their Quarrells among themselves, and the Design charged
upon them of altering the Succession of the Crown.

June—1715.

SINCE the Death of the Queen it was reasonable enough
for me to conclude that I had done with all publick
Affairs and Speculations. Besides the Scene and Station
I am in have reduced my Thoughts into a narrow Compass;
and, being wholly excluded from any View of Favour under
the present Administration, upon that invincible Reason of
having been in some Degree of Trust and Confidence with
the former; I have not found the Transition very difficult into
a private Life, for which I am better qualified both by Nature
and Education.

The reading and enquiring after News having not been one
of my Diversions, having always Disliked a mixed and generall
Conversation, which, however it fell to my Lot, is now in my
Power to avoid; and being placed by the Duties of my Function
at a great Distance from the Seat of Business; I am altogether
ignorant of many common Events which happen in the
World: Only from the little I know and hear, it is manifest
that the Hearts of most Men are filled with Doubts, Fears and
Jealousies, or else with Hatred and Rage to a Degree that there
seems to be an End of all Amicable Commerce between People
of different Parties; and what the Consequences of this may be,
let those consider who have contributed to the Causes; which
I thank God, is no concern of mine.

There are two Points with Reference to the Conduct of the
late Ministry, much insisted on, and little understood by those
who write or talk upon that Subject; wherein I am sufficiently

qualified to give Satisfaction; and would gladly do it; because I see very much Weight laid upon each; and most Mens Opinions of Persons and Things regulated accordingly.

About two Months before the Queen's Death, having lost all Hopes of any Reconcilement between the Treasurer and the rest of the Ministry; I retired into the Country, to await the Issue of that Conflict, which ended as every One had Reason to foresee, in the Earl of Oxford's disgrace; to whom the Lord Bollingbrook immediatly succeeded as first Minister; and I was told, that an Earldom and the Garter were intended for him in a fortnight; and the Treasurer's Staff against the next Session of Parliament, of which I can say nothing certain being then in Barkshire and receiving this Account from some of his Friends; But all these Schemes became soon abortive by the Death of the Queen, which happened in three Days after the Earl of Oxford's Removall.

Upon this great Event, I took the first Opportunity of with-drawing to my Place of Residence; and rejoyced as much as any Man for his Majesty's quiet Accession to the Throne, to which I then thought and it hath since appeared indisputable, that the Peace procured by the late Ministry, had among other good Effects been highly Instrumentall. And I thank God I have been ever since a Loyall humble Spectator during all the Changes that have happened, although it were no Secret to any Man of common Sagacity; that his present Majesty's Choice of his Servants, whenever he should happen to succeed, would be determined to those who most opposed the Proceedings during the four last Years of his Predecessor's Reign; And I think there hath not since happened one Particular of any moment which the Ministers did not often Mention at their Tables as what they certainly expected from the Dispositions of the Court at Hannover, in Conjunction with that Party at Home which upon all occasions publickly dis-approved their Proceedings; excepting only the Attainder of the Duke of Ormonde, which indeed neither they nor I, nor I believe any one Person in the three Kingdoms did ever pretend to foresee; and now it is done, it looks like a Dream,

to those who will consider the Nobleness of his Birth, the great
Merits of his Ancestors and his own, his long unspotted
Loyalty; his Affability, Generosity, and Sweetness of Nature.
I knew him long and well; and excepting the Frailtyes of his
Youth, which had been for some Years over, and that easyness
of Temper which did sometimes lead him to follow the
Judgment of those who had by many degrees less Understanding than himself; I have not conversed with a more
faultless Person; of great Justice and Charity, a true sense of
Religion without Ostentation; of undoubted Valour, throwly
skilled in his Trade of a Souldier; a quick and ready Apprehension, with a good Share of Understanding, and a generall
Knowledge in Men and History, although under some Disadvantage by an invincible Modesty, which however could not
but render him yet more amiable to those who had the Honour
and Happiness of being throwly acquainted with Him. This is
a short imperfect Character of that great Person the Duke of
Ormonde, who is now attainted for high Treason; And therefore I shall not presume to offer one Syllable in his Vindication
upon that Head, against the Decision of a Parliament. Yet this
I think may be allowed me to believe, or at least to hope,
that when by the direct and repeated Commands of the
Queen his Mistress he committed those Facts, for which he
hath now forfeited his Country, his Titles and his Fortune;
he no more conceived himself to be acting high Treason,
than he did when he was wounded and a Prisoner at Landen
for his Sovereign King William; or when he took and burned
the Enemyes Fleet at Vigo.

Upon this Occasion, although I am sensible it is an old Precept
of Wisdom to admire at nothing in human Life, yet I consider
at the same Time how easily some Men arrive to the Practice
of this Maxim by the Help of plain Stupidity or Ill nature,
without any Strain of Philosophy, and although the uncertainty of human Things be one of the most obvious Reflections
in Morality; yet, such unexpected, sudden, and signall Instances
of it as have lately happened among us are so much out of the
usuall Form, that a wise Man may perhaps be allowed to start

and look aside as at a sudden and violent Clap of Thunder, which is much more frequent and more naturall.

And here I cannot but lament my own particular Misfortune, who having singled out three Persons from among the rest of Mankind, on whose Friendship and Protection I might depend; whose Conversation I most valued, and chiefly confined my self to, should live to see them all within the Compass of a Year, accused of high Treason; two of them attainted, and in Exile, and the third under his Tryall, whereof God knows what may be the Issue. As my own Heart was free from all treasonable Thoughts, so I did little Imagine my self to be perpetually in the Company of Traytors. But *the Fashion of this World passeth away*. Having already said something of the Duke of Ormonde, I shall add a little towards the Characters of the other two. It happens to very few Men in any Age or Country to come into the World with so many Advantages of Nature and Fortune, as the late Secretary Bolingbroke: Descended from the best Families in England, Heir to a great Patrimoniall Estate, of a sound Constitution, and a most gracefull, amiable Person: But all these had they been of equall Value, were infinitely below in Degree, to the Accomplishments of his Mind, which was adorned with the choicest Gifts that God hath yet thought fit to bestow upon the Children of Men; a strong Memory, a clear Judgment, a vast Range of Wit and Fancy, a thorow Comprehension, an invincible Eloquence, with a most agreeable Elocution. He had well cultivated all these Talents by Travel and Study, the latter of which he seldom omitted even in the Midst of his Pleasures, of which he had indeed been too great and Criminall a Pursuer; For although he were perswaded to leave off Intemperance in Wine, which he did for some Time to a Degree that he seemed rather abstemious; yet he was said to allow himself other Liberties, which can by no Means be reconciled to Religion or Moralls, whereof I have Reason to believe he began to be sensible. But he was fond of mixing Pleasure and Business, and of being esteemed excellent at both; upon which account he had a great Respect for the Characters of Alcibiades and

Petronius, especially the latter, .whom he would gladly be thought to resemble. His Detractors charged him with some Degree of Affectation, and perhaps not altogether without Grounds, since it was hardly possible for a young Man with half the Business of the Nation upon him, and the Applause of the whole to escape some Tincture of that Infirmity. He had been early bred to Business, was a most Artfull Negotiator, and perfectly understood foreign Affairs. But what I have often wondred at in a Man of his Temper, was his prodigious Application whenever he thought it necessary; For he would plod whole Days and Nights like the lowest Clerk in an Office. His Talent of Speaking in publick, for which he was so very much celebrated, I know nothing of except from the Informations of Others; But understanding Men of both Parties have assured me, that in this Point, in their Memory and Judgment he was never equalled.

The Earl of Oxford is a Person of as much Virtue as can possibly consist with the Love of Power; and his Love of Power is no greater than what is common to Men of his Superiour Capacities; Neither did any Man ever appear to value it less after he had obtained it, or exert it with more Moderation. He is the only Instance that ever fell within my Memory or Observation, of a Person passing from a private Life through the severall Stages of Greatness, without any perceivable Impression upon his Temper or Behaviour. As his own Birth was Illustrious, being descended from the Heirs generall of the Veres and the Mortimers, so he seemed to value that accidentall Advantage in himself and others more than it could pretend to deserve. He abounded in good Nature and good Humour, although Subject to Passion, as I have heard it affirmed by others, and owned by himself; which however he kept under the Strictest Government, till towards the End of his Ministry, when he began to grow sowred, and to suspect his Friends, and perhaps thought it not worth his Pains to manage any longer. He was a great Favourer of Men of Witt and Learning, particularly the former, whom he caressed without Distinction of Party, and could not endure to think that any of them should be his Enemies; and it was his good Fortune that none of them ever appeared to be so, at least if one may judge by the Libels and Pamphlets published against him, which he frequently read by way of Amusement with a most unaffected Indifference; Neither do I remember ever to have endangered his good Opinion so much as by appearing uneasy when the Dealers in that kind of Writing first began to pour out their Scurrilities against me, which he thought was a Weakness altogether inexcusable in a Man of Virtue and liberall Education. He had the greatest Variety of Knowledge, that I have any where met; was a perfect Master of the learned Languages, and well skilled in Divinity; He had a prodigious Memory, and a most exact Judgment. In drawing up any State Paper no man had more proper Thoughts, or put them in so strong and clear a Light, Although his Stile were not always correct, which however he knew how to mend, yet often to save time he would leave the smaller Alterations to others. I have heard that he spoke but seldom in Parliament, and then rather with Art than Eloquence; But no Man equalled him in the Knowledge of our Constitution; the Reputation whereof made him be chosen Speaker to three Successive Parliaments; which Office I have often heard his Enemies allow him to have executed with universall Applause; His Sagacity was such, that I could produce very amazing Instances of it, if they were not unseasonable. In all Difficulties he immediatly found the true Point that was to be pursued, and adhered to it: And one or two others in the Ministry have confessed very often to me, that after having condemned his Opinion, they found him in the right, and themselves in the wrong. He was utterly a Stranger to Fear, and consequently had a presence of Mind upon all Emergences. His Liberality and Contempt of Money were such, that he almost ruined his Estate while he was in Employment; Yet his Avarice for the Public was so great, that it neither consisted with the present Corruptions of the Age, nor the Circumstances of the Time. He was seldom mistaken in his Judgment of Men, and therefore not apt to change a good or ill Opinion by the Representation of Others;

except towards the End of his Ministry. He was affable and courteous, extreamly easy and agreeable in Conversation, and altogether disengaged; regular in his Life, with great Appearance of Piety; nor ever guilty of any Expressions that could possibly tend to what was undecent or prophane. His Imperfections were at least as obvious although not so numerous as his Virtues: He had an Air of Secrecy in his Manner and Countenance, by no means proper for a great Minister, because it warns all Men to prepare against it. He often gave no Answer at all, and very seldom a direct one; And I the rather blame this Reservedness of Temper, because I have known a very different Practice succeed much better; of which among Others the late Earl of Sunderland, and the present Lord Sommers, Persons of great Abilities, are remarkable Instances; who used to talk in so frank a Manner; that they seemed to discover the Bottom of their Hearts, and by that Appearance of Confidence would easily unlock the Breasts of Others. But the Earl of Oxford pleads in Excuse of this Charge, that he hath seldom or never communicated any Thing which was of Importance to be concealed, wherein he hath not been deceived by the Vanity, Treachery, or Indiscretion of those he discovered it to. Another of his Imperfections universally known and complained of, was Procrastination, or Delay; which was doubtless naturall to him, although he often bore the Blame without the Guilt, and when the Remedy was not in his Power; For never were Prince and Minister better matched than his Sovereign and He upon that Article; and therefore in the Disposall of Employments, wherein the Queen was very absolute, a year would often pass before they could come to a Determination. I remember he was likewise heavily charged with the common Court vice of promising very liberally and seldom performing; of which although I cannot altogether acquit him, yet I am confident his Intentions were generally better than his disappointed Sollicitors would believe. It may be likewise said of him, that he certainly did not value, or did not understand the Art of acquiring Friends; having made very few during

M

the Time of his Power, and contracted a great number of Enemies. Some of us used to observe, that those whom he talked well of, or suffered to be often near him, were not in a Scituation of much Advantage; and that his mentioning others with Contempt or Dislike, was no Hindrance at all to their Preferment. I have dwelt the longer upon this great Man's Character, because I have observed it so often mistaken by the wise Reasoners of both Parties; Besides, having had the Honour for almost four Years of a nearer acquaintance with Him than usually happens to men of my Level; and this without the least mercenary Obligation; I thought it lay in my Power, as I am sure it is in my Will, to represent Him to the World with Impartiality and Truth.

Having often considered the Qualities and Dispositions of these two Ministers, I am at a loss to think how it should come to pass that Men of exalted Abilities, when they are called to publick Affairs, are generally drawn into Inconveniencies and Misfortunes, which others of Ordinary Talents avoid; whereof there appear so many Examples both antient and modern, and of our own as well as other Countries. I cannot think this to have been altogether the Effect of Envy, as it is usually imputed in the Cases of Themistocles, Aristides, Scipio and others; and of Sir Walter Rawleigh, the Earls of Clarendon and Strafford here in England: But I look upon it, that God intending the Government of a Nation in the severall Branches and Subordinations of Power, hath made the Science of Governing sufficiently obvious to common Capacities; otherwise the world would be left in a desolate Condition, if great Affairs did always require a great Genius, whereof the most fruitfull Age will hardly produce above three or four in a Nation, among which, Princes, who of all other Mortals are the worst educated, have twenty Millions to one against them, that they shall not be of the Number; and proportionable Odds for the same Reasons are against every one of noble Birth or great Estates: Accordingly we find, that the dullest Nations antient and modern have not wanted good Rules of Policy, or Persons qualified for Administration. But, I take the Infelicity of such extraordinary Men to have been caused by their Neglect of common Forms, together with the Contempt of *little Helps*, and *little Hindrances*; which is made by Hobbes the Definition of Magnanimity; And this Contempt, as it certainly displeases the People in generall, so it giveth Offence to all with whom such Ministers have to deal; For, I never yet knew a Minister, who was not earnestly desirous to have it thought, that the Art of Government was a most profound Science; wheras it requires no more in reality, than Diligence, Honesty, and a moderate Share of plain naturall Sense. And therefore men thus qualifyed may very reasonably and justly think, that the Business of the World is best brought about by Regularity and Forms, wherein themselves excell. For, I have frequently observed more Causes of Discontent arise from the Practice of some refined Ministers, to act in common Business, out of the common Road, than from all the usuall Topicks of Displeasure against Men in Power: It is the same thing in other Scenes of Life, and among all Societies or Communities; where no Men are better trusted, or have more success in Business, than those who with some Honesty and a moderate Portion of Understanding are strict Observers of Time, Place, and Method; and on the Contrary, nothing is more apt to expose Men to the Censure and Obloquy of their Colleagues and the Publick, than a Contempt or Neglect of these Circumstances, however attended with a superiour Genius, and an equall Desire of doing Good; Which hath made me sometimes say to a great Person of this latter Character, that a small Infusion of the *Alderman* was necessary to those who are employed in publick Affairs. Upon this Occasion I cannot forget a very trifling Instance; That one day observing the same Person to divide a Sheet of Paper with a Penknife; the Sharpness of the Instrument occasioned it's Moving so irregularly and crooked, that he spoiled the whole Sheet; Whereupon I advised him to take Example by his Clerks, who performed that Operation much better with a blunt piece of Ivory, which directed by a little Strength, and a Steddy Hand, never failed to go right.

But, to return from this long Digression: About a Fortnight

after the Queen's Death, I came to my Place of Residence, where I was immediatly attacked with Heat enough by severall of my Acquaintance of both Parties; and soon learned, that what they objected, was the generall Sense of the rest. Those of the Church Side, made me a thousand Reproaches upon the Slowness and Inactivity of my Friends, upon their foolish Quarrells with each other for no visible Cause, and thereby sacrificing the Interests of the Church and Kingdom to their private Piques. And that they had neglected to cultivate the Favour and good Opinion of the Court at Hannover: But the Weight of these Gentlemen's Displeasure fell upon the Earl of Oxford; that he had acted a trimming Part; was never throwly in the Interest of the Church, but held separate Commerce with the Adverse Party: That, either from his Negligence, procrastinating Nature, or some sinister End, he had let slip many Opportunities of strengthning the Church's Friends, That he undertook more Business than he was equall to, affected a Monopoly of Power, and would concert nothing with the rest of the Ministers. Many Facts were likewise mentioned, which it may not be now very prudent to repeat; I shall only take Notice of one relating to Ireland, where he kept four Bishopricks undisposed of, though often and most earnestly pressed to have them filled; by which Omission, the Church Interest of that Kingdom in the House of Lords is in danger of being irrecoverably lost.

Those who discoursed with me after this manner, did at the same time utterly renounce all Regard for the Pretender; and mentioned with Pleasure the glorious Opportunity then in his Majesty's Hands of putting an End to Party Distinctions for the time to come; And the only Apprehension that seemed to give them any Uneasiness, was lest the Zeal of the Party in Power, might not perhaps represent their Loyalty with Advantage.

On the other Side, the Gainers and Men in hopes by the Queen's Death talked with great Freedom in a very different Style; They all directly asserted that the whole late Ministry were fully determined to bring in the Pretender, although they would sometimes a little demurr upon the Earl of Oxford; and by a more modern Amendment, they charged the same Accusation without any Reserve, upon the late Queen her self. That, if Her Majesty had dyed but a Month later, our Ruin would have been inevitable. But in that juncture it happened, (to use their own Term, which I could never prevail with them to explain) *Things were not ripe.* That this Accusation would in a short time infallibly be proved as clear as the Sun at Noon day to all the World: And the Consequences naturally following from these Positions were, that the Leaders ought to lose their Heads, and all their Abetters be utterly stript of Power and Favour.

These being the Sentiments and Discourses of both Parties tending to load the late Ministry with Faults of a very different Nature; it may perhaps be either of some Use or Satisfaction to examine those two Points; That is to say, First how far these Ministers are answerable to their Friends for their Neglect, Mismanagement and mutuall Dissensions; and Secondly with what Justice they are accused by their Enemies for endeavouring to alter the Succession of the Crown, in favor of the Pretender.

It is true indeed I have occasionally done this already in two severall Treatises, of which the One is an History, and the other Memoirs of particular Facts, but neither of them fit to see the Light at present, because they abound with Characters freely drawn, and many of them not very amiable; and therefore intended only for the Instructing of the next Age, and establishing the Reputation of those who have been usefull to their Country in the present. At the same Time I take this Opportunity of assuring those who may happen some Years hence to read the History I have written, that the blackest Characters to be met with in it, were not drawn with the least Mixture of Malice or ill Will; but meerly to expose the Odiousness of Vice; For I have always held it as a Maxim, that ill Men are placed beyond the Reach of an Historian, who indeed hath it in his Power to reward Virtue, but not to punish Vice; Because I never yet saw a profligate Person, who seemed to have the least regard in what manner his Name should be transmitted to Posterity: And I knew a certain *Lord not long since dead, who I am very confident, would not have disposed one single Shilling to have had it in his Choice whether he should be represented to future Ages as an *Atticus* or a *Catiline*.

However, being firmly resolved, for *very Materiall Reasons*, to avoyd giving the least Offence to any Party or Person in Power; I shall barely set down some Facts and Circumstances during the four last Years of Queen Anne's Reign, which at present are little known, and whereby those of the Church Party who object against the Unsteadiness, Neglect, and Want of Concert in the late Ministry, may better account for their Faults. Most of these Facts I can bear Witness of my self, and have received the rest from sufficient Authority.

It is most certain, that when the Queen first began to change her Servants it was not from a Dislike of Things but of Persons, and those Persons were a very small Number. To be more particular would be, *incedere per ignes*. It was the Issue of Doctor Sacheverall's Tryall, that encouraged her to proceed so far; And several of the low-Church Party knowing that her Displeasure went no further than against one single Family, did not appear to dislike what was done; of which I could give some †extraordinary Instances. But, that famous Tryall had raised such a Spirit in the Nation against the Parliament, that Her Majesty thought it necessary to dissolve them, which I am confident she did not at first intend. Upon this Resolution delivered by the Queen at Council in a more determinate Manner than was usuall with her, as I was particularly informed by my Lord Sommers then President, some who were willing to sacrifice one or two Persons, would not sacrifice their Cause; but immediatly flew off; and the great Officers of the Court and Kingdom began to resign their Employments, which the Queen suffered most of them to do with the utmost Regret, and which those who knew her best thought to be reall; especially Lord Sommers and Lord Cowper, for whom she had as great a Personall Regard and Esteem as her Nature was capable of admitting, particularly

* Earl of Wharton.   † Duke of Sommerset.

for the former. The new Parliament was called during that
Ferment in the Nation, and a great Majority of the Church
Party was returned, without the least Assistance from the
Court; whether to gain a Reputation of Impartiality where
they were secure; or as Mr. Harley's Detractors would have
it (who was then Minister) from a Refinement of His Politicks,
not to suffer, upon the Account of I know not what wise
Reasons, too great an Inequality in the Balance.

When the Parliament met, they soon began to discover
more Zeal than the Queen expected or desired; She had entertained the Notion of forming a moderate or comprehensive
Scheam, which She maintained with great firmness, nor would
ever depart from untill about half a Year before her Death;
But this neither the House of Commons nor the Kingdom in
generall were then at all inclined to admit, whatever they may
have been in any Juncture since: Severall Country Members
to almost a third part of the House began immediatly to form
themselves into a Body under a fantastick Name of the
October-Club: These daily pressed the Ministry for a thorow
Change in Employments, and were not put off without
Jealousy and Discontent; I remember it was then commonly
understood and expected, that when the Session ended, a
generall Removall would be made; but it happened otherwise,
for not only few or none were turned out, but much Delibera-
tion was used in supplying common Vacancies by Death.
This manner of proceeding in a prime Minister, I confess
appeared to me wholly unaccountable, and without Example;
And I was little satisfied with the Solution I had heard, and
partly knew, that he acted thus to keep Men at his Devotion
by letting Expectation lye in common; for I found the Effect
did not answer, and that in the mean Time he led so uneasy a
Life by Sollicitations and Pursuits, as no Man would endure
who had a Remedy at hand. About the beginning of his
Ministry I did at the Request of severall considerable Persons
take the Liberty of representing this Matter to him; His
Answer was short and cold; That he hoped his Friends
would trust him; that he heartily wished none but those who
loved the Church and Queen were employed; but that all

Things could not be done on a sudden. I have Reason to believe, that his nearest Acquaintance were then wholly at a Loss what to think of his Conduct. He was forced to preserve the Opinion of Power without which he could not act, while in reality he had little or none; and besides he thought it became him to take the Burthen of Reproach upon himself, rather than lay it upon the Queen his Mistress, who was grown very positive slow and suspicious; and from the Opinion of having been formerly too much *directed*, fell into the other extream, and became difficult to be *advised*. So that few Ministers had ever perhaps a harder Game to play, between the Jealousy and Discontents of his Friends on one Side, and the Management of the Queen's Temper on the other.

There could hardly be a firmer Friendship in appearance than what I observed between those three great Men who were then chiefly trusted, I mean the Lords Oxford, Bolingbroke and Harcourt. I remember in the Infancy of their Power, being at the Table of the first, where they were all met, I could not forbear taking notice of the great Affection they bore to each other; and said I would venture to prophecy, that however inconstant our Court had hitherto been, their Ministry would certainly last; For, they had the Church, the Crown, and the People entirely on their side; Then, it happened, that the publick Good and their private Interest had the same Bottom, which is a piece of good Fortune that doth not always fall to the Share of Men in Power: But principally, because I observed they heartily loved one another; and I did not see how their Kindness could be disturbed by Competition, since each of them seemed contented with his own District; so that notwithstanding the old Maxim which pronounceth Court Friendships to be of no long Duration, I was confident their's would last as long as their Lives. But it seems, the Inventer of that Maxim happened to be a little wiser than I, who lived to see this Friendship first degenerate into Indifferency and Suspicion, and thence corrupt into the greatest Animosity and Hatred, contrary to all Appearances, and much to the Discredit of me and my Sagacity. By what Degrees, and from what Causes those Dissentions grew, I shall as far as it may be safe and convenient, very impartially relate.

When Mr. Harley was stabbed by Guiscard, the Writer of a weekly Paper called the *Examiner*, taking Occasion to reflect on that Accident, happened to let fall an idle Circumstance, I know not upon what Grounds, that the French Assassin confessed he at first intended to have Murdered Mr. Secretary St. John, who sitting at too great a Distance, he was forced to vent his Rage on the other: Whether the Secretary had been thus informed, or was content that others should believe it, I never yet could learn, but nothing could be more unfortunate than the Tendency of such a Report, which by a very unfair Division, derived the whole Merit of that Accident to Mr. St. John, and left Mr. Harley nothing but the Danger and the Pain; Of both which although he had a sufficient Share, (his Physicians being often under Apprehensions for his Life) yet I am confident the Time of his Illness was a Period of more Quiet and Ease than he ever enjoyed during the rest of his Administration. This Report was not unresented by Mr. Harley's Friends, and the rather because the Fact was directly otherwise, as it soon appeared by Guiscard's Confession.

While that Minister lay ill of his Wound, and his Life in Question, the Weight of Business fell in some Measure upon the Secretary, who was not without Ambition, which I confess I have seldom found among the wants of great Men; and it was conceived that he had already entertained the Thoughts of being at the Head of Affairs in case Mr. Harley should dye. Although at the same time I must do Justice to Mr. St. John by repeating what he said to me with great Appearance of Concern, (and he was but an ill Dissembler) that if Mr. Harley's Accident should prove fatal, it would be an irreparable Loss; that as Things then stood, his Life was absolutely necessary; that as to Himself, he was not Master of the Scheme by which they were to proceed, nor had Credit enough with the Queen; neither did he see how it would be possible for them in such a Case to wade through the Difficulties they were then under. However, not to be over particular in so nice a Point, thus much is certain, that some Things happened during Mr. Harley's Confinement, which bred a Coldness and Jealousy between those two great Men; and these increasing by many subsequent Accidents could never be removed.

Upon Mr. Harley's Recovery, which was soon followed by his Promotion to an Earldom and the Treasurer's Staff; He was earnestly pressed to go on with the Change of Employments, for which his Friends and the Kingdom were very impatient, wherein I am confident he was not unwilling to comply, if a new Incident had not put further Difficulties in his Way. The Queen having thought fit to take the Key from the Dutchess of Marlborough; it was after some time given to another great *Lady wholly in the Interests of the Opposite Party, who by a most obsequious Behaviour of which she is a perfect Mistress and the Priviledges of her Place, which gave her continuall Access, quickly won so far upon the Affections of Her Majesty, that she had more Personall Credit than all the Queen's Servants put together. [Of this Lady's Character, and Story, having spoken so much in other Papers which may one day see the Light]; I shall only observe, that as soon as she was fixed in her Station, the Queen following the Course of her own Nature, grew daily much more difficult and uncomplying. Some weak Endeavours were indeed used to divert Her Majesty from this Choice, but she continued steady, and pleaded, that if She might not have Liberty to chuse Her own Servants, She could not see what Advantage She had got by the Change of Her Ministry. And so little was Her Heart set upon what they call a High Church or Tory Administration, that several Employments in Court and Country, and a great Majority in all Commissions remained in the Hands of those who most opposed the present Proceedings; Nor do I remember that any Removall of Consequence was made till the Winter following, when the Earl of Notingham was pleased to prepare and offer a Vote in the House of Lords against any Peace while Spain continued in the Hands of the Bourbon Family. Of this Vote the Ministers had early Notice, and by casting up the Numbers, concluded they should have a Majority of ten to overthrow it. The Queen was

* Dutchess of Somerset.

desired and promised to speak to a certain Lord who was looked upon as Dubious, that Lord attended accordingly, but heard not a Word of the Matter from Her Majesty, although She afterwards owned it was not for want of Remembring, but from perfect Indifference. The Treasurer who trusted to Promises, and reckoned that others would trust to His, was by a most unseasonable Piece of Parsimony, grossly deceived; and the Vote carried against the Court. The Queen had the Curiosity to be present at the Debate; and appeared so little displeased at the Event, or against those from whom she might have expected more Compliance; that a *Person in high Station among her Domesticks, who that day in her Presence had shewn his utmost Eloquence (such as it was) against the Ministers, received a †particular Mark of Distinction and Favour, which by his Post he could not pretend to, and was not removed from her Service but with exceeding Difficulty many Months after. And it is certain that this Vote could not have been carried if some Persons very near Her Majesty, had not given Assurances where they were proper, that it would be acceptable to the Queen, which Her Behaviour seemed to confirm.

But when the Consequences of this Vote were calmly represented to Her, that the Limitation specified therein had wholly tyed up her Hands, in case the Recovery of Spain should be found impossible, as it was frequently allowed and owned by many principle Leaders of the Opposite Party, and had hitherto been vainly endeavoured either by Treaty or War: That the Kingdom was not in a Condition to bear any longer it's Burthen and Charge, especially with annuall Additions: That other Expedients might possibly be found for preventing France and Spain from being united under the same King, according to the Intent and Letter of the Grand Alliance: That the Design of this Vote was to put Her Majesty under the Necessity of Dissolving the Parliament, beginning all things a new, and placing the Administration in the Hands of those whom She had thought fit to lay aside, and this by sacrificing her present Servants to the Rage and Vengeance

---

* Duke of Somerset.   † To lead out the Queen.

of the former; with many other obvious Considerations not very proper at this time to be repeated; Her Majesty who was earnestly bent upon giving Peace to her People, consented to fall upon the sole Expedient, that her own Coldness, or the Treasurer's Thrift, and want or Contempt of Artifice had left Her; which was to create a Number of Peers sufficient to turn the Balance in the House of Lords. I confess that in my History of those Times, where this Matter among others is treated with a great deal more Liberty, and consequently very unfit for present Perusall, I have refined so far as to conjecture that if this were the Treasurer's Council, he might possibly have given it upon some further Views than that of avoiding the Consequences of My Lord Notingham's Vote. And what those were, I suppose I may offer without Offence. It is known enough, that from the Time of the Revolution to the Period I am now speaking of, the Favour of the Court, was almost perpetually turned towards those who in the Party Term are called Whigs, or the low-Church; and this was a Space of above twenty Years, wherein great Additions were made to the Peerage; and the Bishop's Bench almost wholly renewed. But the Majority of landed Men still retaining the old Church Principles in Religion and Government, notwithstanding all Endeavours to convert them, the late King was under many insuperable Difficulties during the Course of his Reign; Elections seldom succeeding, so well as to leave the Court side without strenuous Opposition, sufficient to carry many Points against him which he had much at Heart. Upon the late Queen's Succeeding to the Crown, the Church Party who seemed to have grown more numerous under all Discouragements, began to conceive Hopes, that Her Majesty who had always professed to favour their Principles, would make use of their Service: And indeed upon that Foot, things stood for some time; But a new War being resolved on, three Persons who had most Credit with Her Majesty, and who were then looked upon to be at least as high Principled as could possibly consist with the Protestant Succession, having consulted their Friends, began to conceive, that the Military Spirit was much more vigorous in the other Party, who appeared more keen against France, more sanguine upon the Power and Wealth of England, and better versed in the Arts of finding out Funds, to which they had been so long used. There were some other Motives for this Transition of the Ministers at that time, which are more proper for the History above mentioned; where they are faithfully recorded. But, thus the Queen was brought to govern by what they call a Low-Church Ministry, which continued for severall Years; Till at length grown weary of the War, although carried on with great Glory and Success; and the Nation rising into a Flame (whether justly or no) upon the Tryall of Doctor Sacheverall, which in Effect was a generall Muster of both Parties; Her Majesty following her own Inclinations, and those of her People, resolved to make some Changes in the Ministry, and take Mr. Harley into Her Councils. This was brought about, as the Charge against that Minister says, *by the basest Insinuations*; upon which, being a Determination of Parliament, I shall not dispute; although I confess to have received a very different Account of that Matter from a most excellent Lady upon whose Veracity I entirely depend, and who being then in chief Confidence with her Mistress, must needs know a particular Fact wherein She was immediatly concerned and trusted, better than any One Man or Number of Men, except the Majority of a House of Commons.

When the new Parliament met, whose Elections were left entirely to the People without the least Influence from the Court, it plainly appeared how far the Church Party in the Nation outnumbred the other, and especially in the severall Counties. But in the House of Lords even after some Management, there was but a weak and crazy Majority; Nor even could this have been expected, if severall great Lords who were always reputed of the other Party, had not only complyed but been highly instrumentall in the Change, as the Dukes of Shrewsbury and Argyle, the Earls of Peterborough, Rivers, and some others, who certainly came into the Queen's Measures upon other Motives than that of Party. Now, since the Government of England cannot go on while the two Houses of Parliament are in Opposition to each other, and that the People whenever they acted freely would infallibly return a Majority of Churchmen; One of these two Things was of Necessity to be done; Either first, to dissolve that Parliament, and call another of the Whig Stamp by force of a prodigious Expence, which would be neither decent nor safe, and perhaps at that time hardly feisible; or else to turn the Balance in the House of Lords, which after the Success of Lord Nòtingham's Vote, was not otherwise to be done than by creating a sufficient Number of Peers, in order at once to make the Queen and her People easy upon that Article for the rest of her Reign. And this I should be willing to think, was the Treasurer's meaning, when he advised those Advancements; which however I confess I did very much dislike.

But if after all I have said, my Conjecture should happen to be wrong; yet I do not see how the Treasurer can justly be blamed for preserving His Cause, his Friends and himself from unavoidable Ruin, by an Expedient allowed on all Hands to be lawfull; Perhaps he was brought under that Necessity by the Want of proper Management; but when that Necessity appeared, he could not act otherwise without unravelling whatever had been done, which in the Language of those Times would have been called, delivering the Queen and Kingdom back into the Hands of a Faction they had so lately got rid of. And I believe no Minister of any Party would in his Circumstances have scrupled to make the same Step when the *Summa rerum* was at Stake.

Although the Queen was brought into this Measure by no other Motive than her earnest Desire of a Peace; yet the Treasurer's Friends began to press him a-new for further Changes in Employments; concluding from what was past, that his Credit was great enough to compass whatever he pleased. But this proved to be ill Reasoning; For the Queen had no Dislike at all to the other Party, (whatever Personall Piques She might bear to some among them) further than as She conceived they were bent upon continuing the War, to which Her Majesty resolved to put as speedy an End as She could with Honor and Safety to her Kingdoms: And therefore fell with readiness enough into the Methods proposed to Her for advancing that great Work. But in dispensing her Favours, She was extreamly cautious and slow; and after the usuall Mistake of those who think they have been often imposed on, became so very suspicious that She overshot the Mark and erred in the other Extream. When a Person happened to be recommended as usefull for her Service, or proper to be obliged, perhaps after a long delay She would consent; but if the Treasurer offered at the same time a Warrant or other Instrument to Her already prepared, in order to be signed, He was certain to be refused; because he presumed to reckon upon her Consent before hand; and thus the Affair would sometimes lye for severall Months together, although the Thing were ever so reasonable, or that even the Publick suffered by the Delay. So that this Minister had no other Remedy, but to let Her Majesty take her own time, which never failed to be the very longest that the Nature of the Thing could suffer Her to defer it.

When this Promotion was made, Mr. Secretary St. John whose Merits and Pretensions as Things then stood were far superiour to any, was purposely left out, because the Court had need of his great Abilities the following Session in the House of Commons, and the Peace being then upon the Anvil, he was best able to explain and justify the severall Steps towards it; which he accordingly did with invincible Reason and universall Applause. When the Session was over, the Queen thought fit to give him a Title, and that he might not lose his Rank, created him Viscount. There had been an Earldom in his Name and Family lately extinct; (though a Barony fell to a collaterall Branch in the Person of an Infant), and the Secretary being of the same House, expected and desired the same Degree. For he reasoned, that making him a Viscount, would be but rigorous Justice, and he hoped he might pretend to some Mark of Favour; But the Queen could not be prevailed with, because to say the Truth, he was not much at that time in her good Graces; some Women about the Court, having infused an Opinion into her that he was not so regular in his Life as He ought to be. The Secretary laid the whole Blame of this Disappointment upon the Earl of

Oxford, and freely told me, that he would never depend upon the Earl's Friendship as long as he lived, nor have any further Commerce with him than what was necessary for carrying on the publick Service. And although I have good Reason to be assured, that the Treasurer was wholly innocent in this Point, as both himself and Lady Masham then protested to me, yet my Lord Bolingbroke thought the Appearances were so strong, that I was never able to bring him over to my Opinion.

The Divisions between these two great Men, began to split the Court into Parties; Harcourt Lord Chancellour, the Dukes of Shrewsbury and Argyle, Sir William Windham and one or two more adhered to the Secretary, the rest were either Neuters, or inclined to the Treasurer, whether from Policy or Gratitude, although they all agreed to blame and lament his Mysterious and procrastinating Manner in acting; which the State of Affairs at that Time could very ill admit, and must have rendred the Earl of Oxford inexcusable, if the Queen's obstinate Temper had not put him under the Necessity of exerting those Talents wherewith it must be confessed his Nature was already too well provided.

This Minister had stronger Passions than the Secretary, but kept them under stricter Government; my Lord Bolingbroke was of a Nature frank and open, and as Men of great Genius are superiour to common Rules, he seldom gave himself the trouble of disguising or subduing his Resentments, although he was ready enough to forget them. In matters of State, as the Earl was too reserved, so perhaps the other was too free, not from any Incontinency of Talk, but from the meer Contempt of multiplying Secrets, although the graver Councellours imputed this Liberty of Speech to Vanity or Lightness. And upon the whole no two Men could differ more in their Diversions, their Studies, their Ways of transacting Business, their Choice of Company, or Manner of Conversation.

The Queen, who was well informed of these Animosities among her Servants, of which her own dubious Management had been the Originall Cause, began to find and lament the ill Consequences of them in her Affairs both at home and abroad, and to lay the Blame upon her Treasurer, whose greatest Fault in his whole Ministry was too much Complyance with his Mistress, by which his Measures were often disconcerted, and himself brought under Suspicion by his Friends.

I am very confident, that this Alteration in the Queen's Temper towards the Earl of Oxford, could never have appeared, if He had not thought fit to have made one Step in Politicks which I have not been able to apprehend. When the Queen first thought of making a Change among her Servants after Doctor Sacheverall's Tryall, My Lady Masham was very much heard and trusted upon that Point, and it was by Her Intervention, Mr. Harley was admitted into Her Majesty's Presence. That Lady was then in high Favour with Her Mistress, which I believe the Earl was not so very sedulous to cultivate or preserve as if he had it much at heart, nor was altogether sorry when he saw it under some Degree of Declination. The Reasons for this must be drawn from the common Nature of Mankind, and the Incompatibility of Power: But the Juncture was not favourable for such a Refinement, because it was early known to all who had but looked into the Court, that this Lady must have a Successor, who upon Picque and Principle would do all in Her Power to obstruct his Proceedings. My Lady Masham was a Person of a plain sound Understanding, of great Truth and Sincerity, without the least Mixture of Falshood or Disguise; of an honest Boldness and Courage superiour to her Sex; firm and disinterested in her Friendship, and full of Love, Duty, and Veneration for the Queen Her Mistress; Talents as seldom found or sought for in a Court, as unlikely to thrive while they are there; So that nothing could then be more unfortunate to the Publick than a Coldness between this Lady and the first Minister; nor a greater Mistake in the latter than to suffer or connive at the lessening of her Credit, which he quickly saw removed very disadvantagiously to another *Object, and wanted the Effects of, when his own was sunk, in the only Domestick Affair for which I ever knew him under any Concern.

* The Dutchess of Somerset.

N

While the Queen's Favour to the Earl was thus gradually lessening, the Breaches between Him and his Friends grew every day wider, which he looked on with great Indifference, and seemed to have his Thoughts only turned upon finding out some proper Opportunity for delivering up his Staff; But this Her Majesty would not then admit, because indeed it was not easy to determine who should succeed Him.

In the midst of these Dispositions at Court, the Queen fell dangerously sick at Windsor, about Christmas 1713. It was confidently reported in Town, that She was dead; and the Heads of the expecting Party were said to have various Meetings thereupon, and a great hurrying of Chairs and Coaches to and from the Earl of Wharton's House; whether this were true or not, yet thus much is certain, that the Expressions of Joy appeared very frequent and loud among many of that Party; which Proceeding Men of form did not allow to be altogether decent. A Messenger was immediatly dispatched with an Account of the Queen's Illness, to the Treasurer, who was then in Town, and in order to stop the Report of Her Death, appeared next day abroad in his Chariot with a pair of Horses, and did not go down to Windsor till his usuall Time. Upon his Arrivall there, the Danger was over, but not the Fright, which still sate on every Bodies Face; and the Account given of the Confusion and Distraction the whole Court had been under, is hardly to be conceived: Upon which the Treasurer said to me, whenever any Thing ails the Queen, these People are out of their Wits, and yet they are so thoughtless, that as soon as She is well, they act as if She were immortall; I had sufficient Reason both before and since to allow his Observation to be true; and, that some Share of it might with Justice be applyed to Himself.

The Queen had early Notice of this Behaviour among the discontented Leaders during Her Illness. It was indeed an Affair of such a Nature as required no Aggravation, which however would not have been wanting, the Women of both Parties who then attended Her Majesty, being well disposed to represent it in the strongest Light. The result was, that the Queen immediatly laid aside all her Schemes and Visions of reconciling the two opposite Interests, and entred upon a firm Resolution of adhering to the old English Principles, from an Opinion that the Adverse Party waited impatiently for Her Death upon Views little consisting (as the Language and Opinion went then) with the Safety of the Constitution either in Church or State; She therefore determined to fall into all just and proper Methods that Her Ministers should advise Her to for the Preservation and Continuance of both. This I was quickly assured of not only by the Lord Chancellour and Lord Bolingbroke, but by the Treasurer himself.

I confess my self to have been then thorowly perswaded that this Incident would perfectly reconcile the Ministers by uniting them in pursuing one generall Interest, and considering no further than what was fittest to be done; I could not easily foresee any Objections or Difficulties that the Earl of Oxford would make; I had for some time endeavoured to cultivate the strictest Friendship between him and the *Generall, by telling both of them (which happened to be the Truth) how kindly they spoke of each other; and by convincing the latter of what Advantage such an Union must be to her Majesty's Service. There was an Affair upon which all our Friends laid a more than ordinary Weight. Among the Horse and Foot Guards appointed to attend on the Queen's Person, severall Officers took every Occasion with great Freedom and Bitterness of Speech to revile the Ministry upon the Subject of the Peace and the Pretender, not without many gross Expressions against the Queen her self; such as I suppose will hardly be thought on or attempted, but certainly not suffered under the present Powers. Which Proceeding beside the Indignity, begot an Opinion, that Her Majesty's Person might be better guarded than by such Keepers, who after attending at Court or at the Levee of the Generall or first Minister, adjourned to publish their Disaffection in Coffee-houses and Gaming-Ordinaries without any Regard to Decency or Truth. It was proposed that ten or a dozen of the least discreet among these Gentlemen should be obliged to sell their Posts in the Guards; and that two or three who

* The Duke of Ormonde.

had gone the greatest Lengths, should have a Price fixed for their Commissions, somewhat below the Exorbitant Rate usually demanded for a few Years past. The Duke of Ormonde desired but ten thousand Pounds to make the Matter easy to those Officers who were to succeed, which Sum his Grace told me, the Treasurer had given him Encouragement to expect, although he pleaded present Want of Money; And I cannot but say, that having often at the Duke's Desire presst this Minister to advance the Money, he gave me such Answers as made me think he really intended it: But I was quickly undeceived; For, expostulating some days after with him upon the same Subject, after great Expressions of Esteem and Friendship for the Duke of Ormonde; and mentioning some ill Treatment he had received from his Friends; he said he knew not why he should do other People's Work. The Truth is, that except the Duke, My Lord Trevor, and Mr. Secretary Bromly, I could not find he had one Friend left of any Consequence in Her Majesty's Service. The Lord Chancellour, Lord Boling- broke and Lady Masham openly declared against him; to whom were joyned the Bishop of *Rochester, and some others. Dartmouth then Privy Seal, and Powlet Lord Steward stood Neuters. The Duke of Shrewsbury hated the Treasurer, but sacrificed all Resentments to Ease, Profit, and Power; and was then in Ireland acting a Part directly opposite to the Court, which he had Sagacity enough to foresee might quickly turn to Account; so that the Earl of Oxford stood almost single, and every day found a visible Declension of the Queen's Favour towards Him; which he took but little Care to redress, desiring nothing so much as Leave to deliver up his Staff, which however as Conjunctures then stood, he was not able to obtain; his Adversaries not having determined where to place it; Neither was it upon severall Accounts a work so proper to be done while the Parliament sate, where the Ministry had already lost too much Reputation, and especially in the House of Lords. By what I could gather from severall Discourses with the Treasurer, it was not very difficult to find out how he reasoned with himself. The Church Party

* Doctor Atterbury.

continued violently bent to have some necessary Removalls made in the Guards, as well as a further Change in the Civil Employments through the Kingdom. All the great Officers about the Court, or in Her Majesty's Service, except the Duke of Shrewsbury, and one or two more were in the same Opinion; the Queen her Self since her last Illness at Windsor, had the like Dispositions; and I think it may appear from severall Passages already mentioned, that the Blame of those Delays so often complained on, did not originally lye at the Earl of Oxford's Door. But the State of Things was very much changed by severall Incidents: The Chancellour, Lord Boling-broke, and Lady Masham had entirely forsaken him, upon Suspicions I have mentioned before, which although they were founded on Mistake, yet he would never be at the Pains to clear; and as he first lessened his Confidence with the Queen by pressing her upon those very Points for which his Friends accused him that they were not performed; so, upon Her Change of Sentiments after Her Recovery he lost all Favour and Credit with her for not seconding those new Resolutions from which She had formerly been so averse. Besides, he knew, as well as all others who were near the Court, that it was hardly possible the Queen could survive many Months; in which Case he must of Necessity bring upon him the Odium and Vengeance of the Successor, and of that Party which must then be predominant, who would quickly unravel all he had done; Or, if Her Majesty should hold out longer than it was reasonable to expect, yet after having done a Work that must procure him many new Enemies, he could expect Nothing but to be discharged in Displeasure. Upon these Reasons he continued his Excuses to the Duke of Ormonde for not advancing the Money; and during the six last Months of his Ministry would enter into no Affairs but what immediatly concerned the Business of his Office. That whole Period was nothing else but a Scene of Murmuring, and Discontent, Quarrell and Misunderstanding, Animosity and Hatred between Him and his former Friends. In the mean time the Queen's Countenance was wholly changed towards Him, She complained of his Silence and Sullenness, and in return gave him every Day fresh Instances of Neglect or Displeasure.

The Originall of this Quarrell among the Ministers which had been attended with so many ill Consequences, began first between the Treasurer and Lord Bolingbroke from the Causes and Incidents I have already mentioned; and might very probably have been prevented if the Treasurer had dealt with less Reserve, or the Lord Bolingbroke had put that Confidence in Him which so sincere a Friend might reasonably have expected. Neither perhaps would a Reconcilement have been an Affair of much Difficulty, if their Friends on both Sides had not too much observed the common prudentiall Forms of *not caring to intermeddle*, which together with the Addition of a Shrug, was the constant Answer I received from most of them whenever I pressed them upon the Subject. I cannot tell whether my Lord Trevor may be excepted, because I had little Acquaintance with him, although I am inclined to the Negative. Mr. Prior who was much loved and esteemed by them both, as he well deserved, upon the Account of every Virtue that can qualify a Man for private Conversation, might have been the properest Person for such a Work, if he could have thought it to consist with the Prudence of a Courtier; but however, he was absent in France at those Junctures when it was chiefly necessary. And to say the Truth, most Persons had so avowedly declared themselves on one Side or t'other, that these two great Men had hardly a common Friend left except my Self. I had ever been treated with great Kindness by them both; and I conceived that what I wanted in Weight and Credit might be made up with Sincerity and Freedom. The former they never doubted, and the latter they had constant Experience of: I had managed between them for almost two Years; and their Candour was so great, that they had not the least Jealousy or Suspicion of me. And I thought I had done Wonders, when upon the Queen's being last at Windsor, I put them in a Coach to go thither by Appointment without other Company; where they would have four Hours Time to come to a good Understanding; But in two days after, I learned from them Both, that nothing was done.

There had been three Bishopricks for some time vacant in Ireland, and I had prevailed on the Earl of Oxford, that one of them should be divided. Accordingly four Divines of that Kingdom were named to the Queen, and approved by her; But upon some Difficulties not worth mentioning, the Queen's Mandatory Letters to Ireland had been delayed; I pressed the Treasurer every Week while her Majesty was at Windsor, and every day after Her Return, to finish this Affair, as a Point of great Consequence to the Church in that Kingdom; and growing at Length impatient of so many Excuses, I fell into some Passion, when his Lordship freely told me, that he had been earnest with the Queen upon that Matter about ten times the last Fortnight, but without Effect; and that He found His Credit wholly at an End: This happened about eleven Weeks before the Queen dyed; and two Nights after sitting with Him and Lord Bolingbroke in Lady Masham's Lodgings at St. James's for some Hours; I told the Treasurer, that having despaired of any Reconciliation between them, I had only stayd some time longer to forward the Disposall of those Bishopricks in Ireland, which since His Lordship told me was out of his Power; I now resolved to retire immediatly, as from an Evil I could neither help to redress nor endure the Sight of; That before I left them, I desired they would answer me two Questions: First whether these Mischiefs might not be remedied in two Minutes; and Secondly, whether upon the present foot the Ministry would not be infallibly ruined in two Months; Lord Bolingbroke answered to each Question in the Affirmative; and approved of my Resolution to retire; but the Treasurer after his Manner evaded both, and only desired me to dine with Him next Day: However I immediatly went down to a Friend in Barkshire to await the Issue, which ended in the Removall of my Lord Treasurer, and three Days after in Her Majesty's Death.

Thus I have with some Pains recollected severall Passages which I thought were most materiall for the Satisfaction of those who appear so much at a Loss upon the unaccountable

Quarrells of the late Ministry. For indeed it looked like a Riddle, to see Persons of great and undisputed Abilities, called by the Queen to Her Service in the Place of Others with whose Proceedings She was disgusted, and with great Satisfaction to the Clergy, the landed Interest, and Body of the People, running on a sudden into such a common beaten Court Track of Ruin, by Divisions among themselves, not only without a visible Cause, but with the strongest Appearances to the contrary, and without any Refuge to the usuall Excuse of evill Instruments, or cunning Adversaries to blow the Coals of Dissention; for the Work was entirely their own.

I impute the Cause of these Misfortunes to the Queen, who from the Variety of Hands She had employed, and Reasonings She had heard since her coming to the Crown, was grown very fond of moderating Schemes, which as Things then Stood, were by no means reduceable to Practice; She had likewise a good Share of that Adherence to her own Opinions, which is usually charged upon her Sex: And lastly (as I before observed) having received some Hints that She had formerly been too much governed, She grew very difficult to be advised.

The next in fault was the Treasurer, who not being able to influence the Queen in many Points with Relation to Party, which his Friends and the Kingdom seemed to have much at Heart, would needs take all the Blame on himself, from a known Principle of State Prudence, that a first Minister must always preserve the Reputation of Power: But I have ever thought, that there are few Maxims in Politicks which at some Conjunctures may not be very liable to an Exception. The Queen was by no means inclined to make many Changes in Employments, She was positive in her Nature, and extreamly given to delay; And surely these were no proper Qualities for a chief Minister to personate towards his nearest Friends, who were brought into Employment upon very different Views and Promises. Nor could any Reputation of Power be worth preserving at the Expense of bringing Sincerity into Question. I remember, upon a Saturday, when the Ministers

and one or two Friends of the Treasurer constantly met to
dine at his House, one of the Company attacked him very
warmly on account, that a certain Lord who perpetually
opposed the Queen's Measures was not dismissed from a great
Employment, which besides other Advantages gave that Lord
the Power of chusing severall Members of Parliament. The
Treasurer evaded the Matter with his usuall Answer that this
was whipping Day; Upon which the Secretary Bolingbroke
turning to me, said, it was a Strange Thing that my Lord
Oxford would not be so kind to his Friends, and so just to
his own Innocence, as to vindicate himself where he had no
Blame; for to his Knowledge and the Chancellour's (who
was then also present) the Treasurer had frequently and
earnestly moved the Queen upon that very Point without
Effect; Whereupon, this Minister finding himself pressed so
far, told the Company that he had at last prevailed with Her
Majesty, and the Thing would be done in two days, which
followed accordingly. I mention this Fact as an Instance of
the Earl of Oxford's Disposition, to preserve some Reputation
of Power in himself, and remove all Blame from the Queen;
and this to my particular Knowledge was a frequent Case,
but how far justifiable in Point of Prudence, I have already
given my Opinion. However the Treasurer's Friends were
yet much more to blame than Himself, He had abundance of
Merit with them all not only upon Account of the Publick,
the whole Change of the Ministry having been effected without any Intervention of their's, by Him and Lady Masham;
but likewise from the Consequence of that Change, whereby
the greatest Employments of the Kingdom were divided
among them, and therefore in common Justice as well as
Prudence, they ought to have been more indulgent to his
reall Failings, rather than suspect him of imaginary ones, as
they often did, through Ignorance, Refinement, or Mistake:
And I mention it to the Honour of the Secretary Bolingbroke,
as well as of the Treasurer, that having my Self upon many
Occasions joyned with the former in quarrelling with the
Earl's Conduct upon certain Points, the Secretary would

in a little time after, frankly own that he was altogether mistaken.

Lastly I cannot excuse the Remissness of those whose Business it should have been, as it certainly was their Interest, to have interposed their good Offices for healing this unhappy Breach among the Ministers; But of this I have already spoken.

Cap. 2d.

Written above a year after.

Having proceeded thus far, I thought it would be un-necessary to say any Thing upon the other Head, relating to the Design of bringing in the Pretender; For, upon the Earl of Oxford's Impeachment the Gentlemen of the pre-vailing Side assured me that the whole Mystery would be soon laid open to the World, and were ready to place the Merit of their Cause upon that Issue: This Discovery we all expected from the Report of the Secret Committee; But when that Treatise appeared, (whoever were the Compilers) we found it to be rather the Work of a luxuriant Fancy, an absolute State Pamphlet arguing for a Cause, than a dry Recitall of Facts or a Transcript of Letters; and for what related to the Pretender, the Authors contented themselves with informing the Publick, that the whole Intrigue was privately carried in Personall Treatyes between the Earl of Oxford and the Abbot Gautier, which must needs be a Doctrine hard of Digestion to those who have the least Knowledge either of the Earl or the Abbot, or upon what Foot the latter stood at that Time with the English Ministry: I conceive that whoever is at Distance enough to be out of Fear either of a Vote or a Messenger, will be as easily brought to believe all the Popish Legends together. And to make such an Assertion in a publick Report delivered to the House of Commons without the least Attempt to prove it, will some time or other be reckoned such a Strain upon Truth and Probability as is hard to be equalled in a Spanish Romance. I think it will be allowed that the Articles of high Treason drawn up against the Earl were not altogether founded upon the Report, or at least that those important Hints about bringing in the Pretender were more proper Materialls to furnish out a Pamphlet than an Impeachment: Since this Accusation hath no Part even among the high Crimes and Misdemeanours.

But notwithstanding all this, and that the Earl of Oxford

after two Years Residence in the Tower, was at length dismissed without any Tryall, yet the Reproach still went on, that the Queen's last Ministry in Concert with their Mistress were deeply engaged in a Design to set the Pretender upon the Throne. The cultivating of which Accusation I impute to the great Goodness of those in Power, who are so gracious to assign a Reason, or at least give a Countenance for that sudden and universall sweep they thought fit to make on their first Appearance; whereas they might as well have spared that Ceremony by a short Recourse to the Royall Prerogative, which gives every Prince a Liberty of chusing what Servants he will.

There are two Points which I believe my self able to make out: First, that neither the late Queen nor her Ministers did ever entertain a Design of bringing in the Pretender during Her Majesty's Life, or that he should succeed after Her Decease.

Secondly, that if they conceived such a Design, it was absolutely necessary to prosecute it from the first Year of their Ministry; Because for at least a Year before the Queen's Death, it was impossible to have put such a Design in Execution.

I must premise with three Circumstances which have a great Effect on me, and must have the Like upon those among my Friends who have any tolerable Opinion of my Veracity, and it is only to these that I offer them.

I remember, during the late Treaty of Peace, discoursing at severall times with some very eminent Persons of the opposite Side, with whom I had long Acquaintance, I asked them seriously whether they or any of their Friends did in earnest believe or suspect the Queen or the Ministry to have any favourable Regards towards the Pretender. They all confessed for themselves, that they believed nothing of the Matter, and particularly a Person at present in great Employment said to me with much Frankness; You sett up the Church and Sacheverall against us, and We set up Trade and the Pretender against you.

The second Point I would observe is this; that during

the Course of the late Ministry, upon Occasion of the Libels every Day thrown about, I had the Curiosity to ask almost every Person in great Employment, whether they knew or had heard of any one Particular Man (except those who professed to be Nonjurers) that discovered the least Inclination towards the Pretender; and the whole Number they could muster up did not amount to above five or six, among which one was a certain old Lord lately dead, and one a private Gentleman of little Consequence and of a broken Fortune: Yet I do not believe my self to have omitted any one great Man that came in my Way, except the Duke of Buckingham, in whose Company I never was above once or twice at most; I am therefore as confident as a Man can be of any Truth which will not admit a Demonstration, that upon the Queen's Death, if we except Papists and Nonjurers, there could not be five hundred Persons in England of all Ranks who had any Thoughts of the Pretender, and among these, not six of any Quality or Consequence; But how it hath come to pass that severall Millions are said to have since changed their Sentiments, it shall not be my Part to inquire.

The last Point is of the same Strain, and I offer it like the two former, to convince only those who are willing to believe me on my own Word; that having been for the Space of almost four Years very nearly and perpetually conversant with those who had the greatest Share of Power, and this in their Times of Leisure as well as Business, I could never hear one single Word to be let fall in Favour of the Pretender, although I was curious enough to observe in a particular Manner, what passed upon that Subject. And I cannot but think that if such an Affair had been in Agitation, I must have had either very bad Luck, or a very small Share of common Understanding, not to have discovered some Grounds at least for Suspicion. Because I never yet knew a Minister of State, or indeed any other Man so great a Master of Secrecy, as to be able among those he nearly converseth with, wholly to conceal his Opinions, however he may cover his Designs. This I say, upon a Supposition that they would have held on the Mask always before me, which however I have no Reason to believe. And I confess it is with the Expence of some Patience that I hear this Matter summarily determined by those who had no Advantages of knowing any Thing that passed otherwise than what they found in a Libel or a Coffee-house; Or at best from generall Reasonings built upon mis-taken Facts. Now, although what I have hitherto said upon this Point, can have no Influence further than my own personall Credit reacheth, yet I confess I shall never be brought to change my Opinion, till some One who had more Opportunities than I, will be able to produce any single Particular from the Letters, the Discourses, or the Actions of those Ministers, as a Proof of what they alledge; which hath not yet been attempted or pretended.

But I believe there may be severall Arguments of another Nature produced, which can make it very evident to those who will hear Reason, that the Queen's Ministers never had it in their Thoughts to alter the Succession of the Crown.

For, first, when Her Majesty had determined to change her Servants, it is very well known that those whom She appointed to succeed them, were generally accounted Favourers of what is called the Low Church Party, not only my Lord Oxford, Bolingbroke and Harcourt, but a great Majority of the rest: Among which I can immediatly name the Dukes of Shrewsbury, Newcastle and Argyle, the Earls of Peterborough, Rivers, Strafford, Isley and Orrery, the Lords Mansel and Masham, with severall others whom I cannot at present recollect. Whereas, of the other Party the Dukes of Ormonde and Buckingham and the Earl of Dartmouth were the only Persons introduced at first, and very few afterwards: which I suppose will clearly evince, that the bringing in of the Pretender was not the Originall Scheam of such Ministers, and that they were by no means proper Instruments for such a Work.

And whoever knew any Thing of the Queen's Disposition, must believe She had no Inclinations at all in Favour of the Pretender; She was highly and publickly displeased with my Lord Bolingbroke, because He was seen under the same Roof with that Person at an Opera, when His Lordship was sent to

France upon some Difficulties about the Peace: Her Majesty said, that He ought immediatly to have withdrawn upon the Appearance of the Other; wherein, to speak with Freedom, I think her Judgment was a little mistaken. And at her Toilet among her Women, when mention happened to be made of the Chevalier, she would frequently let fall Expressions of such a Nature, that made it manifest how little She deserved those Reproaches which have been cast on Her since her Death, upon that Account.

Besides, I have already said that Her Majesty began those Changes at Court for no other Cause than her Personall Displeasure against a certain Family, and their Allyes; and from the Hope She had to obtain a Peace, by the Removall of some whose Interest it was to obstruct it; That when the former Chancellour, President, and others came to Her, determined to deliver up their Employments, She pressed them somewhat more than became her Dignity to continue in their Stations, of which I suppose my Lord Cowper is yet a living Wittness.

I am forced to repeat what I have before observed, that it was with the utmost Difficulty She could be ever perswaded to dismiss any Person upon the Score of Party, and that She drove Her Ministers into the greatest Distress, upon my Lord Notingham's Vote against any Peace without Spain, for want of speaking to one or two depending Lords, although with the last danger of breaking the Measures She was most fond of towards settling the Repose of Europe. She had besides upon the Removall of the Dutchess of Marlborough chosen *another great Lady to succeed, who quickly grew into higher Credit than all her Ministers together; A Lady openly professing the utmost Aversion from the Persons the Principles and Measures of those who were then in Power, and excelling all even of Her own Sex in every Art of Insinuation: And this Her Majesty thought fit to do in Opposition to the strongest Representations that could possibly be made to Her of the Inconveniencies which would ensue. Her only Objection against severall Clergymen recommended to Her

* Dutchess of Summerset.

for Promotion in the Church, was their being too violent in Party. And a Lady in high Favour with her, hath frequently assured me, that whenever She moved the Queen to discard some Persons, who upon all Occasions with great Virulence opposed the Court; Her Majesty would constantly refuse, and at the same time condemn her for too much Party Zeal.

But beside all this, there never was a more stale or anti-quated Cause than that of the Pretender, at the Time when Her Majesty chose her last Ministers, who were most of them Children or Youths when the King his Father abdicated; They found a Prince upon the Throne before they were of Years to trouble themselves with Speculations upon Govern-ment, and consequently could have no Scruples of Conscience in submitting to the present Powers, since they hardly remembred any Other. And truly this was in generall the Case of the whole Kingdom; For the Adherents of King James the Second were all either dead or in Exile, or sunk in Obscurity, laden with Years and Want; so that if any Guilt were contracted by the Revolution, it was generally understood that our Ancestors were only to answer for it. And I am confident, with an Exception to professed Non-jurers, there was not one Man in ten thousand through England who had other Sentiments. Nor can the contrary Opinion be defended by arguing the prodigious Disaffection at present; because the same Thing hath happened before from the same Causes in our own Country, and within the Memory of Man, although not with the same Event.

But such a Disaffection could hardly have been raised against an absent Prince who was only in Expectation of the Throne; And indeed I cannot but reckon it as a very Strong Argument for the good Disposition both in the Ministry and Kingdom towards the House of Hannover; that during my Lord Oxford's Administration, there was never thrown out the least Reflection against that illustrious House in any Libel or Pamphlet, which would hardly have happened, if the small Party Writers could have thought that by such a Per-formance they would have made their Court to those in Power, and which would certainly have been a very usefull

Preliminary, if any Attempt had been intended towards altering the Succession to the Crown. But however, to say the Truth, Invectives against the absent and with whom we have Nothing to do, although they may render Persons little and contemptible can hardly make them odious: For Hatred is produced by Motives of a very different Nature as Experience hath shewn. And although Politicians affirm it more eligible for a Prince to be hated than despised, yet that Maxim is better calculated for an absolute Monarchy than for the Clymate of England. But I am sensible this is a Digression, and therefore I return.

The Treatyes made by Her Majesty with France and Spain, were calculated in severall Points, directly against the Pretender, as he hath now found to his Cost, and as it is manifest to all the World. Neither could any Thing be more superficiall than the Politicks of those who could be brought to think that the Regent of France would ever engage in Measures against the present King of England, and how the Grimace of an Ambassador's taking or not taking his publick Character, as in the Case of the Earl of Stairs, should serve so long for an Amusement, cannot sufficiently be wondred at. What can be plainer than that the chief Interest of the Duke of Orleans is woven and twisted with that of King George, and this, whether it shall be thought convenient to suffer the young King of France to live longer or no. For in the second Case, the Regent perfectly agrees with our present King in this particular Circumstance, that the whole Order of Succession hath been broken for his Sake, by which means He likewise will be encumbred with a Pretender and thereby engaged upon the strongest Motives to prevent the Union of France and Spain under one Monarch. And even in the other Case, the Chance of a Boy's Life, and his leaving Heirs Male of his Body is so dubious, that the Hopes of a Crown to the Regent or his Children will certainly keep that Prince as long as his Power continues, very firm in his Alliance with England.

And as this Design was originally intended and avowed by the Queen's Ministers in their Treaties with France and

o

Spain, so the Events have fully answered in every Particular. The present King succeeded to these Crowns with as hearty and universall a Disposition of the People, as could possibly consist with the Grief for the Loss of so gracious and excellent a Princess as her late Majesty; the Parliament was most unanimous in doing every Thing that could endear them to a new Monarch: The generall Peace did entirely put an End to any Design which France or Spain might probably have laid to make a Diversion by an Invasion upon Scotland with the Pretender at the Head, in Case her Majesty had happened to dye during the Course of the War: And upon the Death of the late French King, the Duke of Orleans fell immediatly into the Strictest Measures with England, as the Queen and Her Ministers easily foresaw it would be necessary for him to do, from every Reason that could regard his own Interest. If the Queen had dyed but a Short time before the Peace, and either of the two great Powers engaged against us, had thought fit to have thrown some Troops into Scotland; although it could not have been a very agreeable Circumstance to a Successor and a Stranger, Yet the universall Inclinations at that time in England towards the House of Hanover, would in all Probability have prevented the Consequences of such an Enterprize. But, on the other Side, if the War had continued a Year longer than Her Majesty's Life, and the same Causes had been applyed to produce the same Effects upon the Affections of the People, the Issue must inevitably have been either a long and bloody Civil War, or a sudden Revolution. So that no Incident could have arrived more Effectuall to fortify the present King's Title, and secure His Possession, than that very Peace so much exploded by one Party, and so justly celebrated by the other; in continuing to declare which Opinions under the present Scituation of Things, it is not very improbable, that they may both be in Jest.

But if any Articles of that Peace were like to endanger the Protestant Succession, how could it come to pass, that the Dutch who were Guarentees of that Succession, and valued for Zealous Defenders of it, should be so ready with their Offers to comply with every Article, and this for no greater

a Reward than a Share in·the Assiento Trade, which the
Opposers of Peace represented to be only a Trifle. That
the Fact is true I appeal to Monsieur de Buys, who upon some
Difficulties the Ministry was under by the Earl of Notingham's Vote against any Peace while Spain continued in the
Bourbon Family, undertook to make that matter easy, by
getting a full Approbation from the States His Masters, of all
Her Majesty's Proceedings, provided they might be sharers in
that Trade. I can add this further, that some Months after
the Conclusion of the Peace, and amidst all the appearing
Discontents of the Dutch, a Gentleman who had long resided
in Holland, and was occasionally employed by the Ministers
here, assured me that he had Power from the Pensioner to
treat with the Earl of Oxford about sending hither an extraordinary Ambassy from Holland, to declare that the States
were fully satisfied with the whole Plan of the Peace, upon
certain Conditions which were easy and Honourable, and
such as had no Relation at all to the Pretender; How this
happened to fail, I never inquired, nor had any Discourse
about it with those in Power. For then their Affairs were
growing desperate by their Quarrells among themselves, and
by the Earl of Oxfords Declination in the Queen's Favour,
both which became so publick as well as Her Majesty's bad
State of Health, that I suppose those Circumstances might
easily cool the Dutch Politicians in that Pursuit.

I remember to have heard it objected against the late
Ministry as an Instance of their Inclination towards the
Pretender, that they were careless in cultivating a good
Correspondence with the House of Hannover. And on the
other side, I know very well what continuall Pains were
employed to satisfy and inform the Elector and his Ministers
in every Step taken by Her Majesty, and what Offers were
made to his Highness for any further Securities of the Succession in Him and His Family that could consist with the Honour
and Safety of the Queen. To this purpose were all the Instructions given to Earl Rivers, Mr. Thomas Harley, Lord Clarendon, and some Others. But all Endeavours were rendred
abortive by a foolish Circumstance which hath often made

me remember the common Observation of the greatest Events depending frequently upon the lowest, vilest, and obscurest Causes; And this is never more verified than in Courts, and the Issues of publick Affairs, whereof I could produce from my own Knowledge and Observation, three or four very Surprizing Instances. I have seen an old *Bedmaker by officiously going to one Door, when Gratitude as well as common Sense should have sent her to another, become the Instrument of putting the Nation to the Expence of some thousand Lives, and severall Millions of Money. I have known as great an Event from the Stupidity or Willfullness of a beggarly †Dutchman, who lingred on purpose half an hour at a Visit when he had promised to be some where else. Of no greater Dignity was that Circumstance which rendred ineffectuall all Endeavours of the late Ministry, to establish themselves in the good Graces of the Court at Hannover, as I shall particularly relate in another Work. It may suffice to hint at present, that a Delay in conveying a very inconsiderable Sum, to a very inconsiderable French ‡Vagrant, gave the Opportunity to a more industrious Party, of corrupting that Channel, through which all the Idea's of the Dispositions and Designs of the Queen, the Ministers, and the whole British Nation were conveyed.

The Second Point which I conceive my self able to make out is this; that if the Queen's Ministers had with or without the Knowledge of their Mistress entertained any Thoughts of altering the Succession in Favour of the Pretender, it was absolutely necessary for them to have begun and prosecuted that Design as soon as they came into Her Majesty's Service.

There were two Circumstances, which would have made it necessary for them to have lost no time. First because it was a Work that could not possibly be done on a sudden. For the whole Nation almost to a Man, excepting professed Nonjurers, had conceived the utmost Abhorrence of a Popish

---

* Mrs. Foiston necessary woman to the Queen prefered to that employment by My Lady Masham.

† Cary Lord Hunsden born and bred in Holland.

‡ Robethon then at Hanover but in the service of some other German Prince: it is not known how, got in some Credit with the Elector.

Successor. And as I have already observed, the Scruple of Conscience upon the Point of Loyalty was wholly confined to a few antiquated Nonjurers who lay starving in Obscurity. So that in order to have brought such an Affair about in a Parliamentary Way, some years must have been employed to turn the Bent of the Nation, to have rendred one Person odious and another amiable; neither of which is to be soon compassed towards absent Princes, unless by comparing them with those of whom we have had Experience, which was not *then* the Case.

The other Circumstance was the bad Condition of the Queen's Health, Her Majesty growing every day more unwieldy, and the Gout with other disorders increasing on her; so that whoever was near the Court for about the two last Years of Her Reign, might boldly have fixed the Period of her Life to a very few Months without pretending to Prophecy. And how little a Time the Ministers had for so great a Work as that of Changing the Succession of the Crown, and how difficult the very Attempt would have been, may be judged from the Umbrage taken by Severall Lords of the Church Party in the last Year of her Reign, who appeared under an Apprehension that the very Quarrells among the Ministers, might possibly be of some Disadvantage to the House of Hannover. And the universall Declaration both among Lords and Commons at that Time as well in Favour of the Elector as against the Pretender, are an Argument beyond all Conviction that some Years must have been spent in altering the Dispositions of the People. Upon this Occasion I shall not soon forget what a great Minister then said to me, and which I have been since assured was likewise the Duke of Shrewsbury's Opinion: That there could be no doubt of the Elector's undisturbed Succession, but the chief Difficulty lay in the future Disaffection of the Church, and People, and landed Interest, from that universall Change of Men and Measures, which he foresaw would arrive. And it must be to all impartiall Men above a thousand Wittnesses, how innocent Her Majesty's Servants were upon this Article, that knowing so well through what Channels all Favour was to pass upon the Queen's Demise; that by their coming into Power they had utterly and for ever broken all Measures with the Opposite Party; and that in the Beginning of their Administration, there wanted not perhaps certain favourable Junctures, which some future Circumstances would not have failed to cultivate; Yet their Actions shewed them so far from any View towards the Pretender, that they neglected pursuing those Measures which they had constantly in their Power, not only of securing themselves but the Interest of the Church without any Violence to the Protestant Succession in the Person of the Elector. And this unhappy Neglect I take to have been the only Disgrace of their Ministry. To prevent this Evil, was, I confess, the chief Point wherein all my little Politicks terminated: and the Methods were easy and obvious. But whoever goes about to gain Favour with a Prince by a Readiness to enlarge his Prerogative, although out of Principle and Opinion, ought to provide that he be not outbid by another Party however professing a contrary Principle; For I never yet read or heard of any Party acting in Opposition to the true Interest of their Country, whatever Republican Denominations they affected to be distinguished by, who would not be contented to chaffer publick Liberty for Personall Power, or for an Opportunity of gratifying their Revenge: Of which Truth, Greece and Rome, as well as many other States will furnish Plenty of Examples. This Reflection, I could not well forbear, although it may be of little use further than to discover my own Resentment. And yet perhaps that Misfortune ought rather to be imputed to the Want of Concert and Confidence, than of Prudence or Courage.

I must here take Notice of an Accusation charged upon the late Ministry by the House of Commons, that they put a Lye or Falshood into the Queen's Mouth, to be delivered to Her Parliament. Mr. Thomas Harley was sent to the Elector of Hannover with Instructions to offer His Highness any further Securities for settling the Succession in Him and His Family, that could consist with Her Majesty's Honour and Safety. This Gentleman wrote a Letter to the Secretary of State, a little before his Return from Hannover, signifying in direct

Terms, that the Elector expressed himself satisfied in the
Queen's Proceedings, and desired to live in Confidence
with Her. He wrote to the same Purpose to one of the under-
Secretaries, and mentioned the Fact as a Thing that much
pleased Him, and what he desired might be as publick as
possible. Both those Letters I have read; And the Queen, as
She had Reason to suppose, being sufficiently authorized by
this Notice from Her Minister, made mention of that Information in a Speech from the Throne. If the Fact were a Lye,
tis what I have not heard Mr. Harley to have been charged
with. From what hath since passed in the World, I should
indeed be inclined to grant it might have been a Compliment
in His Highness, and perhaps understood to be so by the
Queen; But without Question, Her Majesty had a fair Excuse
to take the Elector according to the Literall Meaning of his
Words. And if this be so, the Imputation of Falshood must
remain where these Accusers of that excellent Princess's
Veracity will I suppose not profess (at least) an Inclination
to place it.

I am very willing to mention the Point wherein as I said
all my little Politicks terminated, and wherein I may pretend
to know that the Ministers were of the same Opinion, and
would have put it in Practice if it had pleased God to let them
continue to act with any kind of Unanimity.

I have already observed how well it was known at Court
what Measures the Elector intended to follow whenever His
Succession should take Place; and what Hands he would
employ in the Administration of his Affairs: I have likewise
mentioned some Facts and Reasons which influenced and
fixed His Highness in that Determination, notwithstanding
all possible Endeavours to divert him from it. Now, if we
consider the Dispositions of England at that Time, when
almost the whole Body of the Clergy, a vast majority of the
landed Interest and of the People in generall were of the
Church Party, it must be granted that one or two Acts which
might have passed in ten Days would have put it utterly
out of the Power of the Successor, to have procured a House of
Commons of a different Stamp, and this with very little

Diminution to the Prerogative, which Acts might have been only temporary. For the usuall Arts to gain Parliaments can hardly be applyed with Success after the Election, against a Majority at least of three in four; because the Trouble and Expence would be too great, beside the Loss of Reputation. For, neither could such a Number of Members find their Account in point of Profit, nor would the Crown be at so much Charge and Hazard meerly for the sake of Governing by a small Party against the Bent and Genius of the Nation: And as to all Attempts of influencing Electors, they would have been sufficiently provided for by the Scheme intended. I suppose it need not be added, that the Government of England cannot move a Step while the House of Commons continues to dislike Proceedings, or Persons employed, at least in an Age where Parliaments are grown so frequent and are made so necessary: Whereas a Ministry is but the Creature of a Day, and a House of Lords hath been modelled in many Reigns by enlarging the Number, as well as by other obvious Expedients.

The judicious Reader will soon comprehend how easily the Legislature at that time could have provided against the Power and Influence of a Court or Ministry in future Elections, without the least Injury to the Succession, and even without the Modern Invention of perpetuating themselves, which however I must needs grant to be one of the most effectuall vigorous and resolute Proceedings that I have yet met with in Reading or Information. For the long Parliament under King Charles the first, although it should be allowed of good Authority will hardly amount to an Example.

I must again urge and repeat, that those who charge the Earl of Oxford and the rest of that Ministry with a Design of altering the Succession of the Crown in Favour of the Pretender, will perhaps be at some Difficulty to fix the Time when that Design was in Agitation; for if such an Attempt had begun with their Power, it is not easy to assign a Reason why it did not Succeed, because there were certain Periods when Her Majesty and Her Servants were extreamly popular and the House of Hannover not altogether so much, upon Account of some Behaviour and Management in one or two of their Ministers here, and some other Circumstances, that may better be passed over in Silence; All which however had no other Consequence than that of repeated Messages of Kindness and Assurance to the Elector. During the last two Years of the Queen's Life, Her Health was in such a Condition, that it was wondered how She could hold out so long: And then as I have already observed, it was too late and hazardous to engage in an Enterprize which required so much Time, and which the Ministers themselves had rendred impracticable by the whole Course of their former Proceedings, as well as by the Continuance and Heightning of those Dissentions which had early risen among them.

The Party now in Power will easily agree that this Design of overthrowing the Succession could not be owing to any Principle of Conscience in those whom they accuse; For they knew very well by their own Experience and Observation, that such Kind of Scruples have given but small Disturbance of late Years in these Kingdoms. Since Interest is therefore the only Test by which we are to judge the Intentions of those who manage publick Affairs, it would have been but reasonable to have shewn how the Interest of the Queen's Ministers could be advanced by introducing the Pretender, before they were charged with such an Intention. Her Majesty was severall Years younger than her intended Successor, and at the beginning of that Ministry had no Disorders except the Gout, which is not usually reckoned a Shortner of Life; and those in chief Trust were generally speaking older than their Mistress; So that no Persons had ever a fairer Prospect of running on the naturall Life of an English Ministry; considering likewise the generall Vogue of the Kingdom at that Time in their Favour; And it will be hard to find an Instance in History of a Sett of Men in full Possession of Power, so sanguine as to form an Enterprize of overthrowing the Government without the visible Prospect of a generall Defection, which (then at least) was not to be hoped for. Neither do I believe it was ever heard of, that a Ministry in such Circumstances durst engage in so dangerous an Attempt without the direct

Commands of their Sovereign. And as to the Persons then in Service, if they may be allowed to have common Sense, they would much sooner have surrendred their Employments than hazard the Loss of their Heads at so great Odds, before they had tryed or changed the Disposition of the Parliament, which is an Accusation that I think none of their Libellers have charged upon them, at least till towards the End of their Ministry, and then very absurdly, because the Want of Time, and other Circumstances rendred such a Work impossible for severall Reasons which I have already related.

And whoever considers the late Queen so little enterprising in Her Nature, so much given to Delay, and at the same time so obstinate in Her Opinions, (as Restiness is commonly attended with Slowness) so great a Pursuer of Peace and Quiet, and so exempt from the two powerfull Passions of Love and Hatred; will hardly think She had a Spirit turned for such an Undertaking; if we add to this the Contempt She often expressed for the Person and Concerns of the Chevalier her Brother, of which I have already said enough to be understood.

It hath been objected against the late Queen and Her Servants as a Mark of no favourable Disposition towards the House of Hannover, that the Electorall Prince was not invited to reside in England; And at the same time it ought to be observed that this Objection was raised and spread by the Leaders of that Party, who first opposed the Council of inviting Him; offering among other Arguments against it the Example of Queen Elizabeth, who would not so much as suffer Her Successor to be declared, expressing Her self, that She would not live with Her Grave Stone always in Her Sight: Although the Case be by no Means Parallell between the two Queens; For in Her late Majesty's Reign the Crown was as firmly settled on the Hannover Family as the Legislature could do it; And the Question was only, whether the presumptive Heir, of distant Kindred, should keep his Court in the same Kingdom and Metropolis with the Sovereign, while the Nation was torn between different Parties, to be at the Head of that Faction which Her Majesty and the Body of Her People utterly disapproved; And therefore the Leaders

on both Sides when they were in Power did positively determine this Question in the Negative. And if we may be allowed
to judge by Events, the Reasons were cogent enough; since
Differences may happen to arise between two Princes the
most nearly allyed in Blood; although it be true indeed that
where the Duty of a Parent is added to the Allegiance of a
Subject, the Consequence of Family Dissentions may not
always be considerable.

For my own Part, I freely told my Opinion to the Ministers;
and did afterwards offer many Reasons for it in a Discourse
intended for the Publick, (but stopped by the Queen's Death)
that the young Grandson (whose Name I cannot remember)
should be invited over to be educated in England; by which
I conceived, the Queen might be secure from the Influence
of Cabals and Factions, the Zealots who affected to believe
the Succession in Danger could have no Pretences to complain,
and the Nation might one day hope to be governed by a
Prince of English Manners and Language, as well as
acquainted with the true Constitution of Church and State;
And this was the Judgment of those at the Helm before I
offered it; neither were they or their Mistress to be blamed
that such a Resolution was not pursued: perhaps from what
hath since happened, the Reader will be able to satisfy himself.

I have now said all I could think convenient (considering
the Time wherein I am writing) upon those two Points which
I proposed to discourse on; wherein I have dealt with the
utmost Impartiality, and I think upon the fairest Supposition,
which is that of allowing Men to act upon the Motives of
their Interests and their Passions; For I am not so weak as to
think one Ministry more virtuous than another, unless by
Chance, or by extraordinary Prudence and Virtue of the
Prince; which last, taking Mankind in the Lump, and adding
the great Counterbalance of Royall Education, is a very rare
Accident; and where it happens, is even then of little use
when Factions are violent; But it so falls out that among
contending Parties in England the generall Interest of Church
and State is more the private Interest of one Side than the
Other, so that, whoever professeth to act upon a Principle

of observing the Laws of his Country, may have a safe Rule to follow, by discovering whose particular Advantage it chiefly is, that the Constitution should be preserved entire in all it's Parts. For there cannot, properly speaking, be above two Parties in such a Government as our's; and one side will find themselves obliged to take in all the Subaltern Denominations of those who dislike the present Establishment, in order to make themselves a Balance against the other; And such a Party composed of mixt Bodies, although they differ widely in their severall Fundamentals of Religion and Government, and all of them from the true publick Interest; yet whenever their Leaders are taken into Power, under an ignorant, unactive, or ill-designing Prince, will probably by the Assistance of Time or Force become the Majority, unless they be prevented by a Steadiness which there is little Reason to hope, or by some Revolution, which there is much more Reason to fear. For abuses in Administration may last much longer than Politicians seem to be aware of; especially where some bold Steps are made to corrupt the very Fountain of Power and Legislature; in which Case, as it may happen in some States, the whole Body of the People are drawn in by their own supposed Consent, to be their own Enslavers; and where will they find a Thread to wind themselves out of this Labyrinth? Or will they not rather wish to be governed by arbitrary Power after the Manner of other Nations? For whoever considers the Course of the Roman Empire after Cesar's Usurpation, the long Continuance of the Turkish Government, or the Destruction of the Gothick Balance in most Kingdoms of Europe, will easily see how Controllable that Maxim is, that, *Res nolunt diu male administrari*; because, as Corruptions are more Naturall to Mankind than Perfections, so they are more likely to have a longer Continuance; For the Vices of Men considered as Individualls, are exactly the same when they are molded into Bodies; nor otherwise to be withheld in their Effects, than by good Fundamentall Laws, in which when any great Breaches are made, the Consequence will be the same as in the Life of a particular Man, whose vices are seldom known to end but with himself.

APPENDIXES

A Modest Enquiry
into the Reasons of the Joy Expressed by a Certain Sett of People, upon the Spreading of a Report of Her Majesty's Death

T HAT this Enquiry is made by a Private Person, and not by Her Majesty's Attorney General; and that such notorious Offenders have met only with an Expostulation instead of an Indictment, will at once be an everlasting Proof of the Lenity of the Government, and of the unprovok'd and groundless Barbarity of such a Proceeding. Amidst the pious Intercessions of Her Majesty's Dutiful Subjects at the Throne of Grace for Her Health and Recovery; That others of them should receive the News of her Death with Joy, and spread it with Industry, will hardly appear probable to any, except to those who have been Witnesses of such vile Practices, not only in Her Majesty's Capital City, but in several other Places of the Kingdom, not only near *Charing-Cross*, but at some other Market-Crosses: That their Passion on such an Occasion should prove too unruly even for the Caution demanded in the Belief of News still uncertain, for the Severity of the Laws, and for the common Decency that is due to the Fall even of the greatest Enemy; that not only those who were Sharers of the common Blessings of Her mild Government, but such as had been warm'd by its kinder Influences; not only these who ow'd their Honours, their Riches, and other Superfluities, but even the Necessaries of Life to Her Bounty; such as eat Her Bread, wore Her Rayment, and were protected under the Shelter of Her Roof, should not be able for a Moment to stifle their eager and impatient

Ingratitude; that this Behaviour should not only appear in those vile and detestable Places which are Dedicated to Faction and Disorder; but that it should infect Her Majesty's Palaces and Chapels (where the accustomed Devotion for Her Health and Prosperity was derided); These, I say, are Facts that might demand a full Proof, could I not appeal to their own Consciences, and the uncontestable Evidence of credible Persons.

I will, for once, suppose some Foreigner, unacquainted with our Temper and Affairs, to be disturb'd in his Walks by some of the Revels made at *Charing-Cross* upon this Occasion, or by chance to stumble into a neighbouring Coffee-House: Would not his Curiosity prompt him to address himself to the Company after the following manner?

'*Gentlemen*, Though I am no *Englishman*, I rejoyce as much at the Fall of a Tyrant as any of you: Sure this Queen *ANNE* exceeded both *Nero* and *Caligula* in Acts of Cruelty. May I beg you to relate to me some Particulars? As for you, *Gentlemen*, who express such unusual Joy, no doubt but there are at this time Multitudes of your Relations and Friends in Prison, who were to be Executed the next Day, if this lucky Accident had not prevented it.'

Give me leave to imagine some poor Disconsolate honest Gentleman, at the same Time accidentally among them, thus answering this Foreigner: 'Alas! Sir, This good Queen, whom they now Report to be Dead, during a Reign of Twelve Years, never shed one Drop of Blood for any Misdemeanors against Her self.'

For. Well, Sir, allowing what you have said to be true; May not the late Administration have been rendered Merciful by the Indulgence of those entrusted with the Execution of the Laws; and yet, the Queen, of whom we are speaking, have been in her own Nature a wicked and cruel Person?

Gent. Alas! Sir, Quite the contrary: This excellent Queen was the greatest Pattern of all Princely and Christian Virtues that ever adorn'd a Throne; Just, Patient, Firm, Devout, Charitable, Affable, Compassionate, the sincerest Friend, the kindest Mistress, the best Wife!

For. Perhaps She was of a different Religion, inclin'd to

Popery, which has been for many Years held in the utmost Detestation in this Country.

Gent. Sir, This Pious Princess, as She was early Educated in the Religion of Her Country; so amidst a Court corrupted both in Principles and Manners, She gave constant Proofs of Her unshaken Perseverance in it; and by Her unblemish'd Life, prov'd as great an Ornament to the Church of which She was a Member, as She was a steady Professer of its Doctrine, and constant Frequenter of its Devotions. To the Protestant Religion She Sacrific'd Her most tender Interests. Where is that boasted Patriot who acted a more generous Part for the Good of his Country in the most perilous Times? And since Providence set the Crown upon Her Head, in what single Instance hath She departed from those Maxims?

For. I confess then I am at a Loss to find out the Cause of so great an Exultation for the Death of so excellent a Princess: But it hath sometimes happen'd, by the Connivance of good Monarchs, that their People have been Oppressed, and That perhaps might be your Case in the late Reign.

Gent. So much otherwise, that no Annals can produce a Reign freer from Oppression. *Our* Gracious Queen *never accepted the Persons of the Wicked, nor overthrew the Righteous in Judgment. Whose Ox or whose Ass did She take? She was always ready to Relieve, but never to Oppress the Poor, the Fatherless, and the Afflicted. Her Heart was not lifted up above Her Brethren; nor did She turn aside from the Commandment to the Right or to the Left.* Her compassionate Mind pity'd even those Countries which suffered by the Power of Her Victorious Arms. Where are the least Effects of the Pride and Cruelty of Queen *ANNE* to be discovered? So impossible is it to brand Her Government with any Instance of Severity, that perhaps it may be more justly Censur'd for Excess of Clemency. A Clemency, the continuance whereof had once brought Her into the utmost Distress, till that tender Regard, which She had always shown for the Liberties of Her Subjects, taught them in Return to struggle as hard for the Liberty of their Sovereign; even for that Common Right of all Mankind, The Liberty of chusing Her own Servants.

P

For. Give me leave to make another Supposition. Princes sometimes turn Liberality into Profusion, squander their Treasure and impoverish their People: May nothing of this Kind be laid to the Charge of the deceas'd Queen?

Gent. You cannot but have heard, that when She came to the Crown, She found a dangerous War prepar'd for Her, which it pleas'd God to bless Her with unexpected Success: When the Purposes seem'd to be answered, for which it was Undertaken, She thought fit to stop the Vital Streams of the Blood and Treasure of Her People, and to put a Period to a War, that now serv'd only to gratify the Covetousness or Ambition of those She was Confederated with, as well as the vast Designs of a Faction at Home; and with Peace to endeavour to settle such a Commerce as might in some measure reimburse Her Subjects of the vast Treasure they had expended. Alas! Here is her Crime: Touching these Points She *is now call'd in Question* by those Gentlemen. As for her own Expences, I wish they had reach'd as far as the Necessaries and Conveniences of Life, which some can testify She has often deny'd Herself, that She might have to give to those who were in Want. If ever Her Liberality exceeded its just Bounds, it was to a Sett of Men who would now use the Riches they enjoy by Her Bounty, to insult Her. Devotion and Business were all the Pleasures of Her Life: When She had any Relaxation from the Latter, it was only by some painful Attack of the Gout. The Cares of Government, no doubt, had prejudiced her Constitution: But Monsters sure are they, that can rejoice for the Loss of a Life worn out in their own Service. I hope you will have the Goodness to believe there are but few of us who deserve this infamous Character. The Bulk of Her Subjects, and many good Christians besides, in other Parts of the World, are, no doubt, daily offering up their ardent Prayers and Vows for the Preservation of so precious a Life.

For. From what you have said, I readily Condemn the unseasonable Joy of those Gentlemen: But Mankind are govern'd by their Interests. You, *Englishmen*, seldom disguise your Passions. A Monarch may have a thousand good

Qualities; but particular Men, who do not feel the benign Influence of them, may be tempted, perhaps, to wish for a Change.

Gent. Give me leave to Whisper you: That Man of Quality, whom you see in such an Extacy, enjoys by Her Majesty's Bounty one of the most advantageous Places of the Kingdom.——That other Gentleman's Coach that stands there at the Door, was bought with Her Majesty's Mony.——The Lac'd Coat, the Hat and Feather that Officer wears, were Purchas'd with Her Pay; and you see Her Arms on his *Gorget.* ——This Noble Person's Relations have been brought from the lowest Degree of Gentlemen, and surfeited with Riches and Honours by Her Majesty: So that She may truly complain, *She has nourish'd and brought up Children, but they have Rebelled against Her.*

For. Truly, Sir, I am amaz'd at what you say; and yet there appears so much Candour and Confidence in your Assertions, that I can hardly suspect the Truth of them. I have travell'd through many a desolate Country, and heard the Groans of many an afflicted People, who would have thought themselves Blest, if the united Virtues of this Lady had been parcell'd out among all their Governors. Those Virtues of Princes that most dazzle the Eyes of Mankind, are often dearly paid for by their People, who are forced to purchase them a Place in the Annals of Fame, at the dear Price of their Blood and Treasure: And I believe they would seldom find fault with them for being peaceably inclin'd. I am a Stranger, and in such a disorderly Night as this, may meet with some Affront, so must bid you Farewel; hoping you will find this melancholy News contradicted.

I may Appeal to any Impartial Reader, whether there is any thing forc'd or unnatural in this Dialogue; and then desire him to pass his Judgment upon the Proceedings of Those who rejoic'd at Her Death. But to return to my Enquiry.

The Circumstances of Queen *Elizabeth* much resemble those of Her present Majesty, with this Difference; That Queen *Elizabeth* was forc'd upon many great and remarkable

Pieces of Severity, from which it has pleased God to free Her present Majesty; I hope, as a particular Blessing upon Her Reign, and Indulgence to Her merciful Temper. Tho' there were many Factions at that time, both of the *Papists* and *Puritans*, to neither of which She gave much Quarter, so that Her very Life was often Conspir'd against by many Setts of Villains amongst the *Papists*; tho' She had no Posterity to revenge Her Quarrels, but, on the contrary, Her Ministry had most Reason to be afraid of the Vengeance of the Successor; yet She carried the Respect and Duty of Her Subjects with Her, even to the Grave. By the wise and close Management of Her Ministry, Her being Sick of the *Small Pox* at *Hampton-Court*, was conceal'd from the People till She was almost Well. Had they known it, it would have been the constant Subject of their Devotions, as every little Disorder of Hers was: Whether from the Fear of Punishment, a Regard to Decency, Love to their Country, or the Sense of their Duty and Allegiance, which were not extinguish'd in those Days; none of those Multitudes which had suffer'd great Hardships, durst Mutter, or ever dream'd of shewing the least Malice or Insolence to Her even in Her Old Age, and the very last Scene of Her Life: And yet She was a true Friend to Peace, it being Her constant Maxim, *That it was more Glorious to prevent a War by Wisdom, than to finish it by Victories.* When She had a mind to break off in the middle of a successful War, in which She was engag'd against a more formidable Power, and a more hopeful Candidate for Universal Monarchy than any that has since appear'd; a War that was manag'd without the help of destructive Funds, and large Issues of *English* Treasure to Foreign States; a War that was carried on with the proper Force of the Nation, *viz.* their Fleets, and rather served to bring in great Quantities of Bullion, than to carry it out: I say, When She had a mind to make Peace, I don't hear that every little Retailer of Politicks presum'd to tell Her, That it was not yet Time to lay down Her Arms; that *Spain* was not yet suffi-ciently reduc'd; that the Balance of *Europe* was not perfectly setled. Indeed Her Captain-General for that War seem'd to reason at the Council-Board with too much warmth for the

Continuance of it; but I don't hear that Her Lord-Treasurer was disgrac'd for advertizing him at that Time, *That the Blood-thirsty Man should not live half his Days:* A Prophecy but too truly verify'd. When She resolv'd to bring down the haughty Spirit of that great Man, I don't read that many People sooth'd him in his Ambitious Projects, except his Flatterers, *Blunt* and *Cuffe,* to whom he spoke these remarkable Words upon the Scaffold, *Ask Pardon of God and the Queen; for you were the Persons that chiefly provok'd me to this Disloyalty.* And happy had it been for him, had he hearken'd to the Lord Keeper, who advis'd him to submit to the Queen his Sovereign, and to remember that Passage of *Seneca: If the Law punish one who is Guilty, he must submit to Justice; if one who is Innocent, he must submit to Fortune.*

I do not find one single Address from either House of Parliament, advising Queen *Elizabeth* to vest her Captain-General in the *Low Countries* with more Power. On the contrary, it is Recorded to her lasting Honour, That she wrote to him *to allay his Aspirings; that she admir'd how a Man whom she had rais'd out of the Dust, should so contemptuously violate her Commands:* desiring the States to divest him of that absolute Authority, to which she had set such Bounds as he should not pass.

When this prudent Queen had demanded and obtained from the *Dutch* the Town of *Flushing,* Castle of *Ramekins,* and the *Isle* of *Brill,* to be Surrendered to Her as Cautionary for Repayment of the Sums She might expend in their Service, I do not find any *Englishman* at that Time pleading the Cause of the *Distressed Provinces,* (which *then* indeed was allow'd to be a proper *Style*) complaining of the narrowness of their Frontier, and remonstrating against this as a hard Bargain: Nor do I remember that Her Successor was thank'd by the Nation for giving up those cautionary Towns, which She thought as Safe in Her own Hands as in those of the best of Her Allies.

This excellent Queen was sometimes indeed attack'd with Pamphlets; particularly by one, Intituled, *The Gulph wherein* England *will be Swallow'd by the* French *Marriage:* For which, *Stubbs* and *Page,* (the one the Author, the other the Disperser)

lost each their right Hand. And to shew that Men in those
Days had both a Sense of their Duty, and their Guilt; when
Stubbs had his right Hand cut off, he immediately uncovered
his Head with the other, and cry'd, *God Save the Queen!*
I never read that during the Time of the Execution, they
were protected by a Mob of *Chimney-Sweepers* hir'd by their
Partisans.

What Cause shall we then Assign of this tumultuous and
excessive Joy of the Party; their Industry to spread, and their
Eagerness to believe, what they so much wish'd? Were all the
Glories and Blessings of Queen *ANNE's* Reign so soon to
be forgotten? Were their Protestations of Loyalty and Affection nothing else but Petitions for Preferment? or did they
proceed only from the fear of *Newgate* and *Tyburn?* Might
not all her Cares and Labours that (in Her Circumstances)
could have no other End but the Welfare of Her People,
have deserv'd one pitying Tear? Could not even (allowing
their own Supposition) Her *mistaken* Zeal for restoring the
Peace and Commerce of Her Subjects, Her Tenderness to their
exhausted Purses, and Her Care to transmit their Liberties
Safe to Posterity, plead for one relenting Thought? Might
not some Regard have been paid to Her Personal Virtues,
and to the rare Example She has left behind Her, of the
constant Practice of all Christian Duties amidst the Grandeur
and Temptations of a Court? No! All these Things, it seems,
were to be the Subject of Mirth, Ridicule, and of the Songs of
Drunkards; and the Death of the Noble, the Pious, the
Fortunate Queen *Anne*, our Countrywoman, Flesh of our
Flesh, and Bone of our Bone, was to be Celebrated as a
Festival of Joy!

And is the Death then of this *Excellent Princess* become so
absolutely Necessary at this Time for the Welfare of Her
People? I should rather imagine, even allowing their Fears and
Jealousies to be well founded, that some Degrees of Prudence,
Temper, and Tenderness for their Fellow-Subjects, might
induce them to Reason after the following manner.

'That it is Good to put an Evil Day far off; that none can
be more Terrible than that which brings Confusion, Disorder,

and perhaps a Civil War; that Providence may find a Way to disappoint our Fears. It is possible the Spirit of Faction may abate, and that even these formidable Enemies of the Succession may vanish, or return to a Sense of their Duty and Danger: That *France* may fall under the Government of a Minor, and have Business enough at Home: Nay, it is possible, the Pretender himself may Die before Her present Majesty: And considering the changeable Conditions of *British* Affairs, it is not improbable that the *Whiggs* may recover their Credit both at Court and in the Country, and then to be sure all Things must go well. Nay, who can tell but that the Successors may think it their Interest to be Kings of *Britain*, rather than Kings of the *Whiggs*.' All or any one of those Things are fully as probable as that the Queen, Lords and Commons, should agree to alter the present Establishment; and much more so than that Her present Majesty should divest Herself of Her Crown and Dignity in favour of a Popish Successor. Let Her live then, and let us still Hope, that Providence, which has honoured Her to be the Instrument of great Blessings as well to *Europe* as Her own People, may continue to do so still. How short and obscure are the Views of Mankind when they look into Futurity! We are at least as often obliged to Providence for denying as for granting, what we most earnestly Desire.

Out of Respect to my Country, I would fain believe the Number of such Miscreants to be but few: What would all the rest of the World think of us else? Would not they look upon us as the most ungrateful, factious, fickle Race of Mortals under the Sun? Histories are full of the dismal Effects of the Government of Tyrannical Princes, and of their fatal Ends; and they are justly set up as Beacons to warn others of the same Rank from the Rocks and Shelves whereon they have split: But are there no Memoirs of the Undutifulness of Subjects, and the fatal Consequences of their factious and ungovernable Tempers? I am afraid the general Current of History will inform us, that Tyrannical Princes have been more punctually obey'd than the Good and the Merciful. Princes read History as well as Subjects; they are quick-sighted enough to make Inferences to justify what they are but too much inclin'd to, the undue Exercise of their Power. *Is it not plain* (say they) *that Monarchs too often suffer by their Indulgence, that the rigorous Exercise of Power is the only Foundation of Obedience? To what purpose then is it to court the fallacious Breath of the changeable Multitude?* I am afraid too many of them reason after this manner; and that the Tyranny of bad Princes is often founded upon the Misbehaviour of Subjects to good Ones. Let such therefore consider what Misery their factious and disobedient Temper may bring upon their Posterity, not only from the direct Influence and Tendency of it, but also by the Appointment of Divine Providence.

For shame then let us not verify the Description which the Ambassador made of us, who being desired by his Master to give a Character of the *English* Nation: As a full Answer to his Demand, presented him with a Medal, on the one side of which the *English* Monarch was pictur'd as a Lion, and all his People about him like Lambs: And on the Reverse, the Monarch like a Lamb, and all the People like Lions.

Let us proceed now to guess at the Source of this unseasonable Exultation. I begin with the common Cant of the whole Party, The Fear of a *Popish Successor* and *Popery*. The Loss of the Duke of *Glocester*, and the want of Hopes of Posterity from Her present Majesty, are Misfortunes never enough to be lamented: But is it not a very ungenerous way of proceeding, instead of Comforting and Supporting their Prince under this Calamity, to Insult and Despise Her for it? To multiply their Affronts and Indignities, because She wants Posterity, who might possibly revenge them? May such ignoble and base Sentiments be far from the Thoughts of every true-hearted *Briton*; and may He who has Commanded us *not to add Affliction to the Afflicted*, never avenge such inhumane and unjust Dealings! But still I am to seek how the Fear of a Popish Successor should operate in Joy for the Death of a Protestant Possessor! This appears no less unaccountable than other Parts of their System of Politicks, a short View of which seems to be this:

That the Protestant Succession is in the utmost Danger.

That in order to strengthen it, a bad Understanding must be kept up between the Successor and Her present Majesty, the Ministry, and all who are vested with Power and Authority in the Nation.

For this end, the Successor must be persuaded that Those are his mortal Enemies; and the Ministry on the other hand must be told that He is coming to Hang them all up.

That they hope the Ministry are firm Friends to the Pretender; that they ought to be so, having no other Game to play; and that they should be sorry to find them otherwise inclined.

That at this Moment the Queen is expiring; and the Guards gone down as far as *Dover* to meet the Pretender. Now Rejoice all true-hearted *Whigs*, at the happy Prospect, the glorious Scene that discloses it self for *Great Britain*.

From these Premises, I think it will be very hard for the most sagacious Man alive to inferr, Which of Three Things are most in Favour with these Gentlemen who are so Trans-ported: *Viz*. Whether the Protestant Successor, the Pretender, or Confusion? I think so far is plain, That either their Suspicion of the Danger of the Protestant Succession is Counterfeit, or that they are for One of the other Two. And indeed what can one gather from their mad and extravagant Discourse, but that it is all Grimace? *Popery is breaking in like a Torrent. Mass will be quickly said in Churches. Clergymens Wives are taking their last leave of their Husbands*, &c. Good God! that ever I should live to see the Protestant Cause abandon'd by a Queen, (who hath Sacrific'd for the sake of it what was perhaps Dearer than her Life) by the Nobility, Clergy and Gentry of the Nation; and the sole Defence of it left to *Ridpath*, *Dick Steele*, and their Associates, with the Apostles of *Young Man*'s Coffee-House! Before I leave this Head, I would desire these Gentlemen, who are constantly making such malicious In-sinuations against Men of Honour and Probity, to remember that the Oath of Abjuration (what they so often quote, and what every honest Man will keep) contains Faith and true Allegiance to their present Sovereign, in as strong Terms as the Renunciation of the Pretender; and that He who Violates the first Part of the Oath, gives but a small Security for his Observation of the latter: Unless they think that which was last swallowed, must be always uppermost.

Another Cause of their Joy upon the Spreading of this false News, is, Their Discontent at the *Peace*. And in this indeed the Queen has Reason to Rejoyce, That She hath no Enemies but such as are Enemies to Peace. But is not the Hopes of a new War an admirable Subject for Joy, a most endearing Token of their Love to the Successor, and one of their new Methods of keeping up his Interest, to represent him to the People as bringing over War in his Train? It is foreign to my present Purpose to enter into a full Discussion of this Subject: But the Quarrelling with the Peace, because it is not exactly to our Mind, seems as if One that had put out a great Fire should be sued by the Neighbourhood for some lost Goods, or damag'd Houses; which happen'd (say they) by his making too much Haste. Let me Advise them in general, not to disrelish Blessings, because they may Want some Ingredients, which their extravagant and sickly Appetites seem to demand; to leave some Part of the Government of the World to its Maker, and not to believe that He is confined to the narrow Maxims of every Whimsical Politician; not to think it impossible, that the same Powers, that have restor'd the Balance of *Europe*, in Opposition to so great a Force, are able to preserve it; and that we have Reason to be in such mighty Dread of a Nation now impoverished and dispirited, (and probably in the Eve of a long Minority, with all the Confusion that attends it) whom we have humbled in all its Pomp and Glory.

May I presume to descend from those high Topicks, and to suppose that the sublime and publick Spirits of these Patriots may have a little Alloy of a baser Passion; and that Self-Interest had some share in this extraordinary Festival. Far be it from me to deny them the due Use of so humane a Passion! Let the Hopes of seeing better Days produce a secret Satisfaction: But may they not be so affected, without being Brutal and Barbarous? They might have enjoyed the pleasant Prospect of the approaching Favours of the new

Monarch, without insulting the Ashes of the Dead! May that Reign be Glorious and Happy! But I shall always believe, that insulting the Memory of Her present Majesty, will be understood as an ill Compliment to Her Successor. The fatal Event of Her Death, 'tis true, puts an End to their Allegiance; but not to the Obligations to Decency and Gratitude. I have heard that Allegiance and Protection are reciprocal; but never that Allegiance and Preferment were so. If this Principle be admitted, we need go no farther for the List of Her Majesty's good Subjects, than *Chamberlayn's* Present State of *Britain:* But even in this particular the rejoycing Party have of all Mankind the least reason to Complain, whose present Insolence and Pride are the Creatures of Her Majesty's Bounty and Indulgence; who have no other Grievance, that I know of, than when they have *taken our Cloak, that we will not give them our Coat also.* And even under this Ministry, the opposite Party, who are so loud in their Complaints and Revilings against it, may appear upon a right Computation, to have their Quota of all the Offices of the Kingdom. Let them for once shew their Modesty, and not grudge the Nation the little that is left: And since they have so great a Share in Possession, and think themselves sure of All in Reversion, suffer the poor Tories to hold their Part during the Period of the Queen's Life.

There remains still another Cause, which I am afraid operates as strongly as any of those already mentioned: It is a common Observation, that the offended Party often forgives; but the offending Party but seldom. It is one of the corrupt Sentiments of the Heart of Man, to hate One the more for having used them ill; and to wish those out of the Way, who, we believe, ought in Justice to revenge the Injuries we have done them. I leave the Application to themselves.

Thus I think I have briefly enumerated the Causes of their Joy: *viz.*

A Prospect of a new Foreign War.

A fair Chance for a Civil War.

The Expectation of the Monopoly of the Government.

The Hopes of having the Tories all Hang'd. And
Their Consciousness that they ought to be so themselves.

At the same time, far be it from me to Charge all who
are called by the Name of Whiggs with such villainous Inclinations and Designs; amongst whom I know there are many
worthy and excellent Persons. I would not willingly be guilty
of a Breach of Charity, which I could wish all Parties were
possess'd of in a greater Measure. I would have every Body,
who is conscious of his Guilt in any of the forementioned
Particulars, to reflect seriously upon what I have hinted at;
both those who *curs'd the Queen in their Heart*, and those who
curs'd her in the open Streets: But of all others *their* Guilt is of
the deepest Dye, who have personal Obligations to Her
Majesty. For my Part, it was with the utmost Detestation
that I observed some, who ow'd much to his late Majesty
K. *William*, treat his Memory with Scorn and Indifference.
Gratitude, as much despised and disus'd as it is, will ever
continue to be a reputable Virtue, as long as Mankind live in
Society; nay, even if they should return to the Woods.

The Melancholy Occasion of Her Majesty's Sickness had
this in common with other ill Accidents; That some Advantage
could be made of it in discovering the impotent Malice and
Factious Purposes of some, who would otherwise have
been more cautious in disguising their Inclinations, 'till they
believ'd they might discover them with Safety, and thereby
make a Merit with the more abandoned Part of their *Faction*.
God be thanked, Her Majesty wants not those faithful Subjects
who will defend both Her Person and Reputation against the
felonious Attempts of such impious Wretches, and who would
serve Her in the last Moments of Her Life with as much
Fidelity and Zeal, as if She had Twenty Sons and Daughters
to inherit after Her. Her Times are in the Hands of that
Almighty Being whose Minister She is, and in whom She
comfortably puts her Trust; who will not shorten the Period
of Her Life one Moment, for all the impatient Curiosity of
those People who are Daily enquiring, *When will She Die?*
So long as they keep off their Hands, let them wish as much
as they think fit: And when it shall please God to give Her

the happy Change of an Earthly for a Heavenly Crown, let this be wrote upon her Tomb: *That in Compassion to the Miseries of Europe, and the Sufferings of Her Own Subjects, after a bloody and expensive War which had lasted 20 Years, She concluded a Peace: And that She might transmit the Liberties of Her People Safe to Posterity, She Disbanded Her Army: By which Glorious Atchievements She acquired the Hatred of a Faction, who were fond of War, that they might plunder their Fellow-Subjects at Pleasure: And of an Army, that they might do this with Impunity.*

The Humble

ADDRESS

Of the Right Honourable the

Lords Spiritual and Temporal

In PARLIAMENT Assembled.

Die Jovis 11 *Martii,* 1713.

WE Your Majestie's most Dutiful and Loyal Subjects, the Lords Spiritual and Temporal in Parliament Assembled, beg Leave humbly to Represent to Your Majesty, That we have begun our Endeavours to Suppress Seditious Papers (which Your Majesty was pleased to take Notice of in Your most Gracious Speech from the Throne) by Applying our selves to Discover the Author, Printer, and Publisher of a Pamphlet, Intituled, *The Publick Spirit of the Whigs, set forth in their Generous Encouragement of the Author of the* Crisis, *with some Observations on the Seasonableness, Candor, Erudition, and Style of that Treatise.* London, *Printed for* John Morphew *near* Stationers Hall. 1714. Which we conceive to be a False, Malicious and Factious Libel, highly Dishonourable and Scandalous to Your Subjects of *Scotland,* tending to the Destruction of the Constitution, and (by making False and Unjust Reflections upon the Union, and the Steps and Motives to it) most Injurious to Your Majesty, who have been pleased often to Declare from the Throne, That the Union of the Two Kingdoms is the peculiar Happiness of Your Reign, in making a full Provision for the Peace and Quiet of Your People, and the Security of our Religion, by so firm an Establishment of the Protestant Succession throughout *Great Britain:* It Appeared to us, by the Confession of the said *John Morphew* at our Bar, That he Published, Sold, and Dispersed that Libel; and by the Examination of several Witnesses on

Oath, That the same was Printed by *John Barber*, a Printer, who, at the time of the Printing the said Seditious Libel, was and yet is Intrusted with Printing the *Gazette*; But the said *John Barber*, in his Examination, Insisting not to Answer any Questions, the Answer to which might tend to Accuse himself, or to Corroborate the Accusation against him, we have not as yet been able to Discover the Author of the said Libel, or who brought the Written Copy thereof to be Printed. And therefore that nothing may be wanting on our Parts, towards the Discovering and Punishing so great a Criminal, as we take the Author of the said Libel to be, we do most humble beseech Your Majesty, That Your Majesty will be Graciously Pleased to Issue Your Royal Proclamation, with a Promise therein of such a Reward as Your Majesty shall, in Your Royal Wisdom, think fit, to any Person who shall Discover and make due Proof against the Author or Authors of the said Libel, As also Your Majestie's most Gracious Pardon to such Person or Persons as shall make such Discovery, of all Crimes and Misdemeanors committed in relation to the Printing, Publishing and Dispersing the said Libel.

Her MAJESTIE'S most Gracious Answer.

My LORDS,

I Thank you for the Concern you shew for *Suppressing all Seditious Libels:*
And have given Order for a Proclamation according as is desired.

FINIS.

A
COPY
OF
Dr. SWIFT'S MEMORIAL to the QUEEN.

APRIL 15, 1714.

THE change of ministry about four years ago, the fall of the Duke of Marlborough, and the proceedings since, in relation to the peace and treaties, are all capable of being very maliciously represented to posterity, if they should fall under the pen of some writer of the opposite party, as they probably may.

Upon these reasons, it is necessary, for the honour of the Queen and in justice to her servants, that some able hand should be immediately employed to write the history of her Majesty's reign; that the truth of things may be transmitted to future ages, and bear down the falsehood of malicious pens.

The Dean of St. Patrick's is ready to undertake this work, humbly desiring her Majesty will please to appoint him her historiographer, not from any view of the profit, (which is so inconsiderable that it will hardly serve to pay the expence of searching offices) but from an earnest desire to serve his Queen and country; for which that employment will qualify him, by an opportunity of access to those places where papers and records are kept, which will be necessary to any who undertake such an history.

TEXTUAL NOTES

A NOTE ON THE COLLATIONS

Only significant verbal differences are regularly listed, although other aspects of the text are described when they seem illuminating. Contractions or abbreviations of names, titles, and places are regularly and silently expanded. Superior letters have been printed on the line. Obsolete forms of letters and figures (e.g., 'ff' for 'F') have been standardized. A few obvious oversights in spelling and punctuation have been silently corrected. In transcriptions of manuscript passages, it has sometimes been convenient to indicate cancelled words by half-brackets (⌈ ⌉) and insertions by half-diagonals (╲ ╱). Doubtful readings are preceded by question marks. Swift and his scribes did not clearly distinguish the capital 'S' from the small 's' in their writing, and the same confusion is often true of other letters; the editors' arbitrary readings are printed without remark. Among the variants are placed some comments on the text, which appear italicized within parentheses. The numbering of the last ten lines on each page is *f.b.*, or from the bottom.

THE IMPORTANCE OF THE GUARDIAN CONSIDERED

First published on or about 31 October, 1713. See facsimile of title-page, p. 3.
A Supplement to Dr. Swift's Works . . . ; ed. John Nichols, London, 1779, 4to, p. [239]. (A reprint of the first edition.)
The present text is printed from the 1713 edition. The footnote on p. 15 is by the editor. There were marginal glosses in the 1713 edition, giving the page numbers of the sources of Swift's quotations; these are silently omitted.

THE PUBLICK SPIRIT OF THE WHIGS

First published on 23 February 1714. See facsimile of title-page, p. 29. At least four authorized 4to editions were published by Morphew in 1714. The first and second are extant in both a cancelled and an uncancelled issue, but all copies of the third and fourth seem to have been cancelled. There were further editions by Morphew and by others in London and Dublin the same year.
The Second Edition, 1714. [Uncancelled, 14c; cancelled, 14d]
The Third Edition, 1714. [14e]
Volume VI. Of the Author's Works. Containing The Publick Spirit of the Whigs; and other Pieces of Political Writings, With Polite Conversation, &c. Dublin: Printed by and for George Faulkner, M,DCC,XXX,VIII. [38]
. . . M,DCC,XLI. [41]
The present text is printed from Faulkner's collected edition, Vol. VI, 1738, and is collated with the first five authorized London editions or issues (14): the first edition, uncancelled (14a) and cancelled (14b); the second edition, uncancelled (14c) and cancelled (14d); and the third edition (14e). In the 1714 editions were marginal glosses giving the page numbers of the sources of Swift's quotations; these are silently omitted.

Page	Line	Present Text	Variants
30		ADVERTISEMENT . . . *Custody*	(*Omitted*) 14
31	10	these	those 41
	4 *f.b.*	*in*	*of* 14
32	3	the most	most 14
	8	supposed 14	suppose 38, 41
	28	because	For 14
33	24	although	though 14
35	15	doeth	does 14
	7 *f.b.*	Tenths	tenth 41
	4 *f.b.*	in his	his 14
36	1	hath	has 14
	2	hath	has 14
	3	except	but 14
	8	understand	understands 14
	3 *f.b.*	doth	does 14
37	1	Hath	Has 14
	1	this 14	his 38, 41
	3	does	doth 41
	10	knoweth	knows 14
	19	reacheth	reaches 14
	22	against	for 14
38	23	ingenious	ingenuous 41
	5 *f.b.*	*Gentleman* 14	*Gentlemen*
39	16	doth	does 14
	2 *f.b.*	*Power*	*Powers* 14
40	12	in the 14	of the 38, 41
	10 *f.b.*	although	though 14
41	17	hath	has 14
43	7 *f.b.*	never was	was never 14
44	6 *f.b.*	although	though 14
45	16	*although*	*though* 14
	3 *f.b.*	come now 14	now come 38, 41
46	19	hath	has 14
	27	*our* 14	*or* 38, 41
47	20	although	though 14
48	27	hath	has 14
⎰48	6 *f.b.*–	After . . . of.	(*Omitted*) 14 b, d, e
⎱51	11		
48	2 *f.b.*	although	though 14 a, c
48	*fn.*	*The . . . observed.	(*Omitted*) 14
49	22	until	till 14 a, c
50	3	this	the 14 a, c
	19	*Union*, he 14	*Union.* He 38, 41
	27	until	till 14 a, c
	3 *f.b.*	hath	has 14 a, c
51	7	although	though 14 a, c
	12	only . . . more	one Thing 14 b, d, e
	8 *f.b.*	*Advertisement* 14, 41	Advertisement 38
52	17	hath	has 14
	18	He tells	tells 14 a, b, c, d; tell 14c
	25	produceth	produces 14; produced 41

Page	Line	Present Text	Variants
	10 *f.b.*	**doing* 14	*doing* 38, 41
	9 *f.b.*	Inconsistencies	Inconsistences 14
	8 *f.b.*	*hath*	*has* 14
	fn.	*Mr. . . . Speaker	(*This note is a marginal gloss in* 14 a, c *and is omitted in* 38 *and* 41.)
53	1	hath	has 14
	5	hath	has 14
	17	Signs 14	Sign 38, 41
	6 *f.b.*	hath	has 14
	1 *f.b.*	*has*	*hath* 14
54	4	happeneth	happens 14
	6	*Hand*	*Head* 14
	9	pleaseth	pleases 14
	14	Advisers 14	Adviser 38, 41
	18	receive	accept 14a (*so B.M. copy* [E.2004]; *others read* receive)
	22	a	an 14
	25	the Writer	this Writer 14
	5 *f.b.*	happen	happens 14
55	22	although	though 14
	5 *f.b.*	hath	has 14
56	11	ever	every 14
57	18	until	till 14
	27	although	tho' 14 a, b, d, e; though 14c
58	13	hath	has 14
	24	how	that 14
	9 *f.b.*–8 *f.b.*	*a Truth* 14	*Truth* 38, 41
	5 *f.b.*	*a Truth* 14	*Truth* 38, 41
	3 *f.b.*	advanceth	advances 14
	3 *f.b.*–2 *f.b.*	deserveth . . . Doth	deserves . . . Does 14
59	2	the same	same 14
	11	hath	has 14
	12	doth	does 14
	5 *f.b.*	hath put	has put 14
	4 *f.b.*	until	till 14
	3 *f.b.*	until	till 14
	1 *f.b.*	until the other	till t'other 14
60	17	pleaseth	pleases 14; pleased 41
	17	it done	done it 41
	5 *f.b.*	although	though 14
	4 *f.b.*	have	hath 14
	fn.	*Mr. . . . so.	(*Instead of this footnote the editions of* 1714 *have a marginal gloss:* †*Close to the* Englishman, *Pag.* 2.)
61	4	*Hand* 14	*Hands* 38, 41
	20	the other	t'other 14
	10 *f.b.*	*hath*	*has* 14
	8 *f.b.*	until	till 14
62	1	hath	has 14
	3	until	till 14
	8	hath	has 14

Page	Line	Present Text	Variants
	9	hath	has 14
	17	*Interest* 14, 38	*the Interest* 41
	27	*the Encouragement*	*Encouragement* 14
	28	until	till 14
63	7	although	tho' 14
	21	*the Doom be* 14, 38	*be the Doom* 41
	23	be	are 14
	28	deduceth	deduces 14
64	12–13	*far . . . So* 14	*near. So* 38, 41
	13	*conquer*	*conquers* 14
	15	*the Mercy* 41	*Mercy* 14, 38
	15	which hath	who has 14
	16	its	his 14
	20	die	dies 14
	21	hath . . . that	has . . . for 14
	22	torment	to torment 14
65	5	**Person*	*Person* 14
	26	*Sunshine*	*Sunshiny* 14
	10 *f.b.*	believe	believes 14
	8 *f.b.*	*stand*	*are* 14
	1 *f.b.*	they be	they are 14
	fn.	**Parker . . .* Chancellor	(*Omitted*) 14
66	2	although	though 14
	2	assert	asserts 14
	12	feasible	feasibly 41
67	11	proposeth	proposes 14
	14	hath	has 14
	4 *f.b.*	hath	has 14
68	11	chargeth	charges 14
	13	until	till 14
	1 *f.b.*	CREATURE	CREATURE. | FINIS. | [*rule*] | *Just Publish'd,* | A Modest Enquiry into the Reasons of the Joy express'd by a | certain Sett of People, upon the spreading of a Report of | Her Majesty's Death. Price 3*d.* Printed for *John Morphew* near *Stationers-Hall.* 14

A DISCOURSE CONCERNING THE FEARS FROM THE PRETENDER

First published in *The Letters of Jonathan Swift to Charles Ford,* ed. D. Nichol Smith (Oxford, 1935), pp. 216–17.

The present text is printed from the holograph manuscript belonging to Lord Rothschild: a sheet folded to make four pages, measuring about $7\frac{7}{16}$ by $11\frac{15}{16}$ inches, with the text on the right-hand half of the first page. In the manuscript the date (without the year) is written between parentheses above the title, toward the right.

Page	Line	PRESENT TEXT	FIRST READINGS OF MS
71	6	which in reason ought	which ought in reason
	9	were	was
72	1	would	will
	3–5	I . . . examine. (*scored through*)	
	4	may be	may ?both ?I . . rs
	4	worth	worth of

SOME FREE THOUGHTS UPON THE PRESENT STATE OF AFFAIRS

First published in 1741. See facsimile of title-page, p. 75. The same sheets used to make an independent pamphlet were also bound in as the last section of *Letters To and From Dr. J. Swift, D.S.P.D. From The Year 1714, to 1738. To which are added, Several Notes and Translations not in the London Edition.* Dublin: Printed by and for George Faulkner, MDCCXLI. The sheets of that volume were in 1746 re-issued with a new title-page, as Vol. VII of the *Works*. When this was reprinted in 1751, some unauthorized revisions were adopted, mainly changing third-person endings from -*s* to -*th*.

At least two copies were made of Swift's original manuscript, which has itself disappeared, probably destroyed by Swift. One copy, sent to Barber and tampered with by Bolingbroke, was almost certainly the one which Faulkner recovered, and printed in 1741; it does not seem to have been preserved. The other remained with Swift and was transmitted through Mrs. Whiteway to Deane Swift and his descendants; it is now in the collection of Lord Rothschild.

This manuscript, in the hand of an amanuensis with revisions by Swift, contains many passages and corrections not in the published version (which is an earlier state) and has never before been printed. It comprises twenty-one folio leaves, measuring about 7⅜ by 12 inches. The text runs from the second leaf recto to the twentieth leaf verso and is paginated from 1 to 38. It covers the right half of each page, the left being reserved for revisions and additions, which are numerous. The first page is endorsed in Swift's hand; see facsimile, facing p. xxv.

The last leaf verso is endorsed in the hand of Mrs. Whiteway:

Some free thoughts upon
the Present State of
Affairs May 1714

As the copy text of the present edition, the manuscript has been collated with the 1741 edition. Corrections or cancelled readings are marked A if due to the amanuensis, S if due to Swift. Manuscript readings which have been replaced by the editor's emendations are marked MS.

The edition of 1741 has the following announcement on the recto of the first leaf after the title-page:

Advertisement *to the* Reader.

ABOUT a Month before the Demise of Queen ANNE, the Author retired to a Friend's House in Berkshire, upon the Ministry quarrelling among themselves, whom he endeavoured to reconcile to each other; but finding his Endeavours fruitless, he wrote the following Pamphlet in his Retirement, and sent it to London to be printed: But before it was ready for Publication, that Princess died, which prevented its Appearance in the World, and in all Probability would have been lost for ever, had not the Printer hereof been in London some Time ago, and got the original Manuscript from Alderman John

Barber, *formerly City-Printer, who had most carefully preserved it, in Order to oblige the Publick some Time or other; which we here do in the most correct Manner, not doubting but it will be agreeable to all our Readers.*[1]

Dublin, May
1741.

Page	Line	PRESENT TEXT	VARIANTS
76	1–12	MEMORANDUM . . . dyed. S	(*Omitted*) 1741
77	3	May —— 1714	(*Omitted*) 1741
	5	never	hardly 1741
	9	has	hath 1741
	18	neither	nor 1741
	20–21	Lewis . . . France,	(*Omitted*) 1741
	23	Examples are not	Nor are Examples 1741
	25	have	than A
	9 *f.b.*	is . . . Subjects: (*The manuscript has, in Swift's hand, a pencilled dash in the margin before* is *and a karat after* Subjects: *but no insertion.*)	
78	3	Yet in	In 1741
	5	Adherence . . . Point (*In the manuscript Swift has pencilled a dash in the margin before* Adherence *and partially underscored* Point.)	
	7	*great S	great A, 1741
	7–8	*the . . . Negotiating.* S	the . . . Negotiating. A
	13	practicing	employing 1741
	15	those in Power	Ministry 1741
	f.n.	*Monsieur Torcy S	(*Omitted*) A, 1741
	25	is ?S	are
	25–26	is . . . supposed	we . . . suppose 1741
	27	so few S	so A, 1741
	9 *f.b.*	point of Credit and Reputation	Decency 1741
	2 *f.b.*	Tis	It is 1741
	1 *f.b.*	and	and are A, 1741
79	1	deduce	deduct
	6	despises	despiseth 1741
	20	Sessions	Session 1741
	21	has	hath 1741
	27	Dispositions	Disposition 1741
	28	most Men	any Man A, 1741; most Man S
	6 *f.b.*	Effects	Part 1741
80	15	and S	& A
	15	which S	(?& *scratched out by Swift for* and, *also scratched out*)
	21	Management	Administration 1741
	22	virtues	great Abilities and Virtues 1741
	22	more S	so A, 1741
	24	has	hath 1741
	25–26	the better . . . be S	(*Omitted*) A
	25–26	Vice . . . may not be	Defect . . . is not certainly 1741

[1] In Swift's *Works* (Dublin, 1751), VII, p. [298], the closing expression is altered from '*all our Readers*' to '*the Reader.*'

Page	Line	PRESENT TEXT	VARIANTS
	27–28	a very small Omission in Appearance	an Omission, in Appearance very small 1741
	9 *f.b.*	disintrepid S	intrepid A, 1741
	8 *f.b.*	that	and that 1741
	8 *f.b.*–3 *f.b.*	that ... related	(*Omitted*) 1741
81	3	And likewise because	Because likewise 1741
	15	Concert	Love 1741
	16	have	*have* 1741
	17	Consequences	Consequence 1741
	27–28	of ... great ... many 1741	of ... great ... great a Number A; *of ... great ... great* a Number S

(*Swift put dashes in the margin of the manuscript before* of *and* while; *he underscored* great *to indicate the repetition.*)

Page	Line	PRESENT TEXT	VARIANTS
	6 *f.b.*	must S	will A, 1741
	5 *f.b.*	Others	those who can better determine 1741
82	8	the chief Managers	those who were to have the chief Part in Affairs 1741
	17	Foot S	? seat A
	17	The Cause of all which	Which 1741
	19–20	the uncertain ... Court,	(*Omitted*) 1741
	19	or S	as A
	20	some ?S	some certain A
	21	which	among themselves, which 1741
	22	Effects	their Effects 1741
	24	which came in	who came in 1741
	25	forced ... act	acting ever since 1741
	26	sides	Side 1741
	28	losing 1741	(losing *altered to* loosing) MS
	7 *f.b.*	alone are	(or, if that was the Case) the *Minister* alone is 1741
	4 *f.b.*	hath	has A
	3 *f.b.*	*in* S	in A, 1741
83	1	upon which	whereon 1741
	2–4	All ... Helm.	(*Omitted*) 1741
	6	no little	little 1741
	7–10	(particularly ... France)	(*Omitted*) 1741
	8–9	have ... quarrelled S	have quarrelled A
	9	Treaty's	? Treatise A
	15	this S	that A
	16	that (*Swift has marked a cross under* that *to indicate a repetition.*)	
	19	that	the 1741
	27	adverse S	other A, 1741
	2 *f.b.*	Offices	Office 1741
	1 *f.b.*	Changes ?S	Changing A
84	1	And that to	To 1741
	4–5	dangerous Consequence	terrible Consequence 1741
	13	Power ... It was	Assistance ... And it is 1741
	14	universall	general 1741
	18	erecting	creating 1741
	22	is ... may	was ... might 1741

Page	Line	PRESENT TEXT	VARIANTS
	24	Party	Parties 1741
	25	can be never	could never be 1741
	26	have	had 1741
	28	proved	appeared to be 1741
85	3	although S	(tho' *altered by Swift to* altho')
	21	their S	the A
	2 *f.b.*	unnecessarily S	necessarily A
86	4	Although S	Though A
	7	true S	usefull A; useful 1741
	10	who	who, at least, 1741
	12	Evil	Thing 1741
	16	further	farther 1741
	24	Queen	—— 1741
	26–27	(and ... so)	(*Omitted*) 1741
	3 *f.b.*	too great a	very great 1741
	2 *f.b.*	too great a	very great 1741
	1 *f.b.*	further	farther 1741
87	9	faint	feint 1741
{ 87	19–	However ... low.	(*Omitted*) 1741
{ 88	12		
88	16–17	mens ... Science	mens Science A
	25	entire	higher A
89	9	although S	though A
	9	appear ?S	appears A, 1741
	12–13	formerly ... dangerous	already very dangerous 1741
	14	by S	with A, 1741
	20	or	nor A
	22	till	until 1741
	22	shall be	be A
	23	may S	shall A, 1741
	24	although S	though A
	25	a	the 1741
	27	necessary	very necessary 1741
	28	the Officers of	(*Omitted*) 1741
	9 *f.b.*	many	most 1741
	8 *f.b.*	his	the 1741
	4 *f.b.*	to	that A
90	8–10	and ... Adversaries	(*Crossed out in MS.*)
	9	till	until 1741
	4 *f.b.*	would be thought S	pretended A; seemed 1741
	1 *f.b.*	*Person S	Person A, 1741
	fn.	*The . . . himself (*editor's asterisk*)	(*Omitted*) A, 1741
91	4	of	to 1741
	20	changes	changeth 1741
	7 *f.b.*	the like S (*Swift has put a pencil mark in the margin before the line beginning* the *and has underscored* like *in pencil, to indicate a repetition.*)	
92	2	now	now most 1741
	5	Time 1741	Times MS
	6	they S	the A

Page	Line	PRESENT TEXT	VARIANTS
	16–17	passive Obedience, Non-Resistance and	(*Crossed out by Swift in MS; a large asterisk is pencilled before the line containing these words.*)
	20–21	and . . . Crown	(*Crossed out by Swift in MS.*)
	24	am far from justifying	do not pretend to justify 1741
	7 f.b.–6 f.b.	might . . . by . . . from	was offered to . . . by 1741
93	10	further	farther 1741
	11	here (*Underscored by Swift in MS., perhaps to indicate that it is unnecessary.*)	
	13	Moment S	Consequence A, 1741
	24–10 f.b.	Wherefore . . . Title	(*Omitted*) 1741
	7 f.b.–6 f.b.	would . . . that (*Swift has put a mark in the margin before the line beginning* would *and has underscored* that *to indicate a repetition.*)	
	5 f.b.	be	to be 1741
94	5	Requests	Request 1741
	7	of all	of 1741
	26	in the same Interest	of the Number 1741
	7 f.b.	Thoughts	while 1741
	4 f.b.	Engagement	Engagements 1741
95	7	hath S	has A
	10	Opinion	Esteem 1741
	19	Principles (*A crossmark is pencilled in the margin before this word.*)	
	27	any	an 1741
	9 f.b.	at	of 1741
96	1	having then	having 1741
	11	may have	hath 1741
	25	would S	would probably A, 1741
	6 f.b.	inconsiderable	small 1741
	6 f.b.	will S	will probably A, 1741
97	1	Prince . . . of (*Swift has written and crossed out* The ?Ah Author *in the margin before the line* Prince . . . of.)	
	1	may in all likelyhood S	will probably A, 1741
	2	enough . . . Prerogative S	depress the Prerogative enough A, 1741
	7	may not perhaps S	will not A, 1741
	9	Hope	Hopes 1741
	9–10	In such . . . Case,	(*Omitted*) 1741
	11	Alteration	Alterations
	16	such a	the 1741
	16	*Secret Committee* S	Secret Committee A
	16	would not	would 1741
	17	Persons	such, 1741
	17–18	might dispose	disposed 1741
	18	The late King	King 1741
	24	we	one 1741
	10 f.b.	Pretences	Pretence 1741
98	3	last	late 1741
	6	desire	desire. | FINIS. 1741

SOME CONSIDERATIONS UPON THE CONSEQUENCES HOPED AND FEARED FROM THE DEATH OF THE QUEEN

First printed in 1765, in Vol. VIII, Part I, pp. 84–87, of Hawkesworth's 4to edition of Swift's *Works* (published by W. Johnston, London). This volume was prepared by Deane Swift, also as Vol. XV–XVI of the large 8vo edition, and XV–XVII of the small 8vo edition. It was reprinted in Dublin by George Faulkner, 1765, as Vol. XII–XIII of his edition of Swift's *Works* in 8vo, 12mo, and 18mo.

The present text is printed from the holograph manuscript in the Forster Collection of the Victoria and Albert Museum, South Kensington (item 515, pressmark 48. G. 6/2). It consists of two folio leaves, measuring about $7\frac{1}{2}$ by 12 inches and paginated by Swift from 1 to [4]; the left half of each page has been kept blank except for alterations. The left side of the verso of the second leaf is headed:

Memoirs.

Just above the middle of the same space, but upside down, is another heading:

On the hopes &
fears \by⁄ ⌐of⌐ the
Queen's Death

Page	Line	PRESENT TEXT	FIRST READINGS OF MS
102	14	by	to me in
	15	the Earl of	the
	26	united Power	Power
	28–29	own Hands	Hands
	4 *f.b.*	disposed of	given
103	5	very few	very
	12	Dangers	Dangerous
	22–23	Encouragement	Argument as an Incitement
	25	dispositions (*First two letters frayed away*)	
	4 *f.b.*	upon	against
104	9	than to	than
	1 *f.b.*	of the	of

MEMOIRS RELATING TO THAT CHANGE WHICH HAPPENED IN THE QUEEN'S MINISTRY IN THE YEAR 1710

First printed in 1765, in Vol. VIII, Part I, pp. [1]–24, of Hawkesworth's 4to edition of Swift's *Works*; this volume was edited by Deane Swift. See the preface to the textual notes for *Some Considerations upon . . . the Death of the Queen*, above.

The manuscript now belongs to the Forster Collection of the Victoria and Albert Museum, South Kensington (item 516, pressmark 48. G. 6/3). It is in the hands of two amanuenses (who probably worked mainly from dictation), with revisions and additions by Swift. The twenty folio leaves measure about $7\frac{1}{2}$ by $11\frac{3}{4}$ inches, and are paginated from 1 to 39 in the upper, outer corners, beginning with the first recto. Only the right half of each page is regularly written on, the left being reserved for alterations.

The scribes' spelling is illiterate and inconsistent, their use of capitals haphazard, and their punctuation too slight to be of use. For the present edition, therefore, the copy text is that of the 1765 4to edition, which was prepared by

Deane Swift, almost certainly from the Forster manuscript. This text has been corrected by the manuscript and collated with Faulkner's 1765 8vo edition. Deane Swift's footnotes are omitted.

In the textual notes, readings taken from the manuscript are marked S if due to Swift, otherwise MS; cancelled readings in the hand of an amanuensis, A; readings from Faulkner's edition, 65F; from the 4to edition published by Johnston, 65J; rejected readings printed by both Johnston and Faulkner, 65.

The verso of the last leaf of the manuscript is endorsed by Swift:

Draught of
[M]emoirs

A modern, heavy paper cover is endorsed in a modern hand:

Swift
ᒥNo. 18ᒣ (1 to 39 on 20 leaves.)
Memoirs relating to that Change which happened
in the Queen's Ministry
in the Year 1710

The first page of the manuscript has no heading other than the following, in Swift's hand:

Oct^br. 1714

Page	Line	PRESENT TEXT	VARIANTS
107	9	though MS	although 65
	10–11	believed . . . enemies	believed by my friends and Given out by my Enemys A
	10	my MS	by my 65
	14	probably	probably be A
	10 *f.b.*	I'm MS	I am 65
	6 *f.b.*–5 *f.b.*	though . . . convinced MS	although I was convinced, by a thousand instances, 65
	4 *f.b.*	has	hath 65F
	1 *f.b.*	greatest curiosity MS	curiosity 65
	1 *f.b.*	Memoirs	my Memoirs A
108	3	ministers	minister MS
	4	themselves MS	they themselves 65
	6	possesses	possesseth 65F
	12	there	yt. A (*Corrected to* there *in what may be Mrs.* Whiteway's *hand.*)
	20	sometimes make S	make so frequent A
	24	were . . . parliament	in both houses of parliament were pleased A
	1 *f.b.*	till	until 65F
109	2	about six weeks S	a quarter of a year A
	4	as the MS	as in the 65
	25	a	her A
	4 *f.b.*	person	family A
	2 *f.b.*	in concert S	inconcert A
	2 *f.b.*	one MS	an 65
110	1–2	employments . . . power S	employments A
	10–11	her reputation MS	reputation 65
	21	though MS	although 65
	6 *f.b.*	her Majesty S	She A

Page	Line	PRESENT TEXT	VARIANTS
111	2-3	who . . . presence,	(*Omitted*) A
	3	into MS	in 65
	5	upon MS	at 65
	12	though MS	although 65
	12	kept S	held A
	12	till	until 65F
	15	mistress MS	friend 65
	16	unacceptable S	acceptable A
	18	though MS	although 65
	21	till his own MS	until his 65
	27	light S	ill A
	10 *f.b.*	a fear MS	fear 65
	5 *f.b.*	of MS	of it 65
	3 *f.b.*	for MS	from 65
112	1	Sunderland	Hertford 65
		(MS *has* H——d, *over which some illegible letters, among them an n, are scrawled. The present identification is confirmed by the allusion to Sunderland on p.* 120, *ll.* 5–8, *below.*)
	4	offices MS	officers 65
	7	though MS	although 65
	10	presiding. But S	in power, and A
	16	lay S	was A
	22	for MS	from 65
113	3-4	them . . . upon MS	them upon 65
	10	and MS	and all 65
	12	had then MS	had 65
	28	November (*New Style. October* 28, *Old Style, which Swift customarily used for events in England*)
114	7	him MS	them 65
	11-12	the Scotch . . . security MS	*the Scotch act of security* 65
	12	to return S	return A
	4 *f.b.*	(as . . . told) S	(*Omitted*) A
115	2	is MS	was 65
	4	his	this A
	21-22	Mr. Harley . . . impeachment S	As I remember Mr. H——y, who came up to towne while the affair of impeaching was under debate A
	8 *f.b.*	of him	upon him A
116	7	though MS	although 65
	9	of what MS	what 65
	21	though MS	although 65
	22	private	privately 65F
	22-23	told her S	told A
	8 *f.b.*	High MS	High-church 65
	4 *f.b.*	moderating	moderate A
	1 *f.b.*	people MS	the people 65
117	1	upon going S	upon A
	2	first	at first 65F
	11	Mr. Harley S	Harley A
	20	hope MS	hoped 65

Page	Line	Present Text	Variants
	23	He S	The Earle A
	26	that the MS	the 65
	9 f.b.–8 f.b.	had already	already MS
	7 f.b.	the Duke S	([The] [Duke] *written in the hand of the amanuensis and scratched out*)
	6 f.b.–5 f.b.	and making complaints in her Majesty's presence S	(*Omitted*) A
118	5–6	Sunderland's	(*First written* Sun—d's, *then written out*) A
	11	Wharton	(Wh *written and scratched out four times*) A
	18	Damn him	(D—mn him *scratched through but written again*) A
	22	Earl of Godolphin	G——n A
119	3	had	have MS
	6	till MS	until 65
	11	views MS	news 65
	12	of it	from it MS
	15	a discourse	those reasons A
	21	times . . . times MS	time . . . time 65
	25	the MS	of the 65
	10 f.b.	Lords	Lord MS
	1 f.b.	has MS	had 65
120	1	first began MS	began 65
	19	great S	much A
	27	exception S	reflection A
	4 f.b.	that S	but A
	3 f.b.	of Lord S	of A
	2 f.b.	above five MS	five 65
121	1	till MS	until 65
{121 {124	5– 8	Being . . . death	(*Scratched out lightly in MS, probably by Swift*)
121	11	was ever MS	ever was 65
	14	a refusal S	refusal A
	21–22	to . . . intent	of such an A
	22	Though MS	Although 65
	25	till MS	until 65
	25–4 f.b.	At . . . withdrew	(*Scratched out heavily in MS, probably by Swift*)
122	21	of S	to A
	22	though MS	although 65
	10 f.b.	the restoring the first-fruits MS	the first-fruits 65
123	11–12	principles . . . faction	late discarded f A
	14	an entirely new MS	entirely a new 65
	20–21	Upon . . . repeat.	(*Scratched through heavily in MS, probably by Swift. Deane Swift prints this sentence in italics.*)
	20	civilities S	(*Omitted*) A
	21	it will MS	*will* 65
	21–22	province . . . of S	province A

Page	Line	Present Text	Variants
	22	several	some A
	9 f.b.–8 f.b.	(Between these two paragraphs in the manuscript there is a broken line.)	
	4 f.b.	the Lord Godolphin's	the Godolphin's MS
124	5	for about MS	about 65
	5	about eight months S	three and thirty weeks A
	8	till MS	until 65
	19	Dartmouth	and D—th A
	19–20	Ailesbury . . . Berkeley	A—y D—th, and P—t, the Lord B—y MS
			A—y, Dartmouth, and P—t; the Lord B—y 65
	27	though MS	although 65
125	1–2	lords and gentlemen	men A
	4	effectual MS	respectful 65
	14–15	That . . . no MS	That no 65
	19	in the House of Commons	in parliament A
	28	of a strict	a strict 65F
	10 f.b.	mismanagements MS	mismanagement 65
	4 f.b.	dispositions MS	disposition 65
126	3	Benson	B—n MS; B—— 65
	3	afterwards Chancellor	Chancellor A
	5	though MS	although 65
	9	sat MS	rose 65
	13	raised, or discovered, S	both discovered and raised A
	14	thereby MS, 65F	hereby 65J
	15	gained MS	gain 65
	15	a reputation S	their reputation A
	19	enough under	under A
	6 f.b.–1 f.b.	Of . . . Guiscard	(*Written in Swift's hand in MS*)
⎰ 126	1 f.b.–	while . . .	(*Written in the hand of the second*
⎱ 128	1 f.b.	Treasurer	*amanuensis*)
127	2–3	discovery MS	a discovery 65
	8–9	seized . . . order S	seized A
	20	otherwise	otherways MS
	20	thick	strong A
	24	wounds	wound MS
	26	seizing him S	seiseng A
	26	chirurgeon MS	surgeon 65
	1 f.b.	was S	he was A
128	7	later	latter 65F
	13–14	which . . . it's	took its A
	24	This S	This peice of A
	10 f.b.	that Mr. S	that A
	5 f.b.	several S	some A
	1 f.b.	and Lord Keeper a Baron S	(*Omitted*) A

AN ENQUIRY INTO THE BEHAVIOUR OF THE QUEEN'S LAST MINISTRY

First published in 1765, in Vol. VIII, Part I, pp. 30-80, of Hawkesworth's 4to edition of Swift's *Works*; this volume was edited by Deane Swift. See the preface to the textual notes for *Some Considerations upon . . . the Death of the Queen*, above, p. 210.

Two manuscripts are extant, both in the collection of Lord Rothschild: a first draft (*A*) in Swift's hand except for the first leaf of the text, which is in the hand of Esther Johnson, with corrections by Swift; and a fair copy (*B*) in the hand of an amanuensis, with corrections by Swift and a few notes in the hand of Martha Whiteway. The leaves, except for an insert, are folio, from about 12 to 12¾ inches long and from about 7¼ to 7⅛ inches wide. The text covers the right-hand half of each page and is written on both sides of the leaves. Numerous revisions appear on the left-hand half and between the lines. There is a catchword in almost every lower right-hand corner, and the lines of the text are filled out by ornamental dashes.

The first draft (*A*) has thirty-two leaves, the first of which bears the title and the rest the text; each ordinary page has 35 to 49 lines. Between the first two leaves of the text are inserted four quarto leaves, from about 7¾ to 8¼ inches long and from about 5⅞ to 6⅜ inches wide, written right across on both sides, with 25 to 32 lines to each page except the eighth (shorter than the others), which carries the brief closing.

The title leaf is blank on both sides save for Swift's endorsement, recto, in the upper right-hand corner:

> An Enquiry
> into the Behavior of the Queen's
> Last Ministry, with Relation
> to their Quarrells among
> themselves, and the Design
> charged upon them of altering
> the Succession of the Crown

Immediately below this, in a bolder and apparently later hand, Swift has added

> Foul Copy

Above and to the right of the endorsement appears the number '3,' probably in Swift's hand.

The next leaf of the manuscript is that in Stella's hand, with corrections by Swift, having 44 lines recto and 49 lines verso. The endorsement appears again, in Swift's hand, at the top of the left-hand column. A number '1,' probably also in his hand, is in the upper right-hand corner; and the rest of the manuscript, skipping the insert, is paginated continuously to '54,' in the upper, outer corners. The insert is similarly paginated in Swift's hand from '1' to '8.' In the lower left-hand recto corners another, apparently modern hand has foliated the entire manuscript in pencil from '1' to '32,' beginning with the title leaf and including the insert (3–6).

The second draft (*B*) has forty-two leaves with 35 to 41 lines on each page. The leaves are paginated in the upper, outer corners from '1' to '84,' probably by Swift. In the lower left-hand recto corners the same hand as in the first draft has foliated the manuscript in pencil from '2' to '43,' indicating (since the text begins with the first page) that there was once a title leaf which is now lost.

This leaf bore an endorsement which was copied by John Forster as follows:

> "An Enquiry &c. This the original Manuscript
> "Corrected by Me, and Given into the Custody of
> "Mrs. Martha Whiteway by Me Jonathan
> "Swift. June 1737——seven. Memdum
> "I send a fair copy of this by the Earl of
> "Orrery to be printed in England. Jonathan Swift."

If there was a second fair copy, it is untraced; Orrery carried his to Dr. William King at Oxford. Swift's note sounds as if it were to the foul draft (*A*), and his description of the manuscripts in a letter of 1728 practically disallows any third copy at that time. Perhaps Forster attached the loose sheet to the wrong manuscript, and the present *B* is simply Orrery's copy returned. And yet Swift may not have meant 'original' quite literally but have had a third, clean manuscript made, for the English printer to use. In either event, only the two drafts are known to-day. The present text is printed from *B*, which was almost certainly the copy text of the first (1765 4to) edition, prepared by Deane Swift.

In the textual notes, readings from the first draft are marked A; from the second, B; and from the 1765 4to edition, C. Cancelled readings are indicated by subscripts, numbered in order of cancellation. Where a reading is revised more than once within a manuscript, *all* the stages are listed, although the last may not be, strictly, a 'variant.' If a revision in *B* is due to Swift, it is marked S.

Only significant verbal differences have been regularly collated, but several other aspects of the manuscripts have been described when they seemed illuminating. In a few places the final letters of a word close to the edge of a page have been frayed away, but the complete spelling is obvious; these have not been specially noticed.

Page	Line	PRESENT TEXT	VARIANTS
131	16–17	having . . . having	(*Underlined by Swift in manuscript* A, *probably to indicate repetition.*)
	16	having not been	not being C
	17	Disliked S	detested A; *detested* B_1
	18	which . . . Lot	which was never my Choice, and A_1
	19	being . . . Function	the Dutyes of my Function having placed me A_1
	21	which happen	which may happen A_1
	9 f.b.	the Hearts . . . Men S	most mens Breasts A, B_1
132	8–9	whom the S	whom A, B_1
	14	became S	were A, B_1
	19	to the Throne S	to his Throne and Kingdom A; to the Throne and Kingdom (and Kingdom *scored through in pencil, probably by Swift*) B_1
	20–21	thought . . . the Peace S	thought the Peace A, B_1
	20	hath	has C
	22	Effects S	Effects of it A, B_1
	24	although S	though A, B_1
	24	were S	was, A, B_1
	25	any Man of common Sagacity	those who knew any thing of our Court A_1

Page	Line	PRESENT TEXT	VARIANTS
	27	most opposed	least approved A₁
	8 f.b.	Ministers	Ministry A₁
	5 f.b.	that Party	those A₁; the Party C
	2 f.b.	Person in	Person of either Party in A₁
	1 f.b.	*(With* foresee *in manuscript* A *the leaf written by Stella ends, and the second leaf begins. Between these two leaves is inserted, on four smaller leaves, the long section from p. 134, l. 3, to p. 139, l. 2 f.b., in this edition.)*	
133	1	to those who will	when I A₁
	2	unspotted	former unspotted A₁
	7	by many degrees less S	less A₁; much less A₂, B₁
	9	faultless	*faultl*ess A
	13	although S	though A, B₁
	17–18	Person . . . , who	Person who was lately Duke of Ormd but A₁
	22–23	when by . . . Mistress he B₂	when he A, B₁; when by the direct and repeated Commands of his Sovereign he B₂
	23	Facts	faults C
	26	Landen	London C
	27	Sovereign	Master A₁
{ 133 { 134	9 f.b.– 2	Upon . . . naturall.	*(This paragraph is a marginal insertion by Swift in manuscript* A.)
	9 f.b.	am sensible	know A₁
	8 f.b.	human Life S	Life A, B₁
134	1	sudden and violent S	violent A, B₁
	2	more naturall S	naturall A, B₁
{ 134 { 139	3– 2 f.b.	And . . . right.	*(In manuscript* A *this section is a four-leaf insertion by Swift, headed in Swift's hand* Ad. P. 3.)
134	7	live	leave A₁
	8–9	in Exile	living in Exil A₁
	12–13	*the . . . away* S	the . . . away A, B₁
	13	the Duke	the late Duke A₁
	14	a little . . . of the	a few words about the A₁
	9 f.b.	had	had so A₁
	8 f.b.	although S	though A, B₁
	8 f.b.	were S	was A, B₁, C
	7 f.b.	for . . . that	to agree that A₁
	7 f.b.	a	such a C
	7 f.b.	seemed S	was A, B₁
	5 f.b.	which	which however A₁
	4 f.b.	whereof	of which A₁
	2 f.b.	esteemed	thought A₁
	1 f.b.	Respect	Esteem A₁
135	13	nothing of except	of but A₁
	15	Point	Point, and A₁
	9 f.b.	more	more perhaps A₁
	8 f.b.	although	though A, B₁
	5 f.b.	began	seemed A₁
	4 f.b.	and to	and began to A₁

R

Page	Line	PRESENT TEXT	VARIANTS
	3 *f.b.*	Pains	while A$_1$
	2 *f.b.*	particularly S	especially A, B$_1$
136	8	that kind of writing S	those kind of writings A; those kind of Writing B$_1$
	10	Man ... Education	Scholar and a Gentleman A$_1$
	16	Although S4	though A; though B$_1$; although S$_1$; yet S$_2$; Yet S$_3$
	16	were S	was A, B$_1$
	17	yet often S	thô A, B$_1$
	18	would leave	left A, B$_1$
	20	than	and A$_1$

27–9 *f.b.* And ... wrong

And ⌐I have heard⌐ others in the ＼one or two／ ＼have confesst very often／ ⌐Part⌐ Ministry ⌐of very often con-⌐

＼to me, that after having condemned his Opinion they found／
⌐fess after condemning his Opinion, that He was in the⌐

＼him in the right and themselves／
⌐right, and they⌐ in the wrong. A

| | 6 *f.b.* | were | was A$_1$ |

6 *f.b.*–5 *f.b.* while ... Employment   in the publick Service A$_1$

(*In manuscript A the second verso of the four-leaf insertion begins with* ⌐Service⌐. *Above the first line of the text is the following paragraph in Swift's hand, crossed out:*)

If the King of a free People will chuse to govern by a Faction inferior in Number and Property to the rest and suspected of Principles destructive to the Religious or Civil part of the Constitution, ＼I do not see how a civil War can be avoyded／ Because the Bulk of the People and of the Landed Interest, who profess the Established ⌐People⌐ Principles will never endure ⌐themselves⌐ to see themselves entirely cut out and rendred incapable of all Employm^{ts} of Trust or Profit, and the whole Power most unnaturally vested in the Hands of a Minority, whose Interest it must of necessity be to alter the Constitution, & oppress their Fellow Subjects.

(*In pencil under this another hand has written* probatum est. *A blank space is left, and then, on the lower half of this page, the sentence begun on the preceding page continues.*)

	3 *f.b.*	Time. He	Time, nor indeed with common Prudence. He A$_1$
	2 *f.b.*	therefore	thereof A$_1$
137	4	Expressions	thing A$_1$; words A$_2$; Expressions A$_3$
	5	could possibly tend	tended in the least A$_1$
	5	undecent	indecent C
	6	least	*lea*st A
	6	although S	though A, B$_1$
	14–15	remarkable	famous A$_1$
	16	discover S	discover to You A, B$_1$

Page	Line	PRESENT TEXT	VARIANTS
	19	hath . . . any	never discovered any A$_1$
	25	although S	though A, B$_1$
	5 f.b.	cannot altogether S	cannot A, B$_1$
138	2	those whom S	those A, B$_1$
	8	Besides	and A$_1$
	11	mercenary	Perso A$_1$
	15	Ministers	great Ministers A$_1$
	18	others S	Men A, B$_1$
	19	whereof	of which A$_1$
	22	as it	as in the A$_1$
	24	Clarendon S	Essex A, B$_1$
	27	sufficiently S	very A, B$_1$
	28	Condition	plight A$_1$
	10 f.b.	if great	if nothing but a great Genius were fit A$_1$
	10 f.b.	Genius, whereof	Genius to manage them whereof A$_1$
	9 f.b.	most fruitfull S	fruitfullest A, B$_1$
	8 f.b.	among which	of which A, B$_1$
	6 f.b.	proportionable	almost the same A$_1$
	4 f.b.	great	overgrown A$_1$
	2 f.b.	or Persons . . . Administration S	nor Persons unqualifyed to administer their Affairs A$_1$; nor Persons qualified for administration A$_2$, B$_1$
139	2	*little Helps . . . Hindrances* S	(*no italics*) A, B$_1$
	4	displeases S	offends A$_1$; discontents A$_2$, B$_1$
	4	giveth S	gives A, B$_1$
	13–18	For . . . may S	who are usually of the Size of those that would have the World think the Art of Governing to be a most profound Science, and are not content to have Things done, unless they be done in their own Way, like a certain antient Lord now alive who will not be satisfyed that you are of his Opinion, unless you confess it is for his Reasons. Men of this Level ⌐and Size¬ in Understanding do A, B$_1$ (Reasons *and* do *are underscored, and* and Size *omitted in manuscript* B.)
	10	reasonably S (*underscored in pencil*)	
	12	by Regularity	by order an A$_1$
	12–13	excell, For, I have frequently observed S$_2$	excell, and think it a diminution to see others lay no weight upon them. And I can affirm from my own Knoledge to have observed A$_1$; excell, and count it . . . observed A$_2$, B$_1$; excell, And, I have frequently observed S$_1$
	14	some refined S	these two, A, B$_1$
	14	act in S	act after their severall Manners in A, B$_1$

Page	Line	Present Text	Variants
	18	Communities; where	Communityes of Men where A₁
	20	moderate S	small A, B₁
	21	and on . . . is	and there is A₁
	23	Publick S	Vulgar A, B₁
	26	sometimes S	often A, B₁
	27	*Alderman* S	Alderman A, B₁
	6 f.b.	so irregularly	very irregular A₁
	3 f.b.	by	with A₁
	2 f.b.	right. (*The four-leaf insertion which began at p.* 134, *l.* 3, *ends here.*)	
140	9	Piques. And that S	Piques, That A, B₁
	12	Part S	Game A, B₁
	18	(Monopoly *is in Swift's hand.*)	
	20	be now	now be C
	22	undisposed	indisposed A
	27	Regard S	the Regard A, B₁
	9 f.b.	Party	all Party A₁
	6 f.b.	Loyalty	Law A₁
	2 f.b.	directly	roundly A₁
	1 f.b.	although	though A₁
141	5	that	*that* A
	7	with (*in pencil*) S	on A, B₁
	7	*Things*	that Things A₁
	7	*Things . . . ripe*	(*no italics*) A
	11	to lose	to be hangd or lose A
	13	These being	This being (*scratched out in margin*) A₁
	20–21	Crown . . . Pretender S	Crown A, B₁
	22	It is S	Tis A, B₁
	9 f.b.	happen	happen to read A₁
	2 f.b.	Because S	For A, B₁
	2 f.b.	saw	knew A₁
142	1	knew	know C
	1	*Lord S	L—d A; Lord B₁
	2	confident	confidence A₁
	2	disposed	disposed of C
	4–5	*Atticus . . . Catiline* S	(*no italics*) A, B₁
	6–7	*very . . .* giving S	very materiall Reasons against giving any A₁; very materiall Reasons against giving A₂; very Materiall Reasons, giving B₁
	13	Most	Some A₁
	13	these	those C
	13	Witness of (of *in pencil*) S	Witness to A, B₁
	14	received S	had A, B₁
	18	*incidere per ignes* S	(*no italics*) A, B₁
	20	knowing	thinking A₁
	21	one single	a particular A₁
	23	†extraordinary S	extraordinary A, B₁
	24	Spirit	Ferment A₁
	27	delivered	declar A₁
	8 f.b.	two	two particular A₁

Page	Line	PRESENT TEXT	VARIANTS
	5 *f.b.*	suffered . . . them S	suffered them A, B₁
	1 *f.b.*	particularly	especially A₁
	fn.	*Earl of Wharton S	(Omitted) A, B₁
	fn.	†Duke of Sommerset (*editor's obelisk*)	(*Omitted*) A, B₁; D Sommerset (*in pencil*) S; Duke of Somerset C
143	1	that	that great A₁
	13	untill S	till A, B₁
	18	a fantastick	the A₁
	22	ended S	was ended A, B₁
	28–29	heard . . . that S	found, that A₁; heard, that A₂, B₁
	6 *f.b.*–5 *f.b.*	About . . . at the	I remember I did the A₁
	2 *f.b.*–1 *f.b.*	those who loved	true friends of A₁
144	1	be	been A₁
	1	on (*in pencil*) S	of A, B₁
	9–10	*directed . . . advised* S	(*no italics*) A, B₁
	12–13	Management of the	managing the A₁
	27	observed	saw A₁
	27	and	then A₁
	9 *f.b.*	his	their A₁
	8 *f.b.*	pronounceth S	pronounces A, B₁
	7 *f.b.*	confident	confident, that A₁
	4 *f.b.*–3 *f.b.*	Indifferency	indifference C
145	1	those	their C
	13	whole	tot A₁
	15	his	his Friends and A₁
	23	in some Measure	in a good part A₁
	24	who was not without	who had the greatest Talents I ever yet found in any one man, and the most improved considering his Age, which at that time did not amount to two and thirty years, neither was he without A₁
	28	Although S	Thô A, B₁
	28	Mr. St John	the Secretary A₁
	8 *f.b.*	fatal, it	fatal, that as Things then stood his life was absolutely necessary, it A₁
	7 *f.b.*	then stood S	stood A, B₁
146	1	which	which A₁; that A₂; which A₃
	2	and these increasing	which encreasing A₁
	6–7	Change of Employments	Changes so long expected A₁; Changes of Employments A₂
	7	for which	which A
	8–9	was . . . comply	might have succeeded A₁
	9	comply, if	comply in his own way; and might have succeeded, if A₁
	12	*Lady wholly S	Lady who was wholly A₁; Lady wholly A₂, B₁
	17–19	[Of . . . Light] S	(*no brackets*) A, B₁

Page	Line	Present Text	Variants
	22	Some . . . used	I have been assured, that the Ministers aware of the Consequence, Endeavors were used A₁
	23	but she	who A₁
	26	got	gotten C
	4 f.b.	Peace	Vic A₁
	fn.	*Dutchess of Somerset S (editor's asterisk)	(Omitted) A, B₁
147	8	carried	was carryed A₁
	11	*Person S	Person A, B₁
	13	Eloquence	Zeal and Eloquence A₁
	13	Eloquence . . . was)	Eloquence such as it was A₁; Eloquence A₂; Eloquence (Such as it was) A₃
	14	†particular S	particular A, B₁
	17	And it	It A₁
	18	carried	carryed as it was A₁
	25–26	as . . . had	as it had A₁
	10 f.b.	bear	bear its Burthen A₁
	5 f.b.	Design	Intention A₁
	3 f.b.	placing	place A₁
	3 f.b.	Administration	Power A₁
	fn.	*Duke of Somerset S	(Omitted) A, B₁
	fn.	†To . . . Queen S	(Omitted) A, B₁
148	10	Perusall	View A₁
	12	than that of	beside A₁
	14	It is S	Tis A, B
	21	old Church S	whig A₁; old High Church A₂ B
	6 f.b.	new War	War A₁
	5 f.b.	had	had then A₁
149	3	been so long	so long been A
	7	govern	govern for severall years A₁
	8	Till at length grown	But the Queen and Nation growing A₁
	9	Success	Success to her Majesty's Arms A₁
	10	rising	growing A₁
	13	resolved	bega reason A₁
	14	the Ministry	her Ministers A₁
	16	by . . . Insinuations S	(no italics) A, B₁
	17	although	I con A₁; Though A₂
	4 f.b.	and some	and Powlet, with some A₁
150	1	Majority	High Church Majority A₁
	8	not	not to be A₁
	9	in order at once to	which would at once A₁
	11	And this	This A₁
	11	should . . . was S	take to have been A, B₁
	12–13	when . . . dislike S₂	if he advancemts A₁; if he advised those Advancemts A₂, B₁; when he advised those Advance-

Page	Line	PRESENT TEXT	VARIANTS
			ments; which however I did confess I did very much dislike S₁
	21	whatever	all A₁
	25	have	would A₁
	27	was (*underlined by Swift in* B)	was A, B₁
	10 *f.b.*	Friends began	Friends concluded from thence that his Credit was great enough to compass whatever he pleased; began A₁
	5 *f.b.*	as	that A₁
	3 *f.b.*	resolved	was resolved A
	3 *f.b.*	as She	as soon as She A₁
	2 *f.b.*	with . . . Kingdoms S	(*Omitted*) A, B₁
151	4	overshot S	often overshot A, B₁
	5	Extream	Extream, not rightly distinguishing betwixt being governed and advised A₁
	5	happened to be	was A₁
	7	perhaps	of the A₁
	8	a Warrant	any Paper A₁; the warrant A₂; a warrant A₃
	9–10	He . . . refused	(*Omitted*) C
	11	before hand	before hand, she would not C
	11	thus	so A₁
	12	severall Months S	Months A, B₁
	12	although S	tho A, B₁
	18	Promotion A, B₁, S₂	numerous Promotion S₁
	21	Session S	Sessions A, B₁
	22	Commons,	Commons, where no Man ever made a more shining Figure A₁
	22	upon	on A₁
	23	best	better A₁
	4 *f.b.*	Graces	Graces, who was least apt because A₁
	3 *f.b.*	having	had A₁
152	4	Service	Business A₁
	4	although S	though A, B₁
	5	that the	the A
	13	inclined to	favored A₁
	14	although S	though A, B₁
	15	in	of A₁
	20	was already S	was A, B₁
	23	Men	great Men A₁
	28	but from	but out A₁
	10 *f.b.*	although S	though A, B₁
153	1	Blame	Fault A₁
	1–2	greatest . . . much	onely . . . great a A₁
	5	Alteration	Change A₁
	7	have made	make C
	8	not S	never A, B₁

Page	Line	PRESENT TEXT	VARIANTS
	8	apprehend	apprehend, nor can at all think it to have been rightly judged A₁
	10	Doctor Sacheverall's S	Sacheverell's A, B₁
	12	Intervention, S	Intervention, that A, B₁
	10 *f.b.*	Talents	all which are Talents A₁
	9 *f.b.*	as	as they are A₁
	7 *f.b.*	Coldness	misunderstanding A₁
	3 *f.b.*	*Object S	Object A, B₁
	3 *f.b.*	and	and *wh*ich he A₁
	2 *f.b.*	which	*wh*ich A
	fn.	*the Dutchess of Somerset S₁ (*editor's asterisk*)	(*Omitted*) A, B₁; the Dutchess of S S₂
154	3	on	upon C
	6	this	*wh*ich A
	13–14	whether this	which whether they A₁
	15	appeared very	were so A₁
	16	which Proceeding	which A₁
	19	and	who A₁
	25	had been	was A₁
	10 *f.b.*	I	and I A₁
	6 *f.b.*	Leaders	Party A₁
	5 *f.b.*	of . . . as	that in its own Nature seemed to A₁
155	2	old English Principles	*Chu*rch A₁
	5–6	either . . . State	either . . . State (*crossed out but rewritten*) A₁
	6	She therefore S	And A, B₁
	9	Lord Chancellour S	Chancellor A, B₁
	12	reconcile	units A₁
	14	further	farther C
	15–16	the Earl of	Ld. A₁
	17	*Generall S	Generall A, B₁
	18	both	each A₁
	19	each	the A₁
	21	an Affair	a Point A₁
	23	appointed	appointed A
	10 *f.b.*	attempted	attempted under the present Powers A₁
	9 *f.b.*	beside	besides C
	4 *f.b.*	any S	the least A, B₁
	fn.	*the . . . Ormonde S (*editor's asterisk*)	(*Omitted*) A, B₁
156	3	a few	severall A₁
	15	except	excepted A
	20	*Rochester S	Rochester A, B₁
	25	might	would A₁
	fn.	*Doctor Atterbury S (*editor's asterisk*)	(*Omitted*) A, B₁
157	5	and . . . more S	(*Omitted*) A, B₁
	6	the Queen	and the Queen A₁
	9	on	of C

Page	Line	PRESENT TEXT	VARIANTS
	21	others . . . Court	others A_1
	9 f.b.	Upon	For A_1
	7 f.b.	during	for A_1
	3 f.b.	Misunderstanding . . . Hatred	Misunderstanding A_1
158	7	prevented	prevented or put an end to A_1
	10	have expected	expect A_1
	12	not	not a little A_1
	13	*not . . . intermeddle* S	(*no italics*) A, B_1
	17	although S	thô A, B_1
	20	Conversation A	Conversation or publick Business A, B_1
	26	t'other	the other C
	26	great Men	Friend A_1
	8 f.b.	Freedom.	Freedom. I had managed between them for almost two Years. A_1
	2 f.b.	where	whether A_1
159	7	mentioning	mentioned A_1
	9	her Majesty	the Queen A_1
	13	fell	grew A_1
	14	that S (*underlined by Swift in* B)	
	17	Nights	day A_1
	18	in	at A_1
	20	despaired	long despaired A_1
	25	nor	nor to A_1
	25	of B_2	of it A, B_1
	9 f.b.	to each	both A_1
	7 f.b.	both	bo*t*h
	6 f.b.	However	But A_1
	3 f.b.	severall	those A_1
160	3–4	with . . . was	whom She had A_1
	6	on	of A_1
	9	usuall	common A_1
	12	to	partly to A
	16–17	She . . . likewise	And having A_1
	20	She	as I before observed, She⸆A_1
	22	in fault	to blame A_1
	24	Kingdom	Nation A_1
	9 f.b.	Conjunctures A, S	Conjectures B_1
	3 f.b.–1 f.b.	Nor . . . Question.	No Reputation of Power could be worth preserving with the Hazard of Sincerity and Truth, A_1
{ 160 { 161	1 f.b.– 23	I . . . Opinion (*Marginal insertion in* A)	
160	1 f.b.	when	for A_1
161	1	one or two S	other A, B_1
	8	Upon which	whereupon A_1
	9	said	said aloud A_1
	13	frequently	frequently pressed A_1
	14	moved	pressed

Page	Line	Present Text	Variants
	21	frequent	very frequent A₂
	23	However the	The A; *The* A₂; Lastly *the* A₃; Again *the* A₄; But *the* A₅; How-*the* A₆ (*In manuscript* A *this is the beginning of a new paragraph.*)
162	7		(*In manuscript* A *the second chapter follows immediately after the first, on f.* 20ᵛ. *Between them, in a different ink from the rest of the page, Swift has written* Cap. 2d. *It is similarly written in the margin but crossed out. In the same margin, in Swift's hand, is an endorsement*: This Chapter seems to have been written about 2 years after the foregoing. *In manuscript* B *as well the second chapter follows immediately after the first, on the same page. The endorsement* Written above a year after *is in Swift's hand. In* C *this endorsement has been altered to* Written about a year after.)
163	1	Cap. 2d.	CHAPTER II. C
	8	to the World	as clear as the Sun at noon day A₁
	8	place the	lay the whole A₁
	11	(whoever . . . Compilers)	we fou A₁
	13	than	rather than A₁
	15	themselves	himself A₁
	16	carried	carried on C
	17	Abbot	Abbé C
	20	Abbot	Abbé C
	21	conceive that	believe A₁
	9 *f.b.*	upon . . . as	of Prophecy or something else, that A₁
164	7	Reason . . . for	Reason for A₁
	11	Liberty	Power A₁
	12	will.	(*New paragraph begun after* will *in* A *but scratched out*: However because I think it a Pity that so gentle and good natured a Proceeding should pass unrewarded)
	13	two	three A₁
	14	neither . . . Queen	the Q A₁
	15	during	either during A₁
	16	should succeed	succeed A₁
	20	Because . . . least	Lastly that for A₁
	23	three	two A₁
	24	on	with A₁
	26	and . . . offer	and these that I offer A₁
	26	these	those C
165	5	that (*underlined by Swift in* B)	that A, B₁
	7–8	did . . . was S	consisted of A, B₁
	8	a private S	private A, B₁
	9	and of S	and A, B₁
	10–11	any . . . Man	one Person A₁
	11	Buckingham	Ormond A₁
	12	most	Most, and perhaps, the Duke of *Ormonde; because I cannot charge my Memory with any

Page	Line	Present Text	Variants
			Thing which passed between ⌜*us*⌝ ＼His Grace and Me↗ upon that Subject. A₁
	13–20	I . . . inquire (*This section is a marginal insertion in manuscript* A.)	
	18	Consequence;	Consequence — — — — A
			But (*new line*) A
	23	own Word	Word A₁
	24	very	been very A₁
	26	hear	observe A₁
	28	although S	though A, B₁
	10 *f.b.*	cannot but	must needs A₁
	4 *f.b.*	among S	with A, B₁
	4 *f.b.*	converseth S	conversed A, B₁, C
	2 *f.b.*	I say	is A₁
166	2	some Patience	patience A₁
	4	found	meant A₁
	15	can	will A₁
	17	alter	change A₁
	18	Her Majesty	the Queen A₁
	20–21	generally . . . Favourers	entirely A₁
	22	Lord	Lords C
	25	Rivers, Strafford	Rivers, ?*Poulet* and A₁; Rivers, ?*Poulet*, Strafford and A₂; Rivers, ?*Poulet* Strafford A₃ (*Swift's question marks*)
	27	of the other Party	on the other side A₁
	10 *f.b.*	introduced	brought in A₁
	9 *f.b.*	bringing	begin A₁
⎰ 166	3 *f.b.*–	Pretender . . . said	Pretender; My Lord Bolingbroke
⎱ 167	2		felt severe marks of her Displeasure, because while he ⌜was⌝ stayd at Paris, he was seen under the same Roof with that Person, at an Opera, and the Queen said A₁
167	2	He	His Lordship A₁
	6	the Chevalier	that unfortunate Person A₁
	6	would frequently	used to A₁
	7	made . . . She	very little A₁
	8	which . . . cast	that have layd A₁
	11–12	for . . . against	with no other ＼⌜view⌝ Cause↗ ⌜but the⌝ ＼than her↗ personall Displeasure ⌜she had⌝ against A
	14	some	*those* A₁
	15	the former S	the A, B₁
	17	became	it became C
	23	greatest	utmost A₁
	25	although	thô it A₁
	26	last	utmost A₁
	9 *f.b.*	*another S	another A, B₁
	8 *f.b.*	higher	greater A₁
	7 *f.b.*	from S	for A, B₁
	3 *f.b.*	the	all the A₁

Page	Line	Present Text	Variants
	2 *f.b.*	which	that A₁
	2 *f.b.*–1 *f.b.*	Her ... Objection	She objected A₁
	fn.	*Dutchess of Summerset S (*editor's asterisk*)	(*Omitted*) A, B₁
168	1	Promotion B	Promotions A, C
	1	was ... being	that they were A₁
	5	constantly	always A₁
	5–6	refuse ... Zeal	refuse it, and reproach her with too much Violence A₁; refuse, and blame her as too violent A₂; refuse, and seem displeased A₃; refuse, and at ʳthatˡ the same time condemn her for too much Party Zeal. A₄
	9	Ministers	Ministry A₁
	10	Children	either Children A
	10	the King his father	King James II C
	11	They found	and therefore found A₁
	11	Prince	King A₁
	12	Speculations upon	Notions of A₁
	18	laden	loaded A₁
	21	with	that with A₁
	22	ten	a A₁
	28	hardly	never A₁
	8 *f.b.*	for	both of A₁
	7 *f.b.*	Kingdom	People A₁
169	4	although	tho A₁
	8	is	seems A₁
	13	in severall Points	almost in every Point A₁
	19	an Ambassador's	a Ministers A₁
	21	so long for	for A₁
	26	no	not C
	27	in this	both in that A₁
	27–31	that ... prevent	of being linked with a Pretender, and thereby in that more generall one of preventing A₁
	10 *f.b.*	will be	is A₁
	1 *f.b.*	Ministers	Ministry A₁
170	3	a	a Desire and a A₁
	4	and excellent A	excellent A, B₁
	8	laid	layd on A₁
	15	could	good A₁
	19	although S	though A, B₁
	9 *f.b.*–8 *f.b.*	that ... Party	that exploded Peace which that Prince's Friends A₁; that Peace and A₂; that Very Peace so much exploded by one Party A₃
	8 *f.b.*	so justly S	so A, B₁
	6 *f.b.*	both be	be both A₁
{ 170 / 171	5 *f.b.*– / 25	But ... Pursuit (*In manuscript* A *this paragraph is a marginal insertion.*)	
170	5 *f.b.*	But if	But if A₁; if A₂; But if A₃

Page	Line	PRESENT TEXT	VARIANTS
	3 f.b.	that (underscored by Swift in B) S	that A, B₁
	1 f.b.	every Article	them A₁
171	3	some	the A₁
	4	was	were C
	6	undertook	offered A₁
	6–7	by getting	and undertook to get A₁
	12	and . . . occasionally S	and occasionally A, B₁
	13	here	in Engla A₁
	15–16	the States . . . Plan of	Publick Approbation of the States of all Her Majesty's Measures in making A₁
	20	For	but A₁
	22	Earl of Oxfords C	Earls A, B₁; Earl's of Oxfords S
	23	Her Majesty's	the Queen's A₁
	27	an Instance	a mark A₁
	8 f.b.	employed	taken A₁
	7 f.b.–6 f.b.	Offers . . . Highness	Offers and Security his Highness could desire A₁
	5 f.b.–4 f.b.	that . . . Queen	(underscored) A
172	1	remember	reflect upon A₁
	1	the greatest	great A₁
	2	the lowest, vilest, and obscurest	slight and mean A₁; the lowest, and vilest and obscurest A₂
	3	And this is	which is A₁
	3	Courts	the Courts A₁
	4	produce	instance A₁
	6	*Bedmaker (editor's asterisk)	Bedmaker A, B
	8	become A₂, C	be A₁; became B
	12	†Dutchman (editor's obelisk)	Dutchman A, B
	13	had promised to be	should have been A₁
	16	at	of C
	17	may	shall A₁
	18	in	of A₁
	19	‡Vagrant (editor's double obelisk)	Vagrant A, B
	21–22	Queen . . . Nation	British Nation A₁
	10 f.b.	Ministers	or her Ministers A₁
	5 f.b.	Circumstances	unanswerable invincible Circumstances A₁
	fn.	*Mrs. . . . Elector. (Editor's asterisk and obelisks. The notes, added in manuscript B, are in the hand of Mrs. Martha Whiteway, who wrote know for known.)	(Omitted) A, B₁
	fn.	Foiston . . . in some	Foisson . . . into some C
173	1	And as	For as A₁; Because A₂; And as A₃

Page	Line	PRESENT TEXT	VARIANTS
	5	Parliamentary	For A_1
	10	*then* S	then A, B_1
	16	without	with A_1
	17	And	And therefore A_1
	19	be judged	appear A_1
	25	Commons	Commons as wel A_1
	28	shall	can A_1
	10 *f.b.*	me	me about that Time, That there could A_1
	4 *f.b.*	he foresaw	by his great Sagacity he saw A_1
174	4	certain	some A_1
	7	that	yet A_1
	13	chief	onely A_1
	18	however	though A_1
	28	the Want	want A_1
	10 *f.b.*	than	rather than A_1
	4 *f.b.*	settling S	the settling A, B_1
	2 *f.b.*	wrote	writ
175	3	He	Mr Harley A_1
	3	wrote	writ C
	6	those	these
	9	were	was A_1
	16–17	must remain	will rest A_1
	18–19	I . . . it	I hope least care to place it A_1
	20	mention	tell A_1; discover A_2; mention A_3
	4 *f.b.*	which	that A_1
	1 *f.b.*	and this with	with A_1
176	1–2	which Acts might have been only temporary S_2	and that onely temporary A_1; which was likewise to be only temporary A_2, B_1; Which Acts might have been onely temporary S_1
	6	such	so *great* A; so great B_1
	16	Ministry	Minister C
	18	as well as by	and A_1
	19	Expedients	Methods A_1
	26	that	that ever A_1
	27–29	For . . . Example	For the long Parliamt undr Charls 1st was not preceded by a Triennial Act. A_1
	9 *f.b.*	I . . . that	(*Omitted*) A_1
	3 *f.b.*	certain	some A_1
177	1	some	some odd A, B_1
	2	that may	which had A_1
	5	Assurance	assurances C
	5	During the	The
	6	the Queen's	Her Majesty's A_1
	10	the Ministers themselves	themselves A_1
	15	could not be	was not A_1
	20	are to	can A_1
	25	intended	lawfull A_1
	9 *f.b.*	Ministry	Ministry than these A_1

Page	Line	PRESENT TEXT	VARIANTS
	6 f.b-5 f.b.	so sanguine as to	who would A₁
	2	in Service	employd A₁
178	8	and . . . because	when A₁
	13–14	Restiness . . . Slowness	resty Animals are commonly the Slowest A₁
	14	Pursuer	Lover A₁
	19	said . . . understood	mentioned some particular Instances A₁
	24	raised	first raised A₁
	25	who S	who A₁; which A₂, B₁
	10 f.b.–9 f.b.	expressing . . . Sight	but call'd such a Declaration her Grave Stone A₁
179	5–6	although . . . where	although where A₁
	5	be S	is A, B₁
	6	Duty to	Duty of A₁
	6	the Allegiance	that A₁
	10	did . . . many	likewise gave A₁
	15	Zealots (*crossed out in manuscript* B *but written again in margin*)	
	16	could	might A₁
	17	Nation	Kingdom A₁
	20–21	I offered it	it was mine A₁
	22	such a	this A₁
	24–29	I have . . . For	(*In manuscript* A *this section is an insertion.*)
	25	those	these C
	10 f.b.	Interests S	Interest A, B₁
	5 f.b.	little	no A₁
	4 f.b.	Factions	Partyes A₁
	3 f.b.	in England S	(*Omitted*) A, B₁
	1 f.b.	so that, whoever	and this I A₁
	1 f.b.	upon	on A₁
{ 179 180	1 f.b.– 1	a . . . have	Principle hath A₁
180	2	discovering	observing A₁
	2	Advantage	Interest A₁
	8–13	And . . . will	and the former will A₁; in which case the former will A₂; in which Case the former, whenever they are taken into Power will A₃; And such a Party composed of mixt Bodyes, ⌈all⌉ although they differ widely in their severall Fundamentals of Religion and Governmt, and all of them from the true publick Interest, yet whenever their Leaders are taken into Power, under an ignorant, inactive, or ill-designing Prince will A₄
	10	their	the C
	24	Or	and A₁
	10 f.b.	Controllable	weak is A₁
	9 f.b.	Maxim	Maxim in the Politicks A₁
	9 f.b.	Res . . . administrari C	Res . . . administrari A, B
	1 f.b.	whose . . . himself	which seldom end but with himself A₁

APPENDIXES

A. A MODEST ENQUIRY INTO THE REASONS OF THE JOY...
    UPON... HER MAJESTY'S DEATH.

London: Printed for John Morphew, etc., 1714.
First published February 4, 1713–14.
The text is printed from Mr. Davis's copy.

B. THE HUMBLE ADDRESS OF THE ... LORDS, etc. (March 11, 1713–
    14).

London: Printed by John Baskett, etc., 1713 (–14).
The text is printed from a photostat of the Bodleian copy (Vet. A3.c.44).

C. A COPY OF DR. SWIFT'S MEMORIAL TO THE QUEEN.

The text is printed from the first publication, 1765, in Vol. VIII, Pt. I,
p. 83, of Hawkesworth's 4to edition of Swift's *Works*; this volume was edited
by Deane Swift. See the preface to the textual notes for *Some Considerations
upon ... the Death of the Queen*, above, p. 210.

INDEX

Abel. *See* Roper

Acheson, Sir Arthur and Lady, Swift visits, xxxvi

Act of Grace, xxxv

Act of Security, 49, 114

Acts of Settlement, xxviii, 34–5, 94; Regents, xxviii–xxix, 97

Addison, Joseph, aid to Steele, xv; friendship with Steele, 5; and Swift, 122

Ailesbury, Thomas Bruce, Earl of, in Saturday Club, 124

Alcibiades, 134

Alexander VI, Pope, 77

Alps, 71

Anne, Duchess of Savoy, and British crown, 54–5

Anne, Queen of England, xxvii, xxix–xxx, xxxviii, 86, 143, 150, and *passim*; accession, 101; and Bolingbroke, 151–2, 166–7; and Catalonians, 62–3; character, 103–4, 110–2, 137, 144, 146, 151–2, 160, 167, 178, 184–97; and Church of England, 39, 166, 187; and Church of Ireland, first-fruits, 121–3; death, xxviii–xxix, xxxvi, 71, 76, 97, 109, 124, 131–2, 140–1, 174, 183–97, desired, by army, 89–90, by Austrians, 58, by Whigs, 53, 140–1, 154–5, 183–97, regretted, 170; and Dunkirk, 10, 18, 23, 25, 60; and French crown, 55; and Godolphin, 101, 111–3; and Hanover, 93–4, 96–7, 174–5, 177; illness, xvi, xxxiii, 90, 98, 154–5, 157, 171, 173, 177, 183–97; and Irish bishoprics, 159; last years, xxxix, 81f., 101f., 108f., 131f., 142f., *History of. See* Swift; libelled, 64, 92; Lords' address to, xxi–xxii, 198–9, her answer, 199; and Marlborough, 101–2, 111–2, 117; and Duchess of Marlborough, 101, 110–2, 146, 167; and Lady Masham, xxxiii, xxxviii–xxxix, 109–10, 112; and Oxford, 101–2, 115–7, 138, 149, 151–8, 171; speech to Parliament, xx; popularity,

176–7; and Portugal, 61–2; and prerogative, 17, 23; and Pretender, 166–7, 178, 191; court of St. James, 95, 159; and Steele, xii, 11, 13, 15, 17, 20, 34, 67, praised by him, 22, his supposed speech, 18, her supposed answer, 18–19; and succession, xxvi, 31, 93, 164–80; and suspension of arms, 57–8, 133; and Swift, criticised by him, xxiv, xxxiii, 146–51, 160, his *Memorial*, xxxi, 200; and Tories, 140, 148–9, 159–60, their ministry, 14, 81–2, 160; and Union, 49, 114; and Whigs, cursed by them, 52, discards them, 81–3, 102–3, 117–8, 153–5, doubted by them, 48, favours them, 121, mistreated by them, 56, 101–2, threatened by them, 41, 45; and William III, 23–5

Antwerp, xi

Arbuthnot, Dr. John, on *Secret History of the White Staff*, xxx

Argument [against] . . . the Abolishing of Christianity. *See* Swift

Argyll, John Campbell, Duke of, xxii, xxviii; and Marlborough, 114–5; in Saturday Club, 124; and Tories, 149, 152, 166

Aristides, 138

Army. *See* Britain, army

Asiento, and Dutch, 171

Atheists. *See* Deists

Athens, 119

Atterbury, Dr. Francis, Bishop of Rochester, 109; and *Examiner*, 123; and Oxford, 156 & *n.*; Swift writes to, xxxv

Atticus, Titus Pomponius, 142

Augustus II, King of Poland, and, as Frederick Augustus I, Elector of Saxony, 61

Austria ('the Empire'), and France, 60–1; and *passim. See also* Bourbon; Charles VI

Austrians (Imperialists), and suspension of arms, 57; and Queen Anne, 58; and Trarbach, 59; and *passim*

S

Ball, Dr. Francis Elrington, xxii
Bank of England, and Whigs, 41
Bar-le-Duc. *See* Stuart
Barber, John, xxiv, xxxii, 76; printed *Publick Spirit of the Whigs*, 199; prosecuted, xxi–xxii
Barcelona, 62
Barrier Treaty, 59
Bavaria, Elector of. *See* Maximilian
Bedford, Hilkiah ('poor Non-juring Clergyman'), and *Hereditary Right of the Crown of England Asserted*, 64–5
Benson, Robert, Chancellor of the Exchequer, and October Club, 126
Berkeley, Charles, Earl of, 119
Berkeley of Stratton, William, Lord, in Saturday Club, 124
'Bessus, Captain' (character in Francis Beaumont and John Fletcher, *A King and No King*), 54
'Bickerstaff, Isaac,' and *Tatler*, 6
Blount, Sir Christopher, 189
Bolingbroke, Henry St. John, Viscount, Secretary of State, xxviii, 109, 112–3, 159, 174, and *passim*; character, 87 ('others'), 134–5, 145–6; dismissal, xxx; Dunton attacks, 32; and Dunkirk, 12; and *Examiner*, 123; and Guiscard, 128, 145; impeachment and flight, xxxi–xxxii, 134; to be Lord Treasurer, succeeding Oxford, 132; opposition to Marlborough and Godolphin, 101, 112–4; and October Club, 126; quarrel with Oxford, 76, 79, 86–7, 128, 132, 144f., 151–2, 155–62, 171; and Pretender, 48, 163–80; and Prior, 158; and Queen, 151–2, 166–7; in Saturday Club, 124; and *Some free Thoughts*, xxiv–xxviii; Steele attacks, 48; Swift's concern for, xxxii, criticism, xxxiii, 87. *See also* Tories, ministry
Borgia, Cesare, 77
Bouchain, investment, 57
Bourbon, House of, and Duke of Savoy, 64; and union of crowns of France and Spain, 58–9, 71, 146–7, 171
Brent, Mrs., Swift's housekeeper, xxxvii
'Brentford, King of' (character in George Villiers, Duke of Buckingham, *The Rehearsal*), 44

Brill, 189
Britain, Great, or England, 78, 149, 168, and *passim*; army, and Tory policy, 89–90, Guards officers, 155–7; constitution, 37, 40, 88–9, 96–8, 114, 136, 155, 179–80, discussed by Whigs, 41; possible war with Scotland, 50; succession of crown, xxvi, 54–5, 63–4, 86, 148, alterable, 52–3; suspension of arms, 57; trade, 60; Union with Scotland: *see* Scotland. *See also* Bank of England; Parliament.
Bromley, William, Secretary of State, and Oxford, 156; attacked by Steele, 48
Buckingham, John Sheffield, Duke of, 165–6
Buckley, Samuel, publisher of *The Crisis*, xvi, xviii, 33
Burghley, William Cecil, Lord, Lord Treasurer, 189
Burnet, Gilbert, Bishop of Salisbury, xvi, xviii, 119; and Steele, 36, 38, 65
Butler, James. *See* Ormonde
Butler, 'Prince,' 64
Button's Coffee-House, 59
Buys, Willem de, 171

Cabinet Council, 47
Caesar, Julius, 180
Calamy, Edmund, xiv *n*
Caligula, 184
Calvin, John, 96
Cambridge, University, 38
Canterbury, Archbishop of, 35. *See also*, Tenison
Castile, 63
Catalonians, 61–3
Catherine de' Medici, Queen of France, 77
Catiline, 142
Chamberlain. *See* Newcastle, Thomas, Duke of
Chamberlayne, Edward and John, *The Present State of Great Britain* (*Magnae Britanniae Notitia*), 195
Chancellor. *See* Harcourt
Character of Richard St——le, xiv
Charing Cross, 183–4
Charles I, King of England, 17, 176
Charles II, King of Spain, will, 54

Charles VI, Emperor of Austria, and, as Charles III, King of Spain ('his Imperial Majesty'), xi, 61-3, and *passim*; and Italy, 60, 64; and War of the Spanish Succession, 58. *See also* Austria; Bourbon

Cholmondeley, Hugh, Earl of, Treasurer of the Household, dismissal desired, 124

Church of England ('the clergy'), xxvi, xxxi, 67, and *passim*; bishops, praised by enemies of episcopacy, 13-4; secular support needed for, 42; criticised by Steele, 15-6, addressed by him, 35-43, supposed answer to him, 38-9; tithes, 35; and Tory policy, 88-9; threatened by Whigs, 42; Whiggish element in, 41, 148

Church of Ireland, bishops, 121-3; bishoprics vacant, 140, 159; convocation, 37; first-fruits, 121-3

Churchill, George, admiral, 113

Clarendon, Edward Hyde, 1st Earl of, 138

Clarendon, Edward Hyde, 3d Earl of, mission to Hanover, 171

Cockpit, 127

Conduct of the Allies. See Swift

Contests and Dissentions. See Swift

Convocation. *See* Church of Ireland

Cowper, William, Lord, Lord Chancellor, 'a Person,' and Marlborough, 56, 114; Queen attached to 'two great Officers,' 103, 142-3, 167

Cranmer, Thomas, Archbishop of Canterbury, 16

Crisis. See Steele

Cuffe, Henry, 189

Dartmouth, William Legge, Earl of, and Oxford, 156; in Saturday Club, 124· and Tories, 166

Daup See Louis XV

Davi. ɔ7

Defoe, Daniel, *Secret History of the White Staff*, xxx

Deists, atheists, and Socinians, praise bishops, 14; threaten church, 42

Denmark, Prince of. *See* George, Prince of Denmark

Dilke, C. W., xiv

Dissenters, xxvi, and *passim*; praise bishops, 14

Douai (Doway), invaded by French, 57

Dover, 193

Drapier. *See* Swift

Druids, 22

Drummond, John, 'a Gentleman,' 171

Dublin, Swift stays a fortnight, ix, leaves, x, returns for oaths, xxviii; exile for Swift, xxx; and *passim*

Dunkirk, demolition, x-xii, xiv, 67-8, British nation 'expects,' 17-18, and Queen Anne, 10, 18, 23, 25, 60, and Steele, 4-25, 59; surrender, 10, 57-8; and *passim*

Dunton, John, attacks Tories, 34; supports Whigs, 31-2; *Neck or Nothing*, 32

Dutch, and Catalonians, 62; and Peace of Utrecht, 170-1; and Queen Elizabeth, 189; and suspension of arms, 57; and Trarbach, 59; and *passim*. *See also* Barrier Treaty; United Provinces; Low Countries

'*Dutch Gazeteer*,' 31

East India Company, and Whigs, 41

Egerton, Sir Thomas, Lord Keeper, 189

Elections, 176; of 1710, 126, 142-3, 149; of 1715, 176; under William III, 148

Elector of Hanover. *See* George I

Elizabeth I, Queen of England, 178, 187-90

England. *See* Britain

'English Tory.' *See* Steele, *Guardian*

Englishman. See Steele

Enquiry into . . . the Queen's Last Ministry. See Swift

Essex, Algernon Capel, Earl of, Constable of the Tower, 102, 117

Essex, Robert Devereux, Earl of ('Captain-General'), 188-9

Eugene, Prince of Savoy, 56

Europe, 39, 167, 188, 191, 194, and *passim*

Examiner, xii, xiv, xvii, xxv, 67, 123-4, and *passim*; and Guiscard, 128, 145; not prosecuted, 14; and *Publick Spirit of the Whigs*, xviii-xix *n*; and Queen's illness, xvi; and Steele, 8, 10–12, 17; and Swift's *History*, xix; defends Tory ministry, 14; and Tugghe's memorial, 8; attacks Whigs, 14. *See also* Swift

Faulkner, George, xxv
Fenwick, Sir John, 34
First Ode of the Second Book of Horace. *See* Swift
Flanders, trade with, xi; war in, 113
Flushing, 189
Flying-Post, xix; attacks Tories, 34; prosecuted, 14; supported by Whigs, 31–2; and Dunkirk, xi. *See also* Ridpath
Foiston. *See* Foyston
Ford, Charles, correspondence with Swift, v, xxiii & *n*, xxiv, xxvii–xxx, xxxiv, xxxvi, xl
Forster, John, xxxvii, xxxviii; Collection (Victoria and Albert Museum), xxix
Foyston, Mrs. Mary, necessary woman to Queen Anne, 172 & *n*
France, 167, and *passim*; and Austria, 60; correspondence with, 127; and Dunkirk, 18, 60; and English clergy, 39; power, 54; princes, and the Pretender, 91; and Steele, 61; succession of crown, 52, 55, 169, 191; suspension of arms, 57; treaty arrangements with, x, xi, xvii, 71, 83, 169–70, Tory opposition to ('the Bill of Commerce'), 21–2; war with, 148–9. *See also* Bourbon; Louis XIV
Frederick, Prince of Wales, grandson of George I, residence in England, 93, 95, 179
Frederick Augustus I. *See* Augustus II
Freind, Dr. John, and *Examiner*, 124
Fuller, William, 'Narrative' concerning the Pretender, 52

Gaultier, François, and Oxford, 163
George, Prince of Denmark, death, 101, 112–3, 121; and Steele, 6; and Whigs, 114
George, Prince of Hesse, and Catalonians, 62
George I, King of England and Elector of Hanover, xxvii, xxviii, xxxv, 67–8, 93–7, 140, 171–2, and *passim*; accession, 132, 170; and France, 169–70; and Oxford, xxxiv, 157; policies, 174–5; popularity, 168–70, 173–7; 'absent Prince,' 168; 'two Princes,' 179; and Queen Anne, 174–5, 177; and the succession, 94, 173–4, memorial concerning, 93; criticised by Swift, v; and Tories, 193; and Whigs, xxix, 93–8, 109, 132, 175–6, 194–5. *See also* Hanover, House of
George II, King of England, 'two Princes,' 179
Germany, 64
Gloucester, William, Duke of, 192
Godolphin, Sidney, Earl of, Lord Treasurer ('first minister'), 102, 118, and *passim*; family, 102; and first-fruits, 121; 'a certain minister,' 49; 'moderating scheme,' 113; and Oxford, 102, 113, 115–6; 'three Persons,' 148; correspondence with Pretender, 48; and Queen, 101, 111–3; removal, 13, 102–3, 111–2, 118, 120, 123; called 'Volpone,' 115; and Whigs, 56, 113–4
Golden Bull, 60
'Gothick Balance,' 180
Greece, 174
Greeks, detestation of tyranny, 37
Guardian. *See* Steele
Guiscard, Antoine de, stabs Harley, xxxi, 126–8, 145
Guiscard, Comte de, Governor of Namur, 127
'Gulliver, Lemuel,' xvi *n*, xl
Gulliveriana. *See* Smedley
Gulliver's Travels. *See* Swift
Gulph wherein England *will be Swallow'd*. *See* Stubbs

Halifax, Charles Montagu, Earl of, and Swift, 119–21
Hampton Court, 116, 188
Hanmer, Sir Thomas, Speaker of the House of Commons, 'honoured' by Steele, 52 & *n*
Hanover, xxviii, 174
Hanover Club, xv
Hanover, Elector of. *See* George I
Hanover, Electress of. *See* Sophia

Hanover, House of, distrust of Queen Anne, 93-4, 96-7, 174-5, 177; residence in England, 93-8, 178-9; succession of British crown in, x, xx, xxvi, xxvii, 64, 71, 192-3, popular support for, 65-6, 168, 170, 172-3, 176-7, and Tory ministry, 40, 47, 86, 90-5, 168-9, and the Union, 49, and Whigs, xvii, 45, 48, 52, 94-6; and Tories, 132, 140, 171-2; and *passim*. *See also* Acts of Settlement; Britain, succession; George I; Sophia

Harbin, George, *Hereditary Right of the Crown of England Asserted*, 64-5

Harcourt, Simon, Lord, Lord Keeper and Lord Chancellor, 166; baron, 128; opposition to Marlborough and Godolphin, 101, 114; relations with Oxford and Bolingbroke, 144f., 152, 155-7, 161; defence of Sacheverell, 45; in Saturday Club, 124

Harley, Robert. *See* Oxford

Harley, Thomas, mission to Hanover, 171, 174-5

Heinsius, Anthony, Grand Pensionary of Holland ('Pensioner'), 171

Hereditary Right. See Harbin; Bedford.

Hertford, Algernon Seymour, Earl of, 102, 117

Hesse, Prince of. *See* George, Prince of Hesse

Hill, Abigail. See *Masham*

Hill, John, 112

Hoadly, Benjamin, on politics, 40-1; aids Steele, xv; praised by Steele, 45

Hobbes, Thomas, on 'magnanimity,' 139; on republicanism, 37

Holland. *See* United Provinces

Honour and Prerogative of the Queen's Majesty, xi-xii

Honywood, Philip, 'two or three,' 155-6

Horace, *First Ode. See* Swift

Horse Guards, xiv

Humble Address. See Parliament, House of Lords

Hunsdon, William Ferdinand Carey, Lord, 172 & *n*

Ilay, Archibald Campbell, Earl of, and Tories, 166

Imperialists. *See* Austrians

S*

Importance of Dunkirk consider'd. See Steele

Importance of the Guardian. See Swift

Ireland, xiii, 118-9, 159, and *passim*; Parliament, House of Lords, 140

'Ironside, Nestor.' *See* Steele, *Guardian*

Isley. *See* Ilay

Italy, and Duke of Savoy, 64; in the War of the Spanish Succession, 58, 63; and *passim*

James I, King of England, and the Union, xix *n*, 48-9

James II, King of England ('the abdicated King'), 65, 168; invasion, 97; religion, 91; restoration, 39; as Duke of York, 96

Johnson, Hester, or Esther (Stella), and Swift's *Enquiry*, v, xxxiv

Kensington, 116 and *passim*

Kent, Henry Grey, Duke of, Lord Chamberlain, 117

King, Sir Peter, at trial of Sacheverell, 40

King, William, Archbishop of Dublin, 'protects' Swift, xxxii

King, Dr. William, Principal of St. Mary's Hall, Oxford, and Swift's *Enquiry*, xxxviii

Landen, 133

Laracor, 'my country-parish,' Swift withdraws to, ix, xxxiii, 121

Lechmere, Nicholas, at trial of Sacheverell, 40

Leicestershire, 121

Leopold, Duke of Lorraine, and the Pretender, 67-8

Leslie, Charles, and the Pretender, 91

Letcombe Bassett, Berkshire ('Upper Letcombe'), Swift at, xxiii, xxix, 76, 132, 159

Letter ... Concerning the Sacramental Test. See Swift

Lewis, Erasmus, appeals to Swift, x; correspondence with Swift, xxx, xxxv; warns Swift, xxxi

Libya, 43

Locke, John, on government, 43

London, xxix, 76, 183, and *passim*; Swift returns to, x, xii; Whigs in, 41

London Gazette, 199

Lorraine, Duke of. *See* Leopold, Duke of Lorraine

Lorraine, Pretender and, xi, 67–8

Louis XI, King of France, 77

Louis XIV, King of France ('the most Christian King'), 53, and *passim*; and Catalonians, 63; death, 170; and Dunkirk, 9–10, 18–19, 60; and Pretender, 54; and Whigs, 9–10. *See also* France

Louis XV, King of France, 169; Dauphin, 54

Low Countries, and Queen Elizabeth, 189; trade with, xi. *See also* United Provinces; Dutch

Lucius Florus, 37

Luther, Martin, 96

Lysander, 77

Maccartney, George, 'two or three,' 155–6

Mainwaring, Arthur, and Steele, 6–7

Mall, London, 128

Man, Jenny, 66

Manley, Mrs. Mary de la Rivière, *Modest Enquiry into . . . Her Majesty's Death*, composition and publication, xvi–xvii, text, 183–97, bibliographical note, 232

Mansell, Thomas, Lord, and Tories, 166

Mar, John Erskine, Earl of, xxi

March Club, 126

Market Hill, Swift at, xxxvi

Marlborough, John Churchill, Duke of, general, benefits from war, 56; captain-generalship for life, 56, 114–5; and Constableship of the Tower, 102, 117; family, 102, 109, 142, 167; 'moderating scheme,' 113; and Oxford, 113, 115–6; 'three Persons,' 148; and Queen, 101–2, 111–2, 117; removal, 13, 109, 200; wealth, 53; and suspension of arms, 57–8; and Whigs, 113–4.

Marlborough, Sarah Churchill, Duchess of, 109, 114; dismissed from Queen's service, 146, 167; Godolphin's mistress, 111; influence upon Queen, 101, 110–11; 'three Persons,'

148; and death of Prince George, 112; and Oxford, xxxv, 115

Marten, John, 9

Marvell, Andrew, *Rehearsall Transpros'd* echoed by Swift, xvii *n*

Mary, Queen of England, wife of James II ('young wife'), 96

Mary, Queen of England, wife of William III, 95

Masham, Abigail, Lady (Mrs. Hill), bed-chamber woman to Queen, 109–10, 112, 152, 159; character, 153; influence on Queen, xxxiii, xxxviii–xxxix; 'a Lady,' 168; 'a most excellent Lady,' 149; 'a person,' 114; and Oxford, 102, 115–6, 153, 156–7, 161

Masham, Samuel, Lord, and Tories, 166

Maximilian II (Maximilian Emmanuel), Elector of Bavaria, 61

Meredyth, Thomas, 'two or three,' 155–6

Milan, held by Austria, 60

Modest Enquiry into . . . Her Majesty's Death. See Manley

Molesworth, Robert, Viscount, defended by Steele, 37

Moore, Sir Norman, *History of St. Bartholomew's Hospital*, xv *n*

Morphew, John, publishes pamphlets, xi, xiv, 198

Mortimer, family, 135

Most humble Address or Memorial . . . of Dunkirk. See Tugghe

Murray, John, xxxviii

Namur, 127

Neck or Nothing. See Dunton

Nero, 184

Newcastle, John Holles, Duke of, 166

Newcastle, Thomas Pelham-Holles, Duke of, Lord Chamberlain, forbids Oxford the court, xxxv

Newgate prison, 190

Newmarket, 118

Non-jurors, xxvi, 91, 165, 168, 172–3

Northumberland, George Fitzroy, Duke of, 102, 117

Nottingham, Daniel Finch, Earl of, 32; attack on Tories, 34; vote against 'Peace without Spain,' 146, 148, 167, 171

October Club, 83–4, 125–6, 143

Orleans, Philip, Duke of, Regent of France, 169–70

Ormonde, James Butler, Duke of, general, 90; character, 132–3; impeachment, flight, and attainder, xxxi–xxxii, 132, 134; and Oxford, 155–7; in Saturday Club, 124; Steele attacks, 47–8; suspension of arms, 57–8, 133; Swift's concern for, xxxii; and Tories, 166

Ormonde, Mary, Duchess of, xxiii

Orrery, Charles Boyle, Earl of, and Tories, 166

Orrery, John Boyle, Earl of, and Swift's *Enquiry*, xxxvii–xxxviii

Oxford, Robert Harley, Earl of, Lord Treasurer, xvi, xvii, xxv, xxix–xxxi, 114, 150, 154, 171, and *passim*; attacked, xv *n*; friendship and quarrel with Bolingbroke, xxiv, 76, 79, 86–7, 128, 132, 138, 144f., 151–2, 155–9, 171; and Bromley, 156; character, 87, 103–4, 110, 135–8, 143–4, 152, 160–1, procrastination, xxvii, 137, secretiveness, 80–1, 85–6, 137; and Dartmouth, 156, 157, dismissed as Secretary of State, 113; dismissed as Lord Treasurer, xxviii, 132; and Dunkirk, 18; Dunton attacks, 32; earldom, 128, 146; and first-fruits, 122–3; forbidden the court, xxxv; and George I, xxxv, 157; stabbed by Guiscard, xxxi, 126–8, 145; and Harcourt, 144f., 152, 156–7, 161; in Hertfordshire, xxxv; and Irish bishoprics, 159; and Lords' vote against peace, 146f.; opposition to Marlborough and Godolphin, 101–2, 113–6; and Duchess of Marlborough, xxxv, 115; and Lady Masham, 102, 115–6, 153, 156–7, 161; and October Club, 125–6; and Ormonde, 155–7; policies, 126, 143; and Pretender, 9, 141, 163–80; and Prior, 158; and Queen, 101–2, 109–10, 115–7, 137, 149, 151–61, 171; Saturday Club, 124, 160–1; and Shrewsbury, 156; and Steele, 6–7, 11–12, 24, attacked by him, 47; and Swift, acquaintance, 122–4, 138, calls for him, x, correspondence with him,

xxxv, criticised by him, xxxiii, 124–5, 140, 143–4, defended by him, xxxiii, 161–2, Swift's concern for, xxxii; and Trevor, 156, 158; and Whigs, 104. *See also* Tories, ministry

Oxford Regiment, 102, 117

Oxford, University, 38

Page, William, 189–90

Pamphilio Pamphili, and 'Prince' Butler, 64

Parker, Sir Thomas, Lord Chief Justice, 40, 65 & *n*

Parliament, xiv, xx, 68, 79, 85, 92, 93, 97, 132, 136, 170, 175–6, and *passim*; acts of, 48–9; Long Parliament, 176; parties, 83–4, 89, 104, 149–50, 176; and Tory ministry, 125–6, 156–7; House of Commons, 89, 174; *Address of Thanks*, xx; Committee of Secrecy, *Report*, 163; impeachment of Oxford, Bolingbroke, and Ormonde, xxxi–xxxiv, 149; impeachment of five Whig lords, 119; and Steele, 13; Tory majority, 83–4, 175–6; House of Lords, xix, 176; Committee on Precedents, xxxiv; creation of twelve peers, 23, 147–51, condemned by Steele, 15, criticised by Swift, xxxix, 150; petitioned by Oxford, xxxiv; and *Publick Spirit of the Whigs*, xxi–xxii, text of *Humble Address* against, 198–9. *See also* Elections; October Club

Partition Treaty, 54

Peace of Utrecht. *See* Utrecht

Peers, creation of twelve. *See* Parliament, House of Lords

Peterborough, Charles Mordaunt, Earl of, xxii, in Saturday Club, 124; and Tories, 149, 166

Peters, Hugh, 41

Petronius, 135

Philip, King of Macedonia, 77

Philip II, King of Spain, 77; 'hopeful candidate,' 188

Philip V, King of Spain ('his Catholic majesty'), 53; and Catalonians, 62–3; renounces French crown, 57

Plato, on government, 43

Poland, succession of crown, 54. *See also* Augustus II

Pope, Alexander, correspondence with Swift, xxxii, xxxvi
Portugal, 61–2
Post Boy, 67
Poulett, John, Earl, xxxvi, 118; and Oxford, 156; in Saturday Club, 124
Prerogative of the crown, 164, 176; Steele and, 13, 15, 17, 23
Present State of Great Britain. See Chamberlayne
Pretender. See Stuart; Britain, succession
Prior, Matthew, xxxi; and Examiner, 124; relations with Oxford and Bolingbroke, 158; correspondence with Swift, xxxv
Privy Council, xxviii
Project for . . . the Reformation of Manners. See Swift
Protestant Succession. See Hanover
Puritans, 188

Queries Relating to the Birth and Birthright of a Certain Person [i.e., the Pretender], attributed to George Hickes, 64

Raleigh, Sir Walter, 138
Rammekins, castle, 189
Read, Sir William, 9
Reasons concerning the immediate Demolishing of Dunkirk, xi
Regents. See Acts of Settlement
Rehearsall Transpros'd. See Marvell
Revolution of 1688, 92, 120, 148
Ridgeway, cabinet-maker, married to Mrs. Brent's daughter, xxxvii
Ridpath, George, 21, 54; and Protestant Succession, 193; and Whigs, 31–2. See also Flying-Post
Rivers, Richard Savage, Earl, Constable of the Tower, 102, 117; mission to Hanover, 171–2; in Saturday Club, 124; and Tories, 149, 166
Robethon, Jean, 172 & n
Roman Catholics ('Papists'), under Elizabeth, 188; and the Pretender, 91–2, 165
Rome, 119, 174; civil wars, 43–4; decline, 180; history, 37
Roper, Abel, xiv, 9. See also Post Boy
Rothschild, Victor, Lord, v, xxiii n, xxxviii

Sacheverell, Dr. Henry, 164; trial, 6, 39, 40, 45, 84, 102, 109–10, 115, 126, 142, 149, 153
Sacramental Test, 102; and Wharton, 121
St. Bartholomew's Hospital, xiv, xv n
St. George, Chevalier de. See Stuart
St. Germain. See Stuart
St. James, court of. See Anne, Queen of England
St. John. See Bolingbroke
St. Stephen's Chapel, 12
Sardinia, succession of crown, 52, 54
Sarum, Bishop of. See Burnet
Saturday Club. See Oxford
Savoy, Duchess of. See Anne, Duchess of Savoy
Savoy, Duke of. See Victor
Saxony, Elector of. See Augustus II
Scipio Africanus, Publius, 138
Scotland, peerage, attacked by Swift, xviii–xxii, 50–1; and succession, 170; in Publick Spirit of the Whigs, 198; revenue, 50; union with England, 49, 114, attacked by Swift, 48f., dissolution proposed, 50; and passim. See also Act of Security
Scots, 'a poor, fierce Northern People,' xxii, 49; possible war with English, 50
Scriblerus Club, xv n
Second Whigg-Letter, from William Prynne, xii
Secret Committee, Report. See Parliament, House of Commons, Committee of Secrecy
Secret History of the White Staff. See Defoe
Sentiments of a Church-of-England Man. See Swift
Septennial Act, 'Modern Invention,' 176
Sheridan, Dr. Thomas, correspondence with Swift, xxxvi
Shrewsbury, Charles Talbot, Duke of, Lord Treasurer, xxviii; Lord Chamberlain, 102, 118; and Oxford, 156; in Saturday Club, 124; on the succession, 173–4; and Tories, 149, 152, 157, 166
Sicily, 64; succession of crown, 52, 54

Smedley, Jonathan, Dean of Clogher and Killala, *Gulliveriana*, xiv

Smith, John, the corncutter, 9

Snow, John, Bailiff of Stockbridge, xii, xiv; Steele's letter to, 4, 5, 34; in *Importance of the Guardian*, 3–25

Socinians. *See* Deists

Somers, John, Lord, Lord President, xxxi, 113, 121, 137; and Marlborough and Godolphin, 114; Queen attached to, 142, 167; and Swift, 119–21; and the Union, 49, 114

Somerset, Charles Seymour, Duke of, 'a certain Lord,' 161; dismissal desired, 124; Queen attached to, 103, 142 & *n*; vote against peace, 147 & *n*

Somerset, Elizabeth (Percy), Duchess of, and Queen Anne, 146 & *n*; 153 & *n*; 167 & *n*

Sophia, Electress of Hanover, 71; death, 93. *See also* Hanover, House of

Spain, 188, and *passim*; and Peace of Utrecht, 146, 167; and Portugal, 61–2; succession of crown, 52, 54, 61; treaties with, 169–70. *See also* Bourbon; Charles II; Philip II; Philip V

Spectator. See Steele

Stair, John Dalrymple, Earl of, Ambassador to France, 169

Stanhope, James, general, praised by Steele, 45; trial of Sacheverell, 40

State and Condition of our Taxes considered, xv *n*

States-General. *See* United Provinces

Steele, Richard, and Addison, xv, 5; attacks on, xi–xii; 'Brother-Scribler,' xiii, 4, 13; and Burnet, 36, 38, 65; character and career, 5–7, 19–22, 65, 68; criticises Church of England, 15–6, his address to clergy, 35–43; their supposed answer, 38–9; and Dunton and Ridpath, 31–2, 193; on education, 37–8; expelled from Parliament, xx–xxi; 'expects' demolition of Dunkirk, 17, 18, 93; Gazetteer, 6; on government, 43f.; guilty of treason, 51–2; letter to 'Nestor Ironside,' x, xiii, 7–10; on liberty, 46f.; literary style, 5–6, 10–1, 22, 32, 35–6, 46–7, 65; M.P. for Stockbridge, xii, 11–12, 18; name spelled

St——, 15 & *n*; and Oxford (Harley), 6–8, 11; and Queen, xii, 11, 13, 15, 17, 20, 34, 67, praises her, 22, supposed speech to, 18, her answer, 18–9; and Swift, controversy begins, x, attacked by him, in *Importance of the Guardian*, xiii–xiv, 3–25, in *First Ode of the Second Book of Horace*, xv–xvi, in *Publick Spirit of the Whigs*, xvii–xx, xxiii, 31–68; and Tugghe's memorial, 8–12; *Crisis*, composition and publication, xv–xvi, 32–3, subscription to, 32–3, condemned by House of Commons, xx–xxi, answered by Swift, xvii–xx, 31–68; *Englishman*, xv, xx–xxi, 7, 32, 37, 51, 67; *Guardian*, xi, xii, 16, letter from 'English Tory' to 'Nestor Ironside,' x, xiii, 7–12, *Importance of Dunkirk consider'd*, xii, 4–25; *Mr. Steele's Apology*, xvii & *n*; *Spectator*, 7, 16, 18, 36; *Tatler*, 6–7, 16, 18, 36

Stella. *See* Johnson

Stockbridge, 3–25; Borough of, xii, 8; Burgess of, 17; Bailiff of. *See* Snow

Strafford, Thomas Wentworth, 1st Earl of, 34, 138

Strafford, Thomas Wentworth, 3d Earl of, xxxi; and suspension of arms, 57; and Tories, 166

Stuart, James, Chevalier de St. George, son of James II, called the Pretender, xi, xviii, xxv–xxvi, 31, 48, 66, 71–2, 83, 155, 191, and *passim*; and Bolingbroke, 48, 166–7; character, 91–2; and clergy, 38–9; court at Bar-le-Duc, 48, 67–8, 71; court at St. Germain, 48; and Dunkirk, 18, 60; imaginary danger, 41, 65–6, 190–2; and Italy, 64; legitimacy, 52; and Lorraine, xi, 67–8; and Louis XIV, 54; and Oxford, 9, 163–80; and Queen Anne, 166–7, 178, 191; and Scotland, 50; in Steele's *Crisis*, 33; and Tory ministry, 31, 39, 71–2, 87, 140, 163–80; unpopularity, 172–3

Stubbs, John, *The Discouerie of a Gaping Gulf Whereinto England Is Like to Be Swallowed*, 189–90

Succession of the British Crown. *See* Acts of Settlement; Britain, succession; Hanover, House of; Stuart

Suidas, 34

Sunderland, Charles Spencer, 3d Earl of, Secretary of State, removal, 102; and Queen, 112, 118; and Swift, 119

Sunderland, Robert Spencer, 2d Earl of, 137

Swift, Deane, and Jonathan Swift's *Enquiry*, xxxviii

Swift, Jonathan, correspondence seized, xxxii; Drapier, xxxvi; and first-fruits, 121–3; and Halifax, 119–21; as historian, xxxix, 56–7, 107–10, 141–2, 200; and historiographer's post, xxxi, xxxix, 110, 200; in Ireland, 109, summer of 1713, ix, after Queen's death, 131–2, 139–40; goes to Laracor, ix, xxxiii; licence of absence, xxviii; and Mrs. Manley, xvi; and Oxford, xxxv, acquaintance with him, 122–4, 138, relations with him and Bolingbroke, 158–9, 165–6; parliamentary attacks on, 108; political evolution, 119–25; on politics and government, 77–81, 120, 131, 138–9, 149–50, 168–9, 171–2, 175–6, 179–80; on 'refinements,' 126; criticism of Queen, xxiv, xxxiii, 146–51, 160; retires to Letcombe Bassett, xxiii, 132, 159; and Steele, controversy begins, x, attacks him, in *Importance of the Guardian*, xiii–xiv, 3–25, in *First Ode of the Second Book of Horace*, xv–xvi, in *Publick Spirit of the Whigs*, xvii–xx, xxiii, 31–68; travels between England and Ireland, x, xiii, 119–22; *Argument [against] . . . the Abolishing of Christianity*, 122; *Conduct of the Allies*, 52; *Discourse concerning . . . the Pretender*, composition, xxii–xxiii, xxvi, manuscript, v, text, 69–72, textual notes, 204–5; *Discourse of the Contests and Dissentions between the Nobles and the Commons*, 119; *Enquiry into . . . the Queen's last Ministry*, composition, xxxi–xl, manuscripts, v, xxxvii, text, 129–80, textual notes, 215–31; *Examiner*, xxv, 123–4; *First Ode of the Second Book of Horace*, xv–xvi; *Gulliver's Travels*, xvi n, xl; *History of the Four Last Years* (*History of the Peace of Utrecht*), ix, xxix, xxx, xxxiii, 141,

148, publication rumoured, xix–xx, manuscript, xxxvii; *Importance of the Guardian*, composition and publication, xiii–xiv, text, 3–25, textual note, 201; *Letter from a Member of the House of Commons . . . Concerning the Sacramental Text*, 121–2; *Memoirs . . . 1710*, 141, composition, xxx–xxxi, xxxiii, manuscript, xxxvii, text, 105–28, textual notes, 210–4; *Memorial to the Queen*, xxxi, text, 200, textual note, 232; *Project for . . . the Reformation of Manners*, 122; *Publick Spirit of the Whigs*, composition and publication, xvii–xx, action of Lords against, xxi–xxiii, text, 27–68, *Humble Address* of Lords against, xxi–xxii, 198–9, 232, textual notes, 201–4; *Sentiments of a Church-of-England Man*, 122; *Some Considerations upon . . . the Death of the Queen*, composition, xxix–xxx, text, 99–104, textual notes, 210; *Some free Thoughts*, composition and publication, xxiii–xxviii, xxx, xl, 76, manuscript, v, text, 73–98, textual notes, 205–9

Tacitus, 88

Tatler. See Steele

Tenison, Thomas, Archbishop o Canterbury, 47

Themistocles, 138

Tiberius, Emperor of Rome, 77

Tithes. *See* Church of England

'Toby,' relative of Abel Roper (pseudonym of author of *Character of Richard Steele*), xiv, 67

Torcy, Jean-Baptiste Colbert, Marquis de, 78 & n

Tories ('the Church party'), 67 and *passim*; and Church of England, 102, 120; and Dunkirk, 18, 22, 60; and *Flying-Post*, 14; and French commercial treaty, 21–2; and George I, 94–7; 'High Tories,' xxv, 83, 120; and liberty, 47; ministry, 1710–14, character, 82, 85, Church of England supports, 39–40, and George I, 132, 171–2, 175–6, and the Pretender, 40, 90–1, 140–1, 163–80, 193, and Queen, 81–2, 160, criticised, xxii, xxiii, 14, 16, 61, by Steele, in *Importance of*

Dunkirk consider'd, 15, 16, 20, by Swift, 77–98, 131–80, by Tories, 140, 143, 156–7, 161–2, by Whigs, 140–1; principles, 91–2, 120; and Protestant Succession, 92–3; and Queen, 148–9, after her death, 140; strength, 175; and Whigs, differences, 71–2, 120; 'Whimsicals,' 82–3, 87–8. *See also* October Club

Tower of London, xxxiv, 17, 35, 102, 117, 164

Trarbach (Traerback), surrender, 59

Treaty of Commerce. *See* France, treaty arrangements

Trevor, Thomas, Lord, relations with Oxford and Bolingbroke, 156, 158

Tugghe, Sieur, his memorial to Queen Anne, 18, 67, answered by Steele, 8–12

Turin, Battle of, 58

Turkey, 180

Tyburn, 190

Union. *See* Scotland

United Provinces, Holland, 58, 171, and Catalonians, 62, and France, 64, and Guiscard, 127; States-General, xi, 71, deputies at Bouchain, 57, at Douai, 57–8; and *passim*. *See also* Dutch; Low Countries; Barrier Treaty

Utrecht, Peace of, xix, xxix, 71, 155, 167, 169–71, 186, 200, and *passim*; and George I, 132; and Gulliver, xvi *n*; in House of Lords, 146f.; and Queen Anne, 23, 146–7, 150–1; and Duke of Savoy, 63–4; and Whigs, 66, 194; *History of. See* Swift. *See also* War of the Spanish Succession

Vanhomrigh, Hester, or Esther (Vanessa), letter from Swift, ix

*V*ere, family, 135

Victor, Duke of Savoy, and British crown, 54–5, 64; and Peace of Utrecht, 63–4

Vienna, stricken by plague, 61

Vigo, 133

Virgil, on government, 43–4

'Volpone.' *See* Godolphin

War of the Spanish Succession, 56–9, 147–51, 186, and *passim*; suspension of arms, 57–8, 133. *See also* Utrecht, Peace of

Wagstaffe, Dr. William, xiv, xv & *n*; *Miscellaneous Works*, xiv

Walls, Thomas, xvi, xxiii

Welsh justice of the peace, 51

West Indies, 63

Westminster-Hall, 47, 64

Wharton, Thomas, Earl of, Lord Lieutenant of Ireland, 113, 121, 154; and first-fruits, 121; indifferent to reputation, 142 & *n*; and Sacramental Test, 121–2; and Swift, 121–2; and fall of Whigs, 118

Whigs, 67, 191, and *passim*; and Church of England, 88, 120, praise bishops, 14; *Examiner* attacks, 14; 'that Faction,' 178–9; and George I, xxix, 93–8, 109, 132; and Louis XIV, 9–10; and Oxford, 104; and the Pretender, 52, 66; attacked in *Publick Spirit of the Whigs*, 27–68; and Queen, 41, 45, 56, 81–3, 101–2, preferred by her and William III, 121, 148–9, her illness, 98, her death, 53, 140–1, 154–5, 183–97; their republicanism, 24; Steele praises, 47; and Tories, differences with, 71–2, charges against, xix, 163–80; their ministry, 81–2, 102, dismissed, 102–3, 108f., 117–8, 142, 148–9, 200; unpopularity, 48

'Whimsicals.' *See* Tories

Whitehall, 64

Whiteway, Mrs. Martha, and the *Discourse concerning . . . the Pretender*, xxvi; and Swift's *Enquiry*, v, xxxvii–xxxviii; and *Some free Thoughts*, xxiv

William I, King of England, 92

William III, King of England, 133; and Church of England, 95–6; death, 119; and French dog-keeper, 23–5; lords justices, 97; memory, 196; and the Union, xix *n*, 49; and Whigs, 148–9

Windsor, ix, 90, 98, 124, 154, 157, 158, and *passim*

Wyndham, Sir William, Bart., 152

Young Man's Coffee-House, 193